A. W. Kinglake

The Invasion of the Crimea

Its Origin and an Account of its Progress down to the Death of Lord Raglan, 3rd ed.,

the Battle of Balaclava - Vol. 4

A. W. Kinglake

The Invasion of the Crimea
Its Origin and an Account of its Progress down to the Death of Lord Raglan, 3rd ed., the Battle of Balaclava - Vol. 4

ISBN/EAN: 9783348019828

Printed in Europe, USA, Canada, Australia, Japan

Cover: Foto ©ninafisch / pixelio.de

More available books at **www.hansebooks.com**

CONTENTS.

THE BATTLE OF BALACLAVA.

CHAPTER I.

CHAPTER II.

CHAPTER II.—*continued.*

CHAPTER III.

CHAPTER III.—*continued.*

CHAPTER IV.

CHAPTER IV.—*continued.*

CHAPTER V.

CHAPTER VI.

CHAPTER VI.—*continued.*

CHAPTER VI.—*continued.*

CHAPTER VI.—*continued.*

CHAPTER VII.

CHAPTER VIII.

CHAPTER IX.

CHAPTER IX.—*continued.*

CHAPTER X.

I.

II.

III.

CHAPTER X.—*continued.*

IV.

V.

VI.

VII.

VIII.

IX.

CHAPTER X.—*continued.*

CHAPTER X.—continued.

CHAPTER X.—*continued.*

XIX.

XX.

CHAPTER XI.

CHAPTER XII.

I.

II.

III.

SUPPLEMENTARY CHAPTER.

APPENDIX.

ILLUSTRATIONS TO VOLUME IV.

BATTLE OF BALACLAVA.

THE BATTLE OF BALACLAVA.

CHAPTER I.

BEFORE entering upon the narrative of a battle in which the English division of horse took a principal part, it seems right to speak of the selections that were made by our governing authorities when they undertook to name the general officers who were to be entrusted with cavalry commands in the army despatched to the East. If a minister were unhappily forced to cast his eyes over a crowd of officers who had none of them rendered war service, and to try to draw out from among them the three or four gifted men who could best be entrusted to act in the field as generals of cavalry, it would be senseless to blame him for failing in so hard a task; but when it 'so happens that within recent years the State has carried on war, there surely is one test of fitness which has such paramount value, that the neglect to apply it can hardly be deserving of pardon, or even, we would say, of indulgence: Has the officer whose name is submitted done recent service in the field?

Has his service been brilliant? Has he shown his prowess in action as a cavalry officer? Has he in any rank, however humble, taken part in cavalry fights? Is he of the age for a cavalry man? Is he either under thirty-five, or else a man so fresh come from the performance of cavalry feats that the question of age may be waived? If the minister finds that all these questions must be answered in the negative by a portion of the candidates, whilst others can answer affirmatively, it would surely appear to follow that he has already effected some progress towards a selection of the right names, because he can thenceforth confine his investigation to the merits of those officers who have served in the field, and eliminate those who have not. To our own countrymen, more especially, the principle might be expected to recommend itself, because it so happened that, notwithstanding the long duration of the peace which had been existing between the great Powers of Europe, England had a superb list of cavalry officers in the early prime of life who had done brilliant service in the field.

Great advantage enjoyed by England in this respect.

Her brilliant list of war-service officers.

Choice made by the Government.

Well, elimination proceeded—a choice was made; but it was with an actually inverting effect that these operations took place. Incredible as it may seem, it is nevertheless true that, in nominating general officers for cavalry commands in the East, the names of the men who had done service in the field were all set aside, and that from the peace-service residue exclusively the appointments in question were made.

The officer entrusted with the charge of our cavalry

division was Lord Lucan. To his want of experience
in the field there was added the drawback of age; for
he had attained to a period of life at which no man
altogether unused to war service could be expected to
burst into fame as a successful cavalry general; but
by nature Lord Lucan was gifted with some at least
of the qualities essential for high command; and his
fifty-four years, after all, however surely they may
have extinguished the happy impulsiveness which is
needed for a wielder of the cavalry arm, can hardly
be said to have impaired his efficiency in the general
business of a commander. He enjoyed perfect health;
he saw like a hawk; and he retained such extraordinary activity of both body and mind, that perhaps
the mention of his actual age makes it really more
difficult than it might otherwise be to convey an
idea of the tall, lithe, slender, and young-looking
officer, pursuing his task of commander with a
kind of fierce, tearing energy, and expressing by a
movement of feature somewhat rare amongst Englishmen the intensity with which his mind worked.
At every fresh access of strenuousness, and especially at the moments preceding strenuous speech, his
face all at once used to light up with a glittering,
panther-like aspect, resulting from the sudden fire
of the eye, and the sudden disclosure of the teeth,
white, even, and clenched.

At an early period of his life, and whilst still almost
a boy, he had the honour to be encouraged in his
career by the Duke of Wellington, and even to receive
words of counsel and guidance from the lips of the

C H A P.
I.

great captain. In later years, he had had the spirit
and enterprise to join the Russian army whilst engaged
in military operations, thus giving himself the advantage of seeing a campaign;* and I cannot but believe
that the time thus spent was more conducing to warlike
efficiency than many a diligent year employed in peace
service at home. Independently of the general advantage derived from a glimpse of reality, Lord Lucan
gathered from his experience of that campaign on the
Danube some knowledge of a more special kind in
regard to Russian troops; and there is reason for inferring that his mode of handling the English cavalry
in the Crimea was in some measure influenced by the
impressions of his earlier days. A quarter of a century before, he had come back from the Danube campaign with a low opinion of the Russian cavalry, but
with a high respect for the infantry—more especially,
it seems, for the infantry when gathered in heavy
column; and he not only carried those opinions with
him to the Crimea, but continued, when there, to hold
them unchanged, and even, perhaps—though unconsciously—to make them the basis of his resolves.

Lord Lucan's intellectual abilities were of a very
high order, and combined as they were with the extraordinary energy of which I have spoken, they
might seem to constitute power. Experience, too, had
shown that he could apply these qualities effectively
to at least one grade of military duty, for at the time

---

* In the war of 1828-9 against the Sultan, Lord Lucan was attached
to the Staff of Prince Woronzoff; and I have heard that he was gra-
ciously chided by the Emperor Nicholas for too freely exposing his life.

when he exercised a Lieutenant-Colonel's command
his regiment was in excellent order.

No military duties in peace-time could suffice to absorb such energies as those which Lord Lucan possessed; and during a period of many years immediately preceding the Russian war, he had engaged himself in the conduct of large agricultural operations, carried on upon his own estates both in England and Ireland. With him, the improvement and culture of land had not been a mere quiet resource for dawdling away the slow hours, but a serious and engrossing business, eliciting sustained energy. In executing his designs for the improvement of his Irish estates, he pressed on, it appears, with a great strength of purpose, which overthrew all interposed obstacles; and that ruthlessness perhaps was a circumstance which might be numbered amongst the reasons for giving him a command, because the innovating force of will which he evidenced was a quality which had at the time a special and peculiar value. At the commencement of operations in the field, it is difficult for any man who is not of an almost violent nature to prepare troops long used to peace service for the exigencies of actual war, by tearing them out of the grooves in which they have long been moving. Of course, the grave task of choosing our cavalry generals was converted, as it were, into guess-work by the determination to take them exclusively from the list of those officers who had never served their country in the field; but apart from that grave objection, and the objection founded on age, Lord Lucan was an

CHAP.
I.
officer from whom much might be reasonably hoped, if the soundness of his judgment could be inferred from the general force of his intellect, and if also it could be taken for granted that he would prove willing and able, after having long had his own way, to accept the yoke of military subordination in the field, and to bear it with loyalty and temper.

Lord Lucan had one quality which is of great worth to a commander, though likely to be more serviceable to a commander-in-chief than to one filling a subordinate post. He had decision, and decision apparently so complete that his mind never hankered after the rejected alternative. His convictions once formed were so strong, and his impressions of facts or supposed facts so intensely vivid, that he was capable of being positive to a degree rarely equalled. When he determined that he was right and others wrong, he did not fail also to determine that the right and the wrong were right and wrong with a vengeance. In summing up before the House of Lords an argument attempting the refutation of a despatch sent home by Lord Raglan, he spoke in a way which was curiously characteristic. He did not dilute his assurances with the language of moderation. 'My Lords,' he said, ' I believe I have now answered every charge con- ' tained in Lord Raglan's letter. I pledged myself to ' refute every accusation; I said that I would not ' leave a word unanswered. I believe I have fully ' fulfilled the undertaking I gave—have not left two ' words together, but have torn the letter to rags ' and tatters.' Coming from Lord Lucan, this lan-

guage was no vulgar brazenry`: it represented the C H A P.
irrepressible strength of his real though mistaken ⌐ I. ⌐
conviction.

From the qualities observed in this general officer
at the time of his appointment, it might have been
difficult perhaps for a minister to infer the peculiar
tendency which developed itself in the field ; but
what happened was—that, partly from the exceeding
vigour of his intellect, partly from a naturally combative, antagonistic temper, and partly, perhaps, from the
circumstance of his having been long accustomed to
rural and provincial sway, Lord Lucan in the Crimea
disclosed a habit of mind which was calculated to en-
danger his efficiency as a subordinate commander. He
suffered himself to become an inveterate critic—an inveterate critic of the orders he received from Headquarters ; and since it happened that his criticism almost
always ended in his coming to a strong disapproval of
his chief's directions, he of course lost that comfort of
mind which is enjoyed by an officer who takes it for
granted that his chief must be right, and had to be
constantly executing orders with the full persuasion
that they were wrongly conceived. Plainly, that was
a state of mind which might grievously impair a man's
powers of action in the field, not only by chilling him
with the wretched sensation of disapproving what he
had to do, but also by confusing him in his endeavours to put right interpretations upon the orders he
received.

It was never from dulness or sloth, but rather
through a misaiming cleverness, that Lord Lucan used

to fall into error. With a mind almost always apparently in a confident and positive state, he brought
it to bear in a way which so often proved infelicitous,
that his command in the Crimea was made on the
whole to appear like that of a wrong-headed man;
but I imagine that this result was in no small measure produced by the circumstance of his being almost
always in an attitude of oppugnancy; and there is
room for believing that under other conditions, and
especially if detached, and acting for the time independently, he might have evinced a much higher
capacity for the business of war than he found means
to show in the Crimea. There, at all events, he was
not at all happily circumstanced; for besides being
wholly unarmed with the authority which is conferred
by former services in the field, he had so yielded to his
unfortunate habit of adverse criticism as to be more
often fretted than animated by the orders which came
down from Headquarters; and, on the other hand, he
had under him a general officer commanding one of
his brigades, who was rather a busy antagonist than a
zealous and devoted lieutenant.

It must be remembered, moreover, that the control
of a large body of cavalry in action carries with it
one peculiar source of embarrassment. If the general
commanding leads a charge in person (as Murat was
accustomed to do), he loses, of course, for a time his
power of personally directing the troops not included
in his first line, and so abdicates during the interval
one of his principal functions as a general. If, on the
other hand, he clings to his power as a general, and

declines to narrow his authority during several critical minutes by taking the part of a leader, he must be
content to forego a large share of the glory which at-
taches to cavalry achievements. He may deserve and
attain the high credit of seizing the happiest moments
for successively launching his squadrons; but in combats of horse, the task of actually leading an attack is
plainly so momentous a business that it, would be
difficult for any man coming new to field service to
build up any lofty repute as a general of cavalry, by
ordering other people to charge.

Therefore, for general as well as for special reasons,
Lord Lucan's command was one of an embarrassing
kind; but despite the inherent difficulties of his position—despite all the hindrances created by himself, and
the hindrances created by others—he was a diligent,
indefatigable commander,—always in health, always at
his post, always toiling to the best of his ability, and
maintaining a high, undaunted, and even buoyant
spirit, under trials the most depressing. He expended
a prodigious industry upon his duties. It may be
that he was not perfectly consequent, or that his
measures were wrong or ill-timed, or, again, that he
was unduly thwarted; for certainly the result seems
to have been that, in proportion to the energy exerted,
his mind left no great trace of its action; but if a
man's power of commanding could be safely inferred
from mere words, the collection which has been made
of Lord Lucan's divisional orders would be a striking example of vigour applied to the management of
cavalry in a time of the heaviest trials. Disliking

CHAP.
I.

apparently every sacrifice, however temporary, of the controlling power, he did not take upon himself to lead in person any cavalry charge; and therefore the degree in which he may have been qualified for that very peculiar kind of duty must of course be a subject of conjecture rather than proof; but his composure under heavy fire was so perfect that, even in an army where prowess evinced in that way was exceedingly general, it did not escape observation. 'Yes, ' damn him, he's brave,' was the comment pronounced on Lord Lucan by one of his most steady haters.

This is not the place for giving the general tenor of Lord Lucan's services as commander of our cavalry in the Crimea;* but I have sought to prepare for my account of the action in the plain of Balaclava, by conveying beforehand some impression of the officer who there commanded our cavalry. Some such glance was the more to be desired because Lord Lucan's abilities were evidently of a higher order than those he found means to disclose by the part he took in the battle.

It should be understood that Lord Lucan did not thrust himself into the command of our division of horse. All he had asked for was to have charge of a single infantry brigade.

The English division of horse numbered two brigades, one of which comprised the Light Cavalry, the other our Heavy Dragoons. The Light Brigade, as we know, was commanded by the Earl of Cardigan.

* The place for that will be the chapter in which I deal with the period of Lord Lucan's recall.

Lord Cardigan, when appointed to this command, C H A P. was about fifty-seven years old, and had never seen I. war service. From his early days he had eagerly Lord Cardigan. longed for the profession of arms, and although prevented by his father's objections from entering the army at the usual period of life, he afterwards—that is, at about twenty-seven years of age—was made a cornet in a cavalry regiment. He pursued his profession with diligence, absenting himself much from the House of Commons (of which he was at that time a member) for the purpose of doing orderly duty as a subaltern in the 8th Hussars. Aided partly by fortune, but partly by the favour of the Duke of York and the operation of the purchase system, he rose very quickly in the service, and at the end of about seven years from the period of his entering the army, he was a lieutenant-colonel.

He had a passionate love for the service—a fair knowledge, it is believed, of so much cavalry business as is taught by practice in England—a strong sense of military duty—a burning desire for the fame which awaits heroic actions—and, finally, the gift of high courage. Lord Cardigan's valour was not at all of the wild, heedless kind, but the result of strong determination. Even from his way of riding to hounds, it was visible, they say, that the boldness he evinced was that of a resolute man with a set purpose, and not a dare-devil impulse. He bore himself firmly in both the duels he fought; and upon the occasion which opposed him to an officer against whom he was bitterly angered, he shot his foe through the body.*

* Without, I think, killing him.

CHAP.
I.

His mind, although singularly barren, and wanting in dimensions, was not without force; and he had the valuable quality of persistency. He had been so constituted by nature, or so formed by the watchful care which is sometimes bestowed upon an only son, as to have a habit of attending to the desires and the interests of self with a curious exactitude. The tendency, of course, was one which he shared with nearly all living creatures; and it was only from the extraordinary proportions in which the attribute existed, and from the absence of any attempt to mask the propensity, that it formed a distinctive peculiarity. When engaged in the task of self-assertion or self-advocacy, he adhered to his subject with the most curious rigour, never going the least bit astray from it, and separating from it all that concerned the rest of creation as matter altogether irrelevant and uninteresting. Others before him may have secretly concentrated upon self an equal amount of attention; but in Lord Cardigan there was such an entire absence of guile, that exactly as he was so he showed himself to the world. Of all false pretences contrived for the purpose of feigning an interest in others he was as innocent as a horse. Amongst his good qualities was love of order; but this with him was in such morbid excess, that it constituted a really dangerous foible, involving him from time to time in mischief. One of his quarrels was founded upon the colour of a bottle; another upon the size of a tea-cup. In each case the grievance was want of uniformity. To his formulated mind the distinction between lawful and right was

imperceptible. A thousand times over it might be C H A P.
suggested to him that he ought not to have been sleeping on board his yacht—a yacht with a French cook
on board—when not only all the officers and men
under him, but also his divisional chief, were cheer-
fully bearing the hardships and privations of camp
life ; but a thousand times over he would answer
that he indulged himself thus with the permission of
Lord Raglan ; and the lawfulness of the practice
being thus established, he never seemed to understand
that there could remain any question of propriety, or
taste, or right feeling.

With attributes of this kind, he was plainly more
fitted to obey than to command. Having no personal
ascendancy, and no habitual consideration for the
feelings of others, he was not, of course, at all qualified to exert easy rule over English gentlemen, and
his idea of the way to command was to keep on commanding. There surely was cruelty in the idea of
placing human beings under the military control of
an officer at once so arbitrary and so narrow; but the
notion of such a man having been able to purchase for
himself a right to hold Englishmen in military sub-
jection is, to my mind, revolting. Lord Cardigan
incurred a series of quarrels, and was removed from
the command of his regiment; but afterwards, by
the special desire of the Duke of Wellington, he was
restored to active service.

There can hardly have been any well-founded
expectation that Lord Cardigan would be able to go
through a campaign without engaging in quarrels;

and never, surely, by action or speech, did he convince the dispensers of military authority that he was a man who would be competent to meet the emergencies of war with the resources of a fruitful mind. I imagine that the first active Bishop or Doctor of Divinity whom the Commander-in-Chief at the Horse Guards might chance to have met on horseback would probably have been much more competent than Lord Cardigan (whose mind worked always in grooves) to discover and seize the right moment for undertaking a cavalry charge. Yet without the attributes of a commander, a man may be a resolute, faithful, heroic soldier; and that surely is the kind of glory—it is glory of no mean kind—which can best be claimed for Lord Cardigan. In despite of all the faults which he had manifested to the world when appointed to the command of the Light Brigade, there still remained good grounds for trusting that, as long as he should be acting in the performance of what he might clearly understand to be his duty, he would perform it with precision, with valour, and, if need be, with unsparing devotion.

Lord Lucan and Lord Cardigan regarded conjointly.

If between Lord Lucan and Lord Cardigan there could be discovered any points of resemblance, these were not of such a kind as to be conducive to harmony. They were, both of them, contentious; and whether from natural gifts, or from long habits of disputation, they had both of them powers of a kind which are commonly developed in lawyers, though not certainly in lawyers of the same quality. Lord Lucan was the able, the cogent, the strenuous,

the daring advocate, whose opponents (especially if C H A P.
they happened to be in the right) were to be not
merely answered but crushed. Lord Cardigan, in his
forensic aspect, was of the species which repeats a
hundred times over in the same words the same version of the same facts, persistently ignores the whole
strength of the adversary's argument, and which also
relies a good deal upon what in the courts are called
'points' and 'objections.' Yet it would seem that
he must have been capable of attaining to a higher
level; for upon one occasion, when undertaking to
defend himself in the House of Commons, he made
what the House regarded as a very good speech.
Lord Lucan and Lord Cardigan were both of them
men possessed with exceeding self-confidence, but a
self-confidence resulting from very different springs
of thought.   Lord Lucan's trustfulness in himself
was based upon the consciousness of great ability,
and upon that rare vividness of impression as well
as that strength of conviction of which we were just
now speaking. He was confident because he was
positive.   On the other hand, Lord Cardigan's assurance was not, I think, founded upon any quality
which could be rightly called self-conceit, but rather
upon the corollary which he drew from the fact of
his having a given command. He was so extravagantly military in his notions, so orderly, so straight-
minded, so given to narrow and literal interpretations, that from the mere fact of his having been entrusted with the charge of a brigade, he inferred
his perfect fitness for the task. By the act of ap-

C H A P. pointing him his Sovereign had declared him fit, and
I. he took the Queen at her word. When we see him,
by-and-by, side by side with a cavalry officer of warlike experience, at a critical moment, we shall learn
to how great an absurdity a man may be brought
by this army-list process of reasoning. So far did
Lord Cardigan carry the inference, that once, I see—
even in writing—when maintaining his view as to
the extent of undisturbed authority which should be
possessed by the commander of a brigade, he made
bold to bracket himself, as it were, for the purpose of the discussion, with no less a man than
Sir Colin Campbell, basing one of his arguments
upon the tacit assumption, that because Sir Colin
and he both commanded brigades, they were both
of them, therefore, entitled to the same degree of
latitude.

It was hardly to be expected with confidence that
officers appointed to high cavalry commands without
having earned them by serving their country in the
field would all at once show themselves able to put
sound constructions upon the orders which were to
guide them in the presence of the enemy; and the
personal qualities of Lord Lucan and Lord Cardigan
were not of such a kind as to supply in this point the
absence of warlike experience. With Lord Lucan
the danger was, that his fertile and vigorous mind
might bring him into some elaborate and subversive
process of reasoning. If, for instance, we should hear
him informed that he is to be supported by infantry,
we must be prepared to find him convinced that the

infantry is to be supported by him. On the other C H A P.
hand, Lord Cardigan's endeavours at construing or- I.
ders were sure to be characterised by an exceeding
rigidity, which might be preposterous in one instance,
in another superb. If ordered to hold a position, he
might think himself planted as fast as a sentry at the
gate of a palace. If ordered to advance down a valley
without being told where to halt, he might proudly
abstain from supplying the omission, and lead his
brigade to destruction.

Lord Lucan was the brother-in-law of Lord Cardigan ; but so little beloved by him that in the eyes
of cynical London, an arrangement for coupling the
one man to the other seemed almost a fell stroke
of humour. It might have been thought that, in a
free country, the notion of carrying official perverseness to any such extreme length as this must have
been nipped in the bud. It was not so. If England
was free, she was also very patient of evil institutions,
as well as of official misfeasance. She trusted too
much to the fitful anger of Parliament, and the chances
of remonstrance in print.

In justice to Lord Cardigan—because tending to
account for, and in some measure palliate, the act
which will be presently mentioned—it should be
stated that, some short time before the embarkation,
he had had to endure a bitter disappointment, under
which he continued to smart during the first two
weeks of the invasion. Lord Lucan was to have
been left in Bulgaria, and, under that arrangement,
Lord Cardigan in the Crimea would have been com-

mander of our cavalry during several momentous days, without being liable to any interference except from Lord Raglan himself; but Lord Lucan successfully insisted upon his claim to be present with the portion of the division which was likely to come first into the presence of the enemy; and accordingly Lord Cardigan, though commanding the Light Brigade, had over him his divisional general, and was therefore in a measure annulled.

Lord Cardigan's attitude of antagonism to Lord Lucan.

Lord Cardigan was not a man who would have consciously suffered himself to become at all insubordinate; but, whilst writhing under the torture inflicted by the annulling presence of his divisional general, he brought himself to imagine that the custom of the service set something like bounds to the overruling authority which should be exercised by a divisional general over his brigadier, and that in some matters at least—as, for instance, in the arrangements of his camp—the brigadier had a right to expect that he would be left to his own discretion.

Accordingly, and at a period of the campaign when it might be imagined that the eternal claims of self would, for a time, be superseded by the warlike ardour of a cavalry leader, Lord Cardigan applied his mind to the object of protecting himself from the inter-

Lord Cardigan's complaint in writing.

ference of his commanding officer. He drew up in writing a lengthy string of complaints on this subject, and submitted them to Lord Raglan.

Lord Raglan's severe answer.

Lord Raglan judged it his duty to answer this appeal with some severity. In a paper which was addressed, it seems, to Lord Cardigan, but meant to

be communicated also to Lord Lucan, the Commander C H A P.
of the forces thus wrote :—   I.

'BALACLAVA, *Sept.* 28, 1854.

' I have perused this correspondence with the deep-
' est regret, and I am bound to express my con-
' viction that the Earl of Cardigan would have done
' better if he had abstained from making the repre-
' sentation which he has thought fit to submit to
' my decision.

' I consider him wrong in every one of the instances
' cited. A general of division may interfere little or
' much with the duties of a general of brigade, as he
' may think proper or see fit. His judgments may be
' right or wrong, but the general of brigade should
' bear this in mind, that the lieutenant-general is the
' senior officer, and that all his orders and sugges-
' tions claim obedience and attention.'

Lord Raglan, however, determined to try whether
it were possible that words of entreaty from himself,
addressed alike to Lord Lucan and Lord Cardigan,
might either allay the animosity existing between
them, or render it less embarrassing to the public
service ; and accordingly, in the same paper, he addressed to both these Generals the following appeal :
' The Earl of Lucan and the Earl of Cardigan are
' nearly connected. They are both gentlemen of high
' honour and of elevated position in the country, in-
' dependently of their military rank. They must per-
' mit me, as the Commander of the Forces, and, I may
' say, the friend of both, earnestly to recommend to

Lord Rag-
lan's ap-
peal to the
good feel-
ings of
Lord
Lucan and
Lord Car-
digan.

CHAP.
I.

'them to communicate frankly with each other, and 'to come to such an understanding as that there 'should be no suspicion of the contempt of authority 'on the one side, and no apprehension of undue inter-'ference on the other.'   (Signed)   'RAGLAN.'

It must not be supposed, however, that the relations between these two officers involved them in unseemly personal altercations. Lord Lucan with great wisdom and tact took care that the more unwelcome communications which he from time to time made to his brigadier should be either in writing, or else conveyed by the mouth of another; and Lord Cardigan on the other hand had a sense of propriety in such matters, and was not without power of self-restraint.

Inquiry
as to the
causes
which ren-
dered it
possible
for the
Govern-
ment to
do as it
did.

But now, why did it happen that England, having under her eyes a brilliant list of cavalry officers from whom she might make her choice, determined to exclude all those who had served in the field, and to place in the respective commands of which we have been speaking two peers between fifty and sixty years old who had neither of them rendered war-service? One answer is this: There was a divided responsibility. We heard what happened to London when the War Office and the Horse Guards—the clerk and the counter-clerk—differed; but this selection of cavalry officers was the result of agreement, or rather, one may say, of a process which goes by the name of 'compounding.' From ancient treaties of peace between the two sides of Whitehall it re-

sulted that the Commander-in-Chief at the Horse
Guards was the authority for advising the appointment and taking the Queen's pleasure upon it; but
that the authorities responsible to Parliament, or,
in other words, the Ministry, might take upon themselves to interpose; and that if they should do so,
and do so persistently, then, painful as the surrender would be, their objection should be allowed to
prevail.

From this division of power there followed, of course,
a corresponding alleviation of responsibility. Lord
Hardinge could say that the proposed nominations had
been brought to the cognisance of the Ministry, without causing them to interpose their authority as a
positive bar to the proceeding. The Ministry, on
the other hand, could declare—as, indeed, the Duke
of Newcastle very constantly did—that they strongly
disapproved the appointments, and never would have
made them if they had the full power in their hands;
but that, still, they did not feel it absolutely incumbent upon them to take the somewhat strong measure
of interposing.

In the present condition of our State arrangements,
one of the best and most graceful uses of an aris-
tocracy is to supply the country in time of war with
commanders who have attained to distinction in presence of the enemy, and yet are sufficiently youthful.
For a nation to build its hopes upon so narrow a basis,
instead of fairly searching out from among the whole
community those men who may seem the best qualified to lead its forces, this, no doubt, must be looked

CHAP.
I.
upon as a rude, quaint practice, which is only saved from being preposterous by the fact that no more rational method has hitherto found acceptance; but in the mean time, the practice, as thus understood, has its value. The adventitious circumstances combine with personal merit, and lift a man into command at the age best adapted for the purpose; so that the qualities of a Wellesley, for instance, may come to be recognised at thirty instead of at sixty—a difference material to the individual, but unspeakably important to the country; and in that way (until a better method can be discovered) the legitimate ambition of powerful or wealthy families may subserve the true interests of the State. If Lord Lucan and Lord Cardigan had been two nobles of the age of some thirty-three yeers, who had fought side by side on the banks of the Sutlej, who had inspired their commanders with a high idea of their warlike qualities, and who, by aid of these circumstances combining with their family pretensions, had attained to such military rank and distinction as to be recognised, and deserving candidates for high commands, then, indeed, a country which had not yet hit upon any better mode of attaining the object would have had reason to be grateful for the existence of a system which supplied and raised into eminence, at the right time of life, men capable of wielding authority in the field. Far from resting upon any such basis, these appointments deprived the country of the inestimable advantage of seeing her squadrons entrusted to men in the prime of cavalry life who had gloriously served in the field, and com-

mitted a superbly great stake to two peers of the ages C H A P. of fifty-four, and fifty-seven, who, so far as concerns I. that teaching which is imparted by responsible war-services, were now to begin their education, and begin it in the enemy's presence.

However, these two general officers were both of them brave men, and in that, at all events, there was a basis for hoping that, in spite of any misfortunes re-sulting from the appointments in question, the honour of the service would be sustained. It may be that, in professing to judge of the seed which was sown in the spring, one is governed too much by observing the harvest that was reaped in the autumn ; but certainly this double selection of generals does seem as though it were fitted—and that without much help from for-tune—to involve the English Light Cavalry in some ruinous, yet brilliant disaster.

There is a circumstance which tends in some meas-ure to account for dereliction of duty on the part of those who were preparing our army for foreign service. Men who might be supposed the most competent to form an opinion, were persuaded that the force would be used as a support to negotiations, and not for actual warfare.*

The officer appointed to the command of the General Scarlett. Heavy Dragoons was Brigadier-General the Honour-able James Scarlett. He was fifty-five years of age,

* I do not include the Duke of Newcastle amongst those who enter-tained the impression, but certainly the communications made to Lord Raglan—communications extending down to the eve of his departure for Paris—compelled him almost to believe that the period of foreign service would be extremely brief.

CHAP. and he too, like Lord Lucan and Lord Cardigan, had
  I.   never done service in the field; but besides those
soldierly qualities of which we shall be able to judge
when we see him engaging the enemy, he was gifted
with two quiet attributes, which enabled him to
appreciate the deficiency, and do all that man could
to supply it.

He had modesty as well as good sense; and knowing that experience, valuable in almost all undertak-
ings, is especially valuable in the great business of
war, he did not for a moment assume that, by the
magic virtue of his mere appointment to a command,
he became all at once invested with the knowledge or
the practical skill which men acquire in the field; and
he therefore determined, if he could, to have men
at his side who knew of their own knowledge what
fighting was, and had even won high distinction.

The officer whom Scarlett chose as his aide-de-
camp, was Lieutenant Alexander Elliot. Before the
period of his entering the Royal Army Elliot had
served five years in India. He was in the Gwalior
campaign, and at the battle of Punniar commanded
a troop of the 8th Bengal Light Cavalry. With the
same regiment he went through the whole of the
eventful and momentous struggle which we call the
first Sutlej campaign. He commanded a squadron
at the great battle of Ferozeshah; and at a time
when the 62d had been driven back and almost
annihilated, he executed a desperate charge, and with
his standard-bearer and five troopers penetrated into
the Sikh entrenchments. In recognition of his bril-

liant cavalry service in that war, Lord Hardinge C H A P. appointed him to a command in his body-guard, and I. made him honorary aide-de-camp. Being afterwards constrained to leave India by the state of his health, he entered the Royal Army, and it was owing to this necessitated change that he bore no higher rank than that of lieutenant. With all the special knowledge and instincts of a brilliant cavalry officer, he had qualifications of a more general kind; and if there had been at the time of the invasion a minister so strong and so resolute as to be able to do the thing which is right, a man such as Elliot would have been eagerly laid hold of and entrusted with high cavalry command.

But this was not all that Scarlett was able to do towards arming himself with the experience of men who had done good service in war. Colonel Beatson had fought under Evans in Spain, and had afterwards risen to high distinction in India. Being for the time in Europe, and yielding to the warlike impulses of his nature, he had laid aside those considerations of military rank which might have governed a lower order of mind, and consented to be attached to General Scarlett's Staff as his extra aide-de-camp. Lord Lucan, with that unhappy perversity which was so constantly marring his cleverness, opposed himself to this last arrangement of Scarlett's, and declared, it seems, that Colonel Beatson must not be considered as having any recognised position in the army.

I have said that if General Scarlett enjoyed the immense advantage of having two such aides-de-camp as these, he owed the happy idea of thus strengthen-

CHAP.
I.

ing himself to his own wisdom and modesty; but it is worth while to say that that last quality of his had a tendency to withdraw our brigade of Heavy Dragoons from its · due share of public attention. Concurring with other known causes, General Scarlett's quiet unobtrusiveness did much to prevent his fellow-countrymen from acquainting themselves so fully as they might otherwise have been eager to do with the fight between his brigade and the main body of the Russian cavalry.

On the day of the battle of Balaclava it was not the destiny of General Scarlett to have to act under any great complexity of circumstances, nor to give rise to any kind of public controversy, and it will therefore be easy to see and to understand him in action without having a preliminary knowledge of the man; but in truth his achievement corresponded so closely with the noble and heroic simplicity of his character, that the account of what he did will not fail to carry along with it a true indication of his quality. We shall see him lead his great charge.

CHAPTER II.

THE strength and compactness of the position taken up by the Allies on the Chersonese upland was not at all shared, as we know, by the scanty detachment of infantry which Lord Raglan had been able to spare for the defence of Balaclava. Stationed apart in the plain below, this small force was in such local relation to the Allied army on the Chersonese as to be lying outside, and at the foot of the natural castle from which the main body looked down.*

CHAP. II.

The isolated position of the forces defending Balaclava.

Yet Balaclava was the storehouse, the arsenal, the port, whence the English drew all their supplies; and such was the anomalous character of the arrangements which Lord Raglan had been forced to adopt, that, instead of being safely ensconced in the rear of the main Allied camp, the material sources of the English strength lay inviting the enterprise of Prince Mentschikoff's field army, and in charge, so to speak, of an outpost.

It, however, seemed feasible to construct a system of field-works which would enable the troops left out in the plain below to withstand an attack for such

Increasing strength and boldness of the Russians

* See vol. III. chap. xiii. p. 291, et seq.

C H A P.
II.

in the
valley of
the Tcher-
naya.
time as to allow of the needed reinforcements coming down to their aid from the upland; and the English were quickened in their sense of the importance belonging to this part of their task, by the always increasing strength and boldness of the Russian force which had begun to show itself in the direction of Tchorgoun so early as the 7th of October.

Before hearing of the battle of the 25th of October, it is well to have an idea of the ground upon which the security of Balaclava depended, and the arrangements which had been made for its defence.

The string of houses constituting Balaclava extended along a narrow ledge between the eastern side of the little harbour and the western acclivities of Mount Hiblak. Except at the gorge of Kadiköi towards the north,* and the narrow strait towards the south leading crookedly into the Euxine, both the town and the harbour were surrounded in all directions by steep lofty hills; and the hills towards the west being a continuation of that Chersonese upland where the main Allied armies lay camped, were within the unquestioned dominion of the invaders.

Partly from this cause, and partly from their command of the sea—including the small but deep harbour, which brought ships of the line close up to the town—the English, at Balaclava, were secure against any attack coming either from the west or the south; and again, towards the east, the ground was not only steep and commanding, but otherwise favourable for defence. Accordingly, from a part of the sea-cliff which is one mile east of Balaclava, and thence north and north-west to the Church of St Elias, in the neighbourhood of Kadiköï, a curve could be drawn, extending along a distance of between two and three miles, in which nature had done so much for the defence that, by expending upon it a moderate amount of labour, and arming the works there constructed with a few naval guns of position, our Engineers were enabled to place all this portion of the inner line in a fair state of security, without diverting from the duties of the siege any very large body of men.* A few of the guns in position near the church were manned, it seems, by the Royal Artillery, but all the rest of them by our Marine Artillery ;† and the only bodies of infantry which this line of more than two miles absorbed, were the 1200 marines from our fleet, under the command of Colonel Hurdle, with two companies of the 93d Regiment.‡

Towards the north, the hills opened, and the place could be approached by the gorge of Kadiköï ; but even there, at intervals there were spurs thrown out from the neighbouring acclivities which offered good sites for several small field-works, and by taking advantage of these, our Engineers completed their inner

CHAP. II.

The inner line of defence.

---

* The number of guns in battery along this inner line of defence was, I think, 26. The Engineers were confident in the security of the 'inner line,' and at times certainly Sir Colin Campbell shared their belief ; but I gather that he was brought into an anxious state of mind by the peculiar responsibility which weighed upon him, and his language in regard to the security of the position was not always the same.

† I now gather that *all* the guns in position along the 'inner line of defence' were manned by the Marine Artillery.—*Note to 2d Edition.*

‡ Our Engineers put the length of the line, taken altogether, at 'about three miles.'—Official Journal, p. 41.

line of defence. The troops on which Sir Colin Campbell relied for the defence of the gorge were the main body of the 93d Highlanders, with a battalion of Turks and a battery of field-artillery.

There was a frigate* in the harbour, and (besides a score or two of English soldiers, having duties of some kind which brought them to Balaclava on the day of the battle) there lay in the town some eighty or a hundred English soldiers, who, although invalided, were not so prostrate as to be unable to handle a musket.

So great was the confidence which most of our people reposed in the strength of this inner line of defence, in the quality of all the troops which manned it, and in the prowess of the veteran soldier who commanded the garrison, that the safety of the ground thus covered cost them little or no uneasiness; and, as a not inexpressive sign of the quiet efficiency with which this part of the defence was made good, I may mention that an officer holding a very high and responsible command, and one, too, which did not at all tend to divert him from this part of the Allied position, was long able to remain unacquainted with the very existence

---

* So called by Sir Colin Campbell, but the 'Wasp' was in fact a corvette; and with the exception of a gunner and a few men in charge, she had no crew on board. The 'Diamond' was lying also in the harbour, but she neither had guns nor crew on board, and was in charge, it seems, of a single ship-keeper. Captain Patison, R.N., commanding the 'Simoom,' a troop-ship, was the senior naval officer in the harbour. When he became aware that there was likely to be an attack, he ordered his first lieutenant, Lieutenant Selby, to collect the working parties, and get them on board the 'Wasp,' thereby enabling the corvette, if called upon, to deliver fire from her starboard broadside; and he also directed that one watch should follow him ashore, and take part in the land defence.—*Note to Second Edition.*

of the inner line of defence, and to hear of it for the first time some ten years after the peace. To him in the Crimea this inner line of defence was what oxygen is to a peasant—a blessing unperceived and unheard of, on which his existence depended.

The gorge of Kadiköi opens out into a large tract of ground which, though marked in some places by strong undulations, by numberless hillocks, and even by features deserving the name of 'heights,' is yet, upon the whole, so much lower, and so much more even than the surrounding country, as to be called 'the plain of Balaclava.'

This tract of comparatively low ground is the field of the engagement, which we are accustomed to call the battle of Balaclava, but it lies a mile north of the town.* It has an average length of about three miles, with a breadth of about two, and is hemmed in on almost all sides by ground of from some 300 to 1000 feet high; for, on the north of the plain, there are the Fedioukine Hills; on the east, Mount Hasfort; on the south, the Kamara Hills and Mount Hiblak; on the west, the steep buttresses of the Chersonese upland.

The distinctive feature of the basin thus formed is a low ridge of ground, which, crossing the so-called 'plain' in the direction of its length—or, in other terms, from east to west—divides it into two narrow valleys. So completely has this range of heights bridged over the plain, that it served as a natural

* See the map; but a glance at the diagram on the following page may aid towards an apprehension of the general features of the field.

C H A P. viaduct, enabling the designer of the Woronzoff road
   II.   to carry his trace-line across from the Kamara Hills on
the east to the Chersonese uplands on the west without letting it ever descend to the general level of the

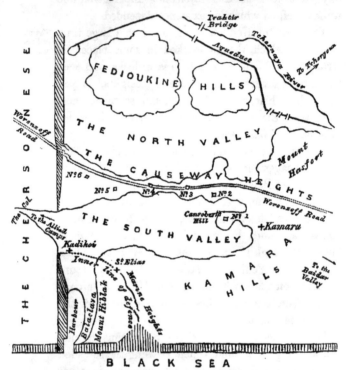

ground which had to be traversed ; and therefore it is
that the features which constitute this ridge are distinguished as the 'Causeway Heights.'

From the foot of the Chersonese the North Valley
sloped down in an eastern direction till it reached

the embankment of the aqueduct, there crossed, it C H A P.
II.
appears, by three bridges. A yet farther descent of
only a few yards down the valley brought a rider to
the left bank of the river Tchernaya, and to fords
by which he might cross it. On the other side of the
river, and at a distance of less than a mile, there
stood the village of Tchorgoun, where Liprandi, as we
know, had established his Headquarters, and gathered
his main strength. This North Valley is ground on
which the memory of our countrymen has brooded.
It was the scene of the Light Cavalry charge.

The South Valley is on the Balaclava side of the
' Causeway Heights.' At its eastern extremity there
is a knoll between 500 and 600 feet high, which, being
joined to the Kamara Hills by a neck of high ground,
juts out over the valley as a promontory does over
the sea, and for a feature thus conspicuous men soon
found a name. They called it ' Canrobert's Hill.' At
the opposite or western extremity of this valley, the
road connecting Balaclava with the Chersonese passed
up by way of the ' Col.' It is with the slope of a hillside descending into this South Valley, and with the
glory of Scarlett's Dragoons, that England will have
to associate her memory of the one great fight between cavalry and cavalry which took place in the
course of the war.

It was of so much moment to secure Balaclava from Concep-
tion of the
outer line
of defence.
disaster, that there could not but be a desire to pre-
vent the enemy from coming within the limits of the
South Valley ; and considering, on the one hand, the
inconvenience of diverting troops from the siege for

merely defensive purposes, and, on the other, the
configuration of the ground in the plain of Balaclava,
men thought that what was wanting in bayonets might
possibly be eked out with the spade ; and this idea was
the more readily pursued because it happened that, in
part from the confidence of the Sultan, and in part
from the graciousness of the French Commander, Lord
Raglan had obtained the services of some 3000 Turkish
soldiers, who might first be employed in constructing
the requisite earthworks, and then in manning them.
Our Engineers saw that by throwing up a slight work
on Canrobert's Hill, and a chain of little redoubts on
the bosses or hillocks which mark at short intervals
the range of the Causeway Heights, there might be
formed an entrenched position which would enable
a force of moderate strength to hold the ground
against one much more numerous; and it is evident
that the design would have had a great value if the
position of Balaclava, when expecting an attack from
20,000 or 25,000 men, had had a small army of
10,000 or 12,000 men to defend it. But this was
not the real exigency ; for, on the one hand, the
Allies, if they could have time to come down, were
in no danger at this period of being outnumbered in
the plain ; and, on the other hand, there was not only
no army at Balaclava of such strength as to be able
to defend an entrenched position like that which
might be formed on the line of the Causeway Heights,
but actually no army at all, and no force of any kind
that could be charged to support the men placed in
the intended works, save only a division of cavalry,

with a single troop of horse-artillery.   Our Engineers C H A P.
formed an entrenched position which could only have ____II.____
strength upon the supposition that several thousands
of the Allied infantry would have time to come down
and defend it. Yet unless there should be a more
than English vigilance in the plain of Balaclava, and
unless, too, our Division of Cavalry should be so bril-
liantly wielded as to be able to check and disconcert
for some hours the marches of the enemy's columns,
there was no good ground for imagining that the
strength of this 'outer line,' or the prowess of the
brave Osmanlis who were to be placed in its earthworks, could fairly be brought into use.

It would seem, therefore, at first sight, that General de Todleben's severe criticism of the outer line of
defence must have been well enough justified; but
the truth is, that the scheme was never recommended
by our Engineers as a really trustworthy expedient.
They chose it apparently as a makeshift which might
more or less baffle a hitherto unenterprising enemy;
and, at least, their plan had the merit—the then truly
enticing merit—of diverting no English forces from
the great business of the siege; for if the outer line
of defence had not been adopted, our cavalry, with
its attendant troop of horse-artillery, would still have
been camped in the plain.

On Canrobert's Hill there was thrown up a slight   The works
breastwork, with its salient towards the north-east;   ing the
and along the whole line of the Causeway Heights   outer line
there were formed as many as five other earthworks,   of defence.
each smaller and weaker than the one on Canrobert's

CHAP.
II.

Hill. Of these six works some were open at the gorge, and some closed, but they used to be all called ' redoubts.' *

The work on Canrobert's Hill was known as the Redoubt Number One, and the five other works were distinguished by successive numbers; † but the one which, in this way, received the name of Number Three, was sometimes also called ' Arabtabia.'

Slight nature of the works.

The works were executed by Turkish labour under the direction of an English Engineer officer.‡ They were of very weak profile, and a horseman, as was proved by the Cossacks, could well enough ride through and through them. Indeed, one of the works was begun, completed, and armed in a single day.

Armament of the works.

The work on Canrobert's Hill was armed with three 12-pounder iron guns, supplied by Dundas from our

---

* Practically—I am not speaking of what might be found in books or in the impressions of formulated people—the word redoubt has two meanings. In its most confined sense it means a work which is not open at the gorge ; but in the everyday language of those military men who are not professing to describe in a special and distinctive way, any kind of field-work, whether open or not at the gorge, is commonly called a ' redoubt.' Like, for instance, the word ship (which may either be used in a very general sense, or else may be taken to designate a three-masted vessel of a particular rig), the word 'redoubt' has practically two meanings, one general the other distinctive. Lord Raglan—the most accurate of men in his language—constantly used the word 're-' doubt' in its general sense, applying it indiscriminately to works which were open at the gorge as well as to those which were not.

† I adopt the nomenclature which obtained so generally as to render any other inconvenient ; but I may usefully mention that some—and amongst them Lord Raglan—did not include the work on Canrobert's Hill in the numerical designation. With them the work commonly called Number Two would be Number One, and so on.

‡ Lieutenant Wagman, I believe ; but I hear Captain Stanton also took some part. The work completed in a single day was the ' Number ' Two.'

fleet; and the three redoubts next adjoining it—that CHAP.
is, the Redoubt Number Two, the Arabtabia or Re- II.
doubt Number Three, and the Redoubt Number Four
—were each of them armed with two guns of the same
sort and calibre.* The two other works—namely,
the Redoubt Number Five and the Redoubt Number
Six—were unarmed on the day of the battle.

The works were manned by Turkish troops, one How
battalion of these being posted on Canrobert's Hill, manned.
and a half battalion or wing in each of the Causeway
redoubts.†

The work on Canrobert's Hill was perilously ex- The
posed to any artillery which might be placed in Height
battery on the neighbouring ridge of Kamara; and possession
no arrangements were made for preventing the enemy of the
enemy.
from seizing this vantage-ground, for the ridge of
Kamara was itself overtopped by crests ranging
higher and higher in the direction of Baidar; and
it was judged that to attempt to hold more ground
would be to add to the weakness of this outer line.
As it was, the line of these six earthworks extended Extent
and re-
over a space of more than two miles; and Can- moteness
robert's Hill was so distant from the ground whence outer line.
supporting forces might be expected to come, as

* There is a difference between the various authorities which record
the number and place of these guns, Lord Raglan putting them at seven,
Todleben at eleven, and others at intermediate numbers. I put them,
as may be seen, at nine—'Journal of Operations.' The difference is an
immaterial one.

† From information communicated to me by Mr Henry Stanley I
have reason to believe that a French officer at the time remonstrated
against the plan of leaving the Turks unsupported in such a position.—
Note to Second Edition.

CHAP.
II.

The force immediately available for supporting the Turks.

Sir Colin Campbell's confidence in the maintenance of the position.

to offer the enemy a licence of some hours' duration for any enterprise in the plain of Balaclava upon which he might think fit to venture.*

The only force immediately available for attempting to give any support to the Turks was the division of English cavalry, which, along with its attendant troop of horse-artillery (commanded by Captain Maude), was under the orders of Lord Lucan. This division of cavalry comprised some 1500 sabres, and was in high order. It lay camped on the southern slopes of the Causeway Heights, at a distance of not much less than two miles from Canrobert's Hill, but it kept an outlying picket at a spot near the heights of Kamara.

Such, then, was the outer line of defence; and this—only this—was the force which, except after the lapse of some hours, could be expected to come and support it.

It is strange, but still true, that for some time before the 25th of October, Sir Colin Campbell had been every day growing more and more confident in the strength of the position. There were moments, no doubt, when he spoke more distrustfully, but in his report of the 20th of October, sent up to Headquarters, he wrote: 'I think we can hold our own ' against anything that may come against us in day- ' light. I am, however, a little apprehensive about ' the redoubts if seriously attacked during the night;'

---

* The distance from Canrobert's Hill to the camp of the nearest English division of infantry was only about four miles going straight; but we shall see that, from the moment of first giving the alarm to that when an English division could be got down to even the more western part of the plain, some hours elapsed.

and, in a later report, he said, 'I fancy we are now 'very strong as well as secure.'

It could not but be that, when so wary and anxious a soldier as Sir Colin reported the position secure, he would more or less impart his own trustfulness to Headquarters ; and it is not to be wondered at that, when thus assured, Lord Raglan abstained from weakening his scant resources by sending down any further detachments of infantry.

This necessarily communicated to Lord Raglan.

The Turkish redoubts, though capable of supplying useful aid to an army, had no such means of independent self-defence as to warrant the notion of their holding out without support ; and it is evident that, in the absence of infantry, nothing short of a vigilant and brilliant use of the cavalry arm would enable the Turks to withstand a determined attack. I cannot say whether Sir Colin Campbell's sense of security was in any high degree founded upon the cavalry, or whether, for once, he went along with the herd in his estimate of what could be insured by a little upturn of the soil with a few Turks standing behind it.

Uncertainty as to the sources of Campbell's confidence.

A main defect in the arrangements of the Allies was the one under which it resulted that those divisions of infantry on the Chersonese which lay the nearest to the plain below were not the troops of the nation which undertook to defend Balaclava. Bosquet, with two divisions, was so posted on the edge of the Chersonese upland, that, judging from their position alone, his troops might have been naturally looked to as the first to descend into the plain for the defence of Balaclava ; and, besides that General Bosquet was an ardent soldier,

CHAP.
II.

and a man most loyal in action, there is no reason for supposing that mere difference of nationality alone would have made the French slow to come down to the aid of Sir Colin Campbell ; but the fact of the interposed force being under the orders of a commander other than Lord Raglan, made a dangerous break in the chain by which the Allies held together. It was only by persuading General Canrobert to allow it, that the nearest of the battalions on the Chersonese could be made to partake in a battle upon the plain of Balaclava ; and the exceeding scantiness of the infantry force which Lord Raglan had been able to spare for the immediate defence of the place made it a thing of great moment that the promptest possible despatch of reinforcements should not be left dependent upon the result of persuasions addressed to an independent commander, more especially where the commander whose assent thus had to be gained was a man of a hesitating and anxious temperament.

Inherent weakness of the outer line.

Collateral arrangements which tended to increase the probability of a disaster.

Independently of the inherent fault that there was in this outer line of defence, the collateral arrangements were far from being calculated to avert a disaster.

One important omission was this : In all the works constituting this outer line, the Turkish soldiery were left without that strengthening help which might have been afforded them by the presence in each redoubt of one or two Englishmen accustomed to rule Orientals ; and the want was in no way supplied by sending, instead, a non-commissioned officer of artillery.* Then,

---

* In the mere mechanical business of working a gun the Turkish Topdji is likely to be quite as well skilled as an English artilleryman.

again, since the cavalry was much looked to as an arm C H A P.
to ward off for some time any Russian attack, it would _II._
have been well to avoid a severance of authority by
placing under one commander the whole of the forces,
whether horse, or foot, or artillery, which were charged
with the defence of Balaclava; for excellent as was
the understanding between Lord Lucan and Sir Colin
Campbell, their concord was no equivalent for the advantage which belongs to absolute unity of command.

Above all, if the plan of defence were to rest at all
on our cavalry, there was cogent need of an effort to
neutralise in some measure the vice of Lord Hardinge's peace - service appointments, and to make
arrangements for giving more or less of initiative
power in the field to men such as Morris and Elliot,
who were practised in war, and knew by their own
experience what it was to lead squadrons in battle.
No such effort was made.

It was against these defences of Balaclava that Mentschikoff's pur-
Prince Mentschikoff now resolved to direct an attack. pose of
assailing
So early as the night of the 13th of the month, Colo- the defences of
nel Rakovitch, with three battalions, four guns, and a Balaclava.
couple of hundred Cossacks had ventured down from The forces
collected
the Mackenzie Heights; and having been suffered at for this
enterprise.
break of day on the following morning to take pos-

What is wanted for converting a herd of Turks into a formidable body
of warriors is the presence of a resolute man or boy of a higher station
in life, who will undertake to lead them. The singular power that can
be exerted over a Turkish force by a fearless English gentleman is
spoken of, *ante*, vol. II. chap. ii. Notwithstanding all that had been
achieved in the defence of Silistria and on the field of Giurgevo, there
was an entire neglect of the means which there produced such brilliant
results.

CHAP. session of the village of Tchorgoun, he there estab-
 II.   lished the nucleus of a force complete in all arms,
which thenceforth began to gather in the valley of
the Tchernaya. On the 23d, this force had been
definitively constituted as the ' Detachment of Tchor-
' goun,' and placed under the command of General
Liprandi. The force comprised 17 battalions of foot,
30 squadrons of horse,* and 64 guns. But besides the
troops under the orders of Liprandi, there was a distinct force, commanded by General Jabrokritsky, and
comprising some 8 battalions,† 4 squadrons of horse,
and 14 guns, which had orders to co-operate with the
Detachment of Tchorgoun. Altogether, therefore,
the force set apart for the attack upon the defences
of Balaclava comprised 25 battalions, 34 squadrons of
horse, and 78 guns. The numerical strength of the
force is not to be learned with strict accuracy;‡ but
it seems to have amounted to about 25,000 men.§

* 20 squadrons of regular cavalry, and 10 'sotnias' (or, as I call them,
'squadrons') of Cossacks. A 'sotnia' imported about the same number
of horsemen as a 'squadron.' General de Todleben is careful to make
all possible 'deductions from strength,' but he acknowledges that each
squadron and each sotnia had a strength in *effectives* of 100 horsemen,
p. 387.

† Literally, 7 and ⅘ths.

‡ Because, at the period in question, the 'morning states' of the infantry had been left uncorrected since the beginning of the month, and
the 'states' of the cavalry were wanting altogether.—Todleben, p. 388.

§ On the 25th of October 1854 the most recent 'states' of the infantry
strength were those which had been furnished at the beginning of
the month; and these, together with the estimated reckoning of the
cavalry (of which no 'states',had been prepared), give a total of 23,425,
without counting the artillerymen, who (at 30 men for each gun) would
number 2340, making, altogether, 25,725 ; but it is right to say that
General de Todleben (by making a guess at the deductions from strength
which may have occurred since the beginning of the month, and by

For a sound appreciation of the battle of Baláclava, it would be well to know what was the object contemplated by the assailant. His primary design was to seize the outer line of defence and the camp of the 93d Highlanders, as well as the camp of the Turks established near Kadiköi.* It is plain, however, that the enterprise of an assailant who might attain to so much as that would be strangely collapsing if he were to stay his victorious advance without doing all he could to bring ruin upon the English in the small crowded port from which they drew their supplies; and the possession of a spot from which it would have been practicable to shell Balaclava must needs have been coveted. The destruction of the root which the English had taken in Balaclava may therefore, perhaps, be regarded as the real, though ulterior object of the intended attack.

The force destined for the attack upon the Turkish redoubts was divided into three columns. The left column was commanded by General Gribbé, the centre column by General Semiakine, the right column by Colonel Scudery; and, with that last force, General Jabrokritsky's detachment was in close co-operation. Gribbé was to issue from the direction of the Baidar valley, seize the heights of Kamara, and thence take part in the attack directed against Canrobert's Hill. General Semiakine, at the same time, was to advance against Canrobert's Hill, and the Redoubt Number

C H A P.
II.

The object of the contemplated attack.

Distribution of the Russian force into three distinct bodies, and the duties assigned to each.

reducing the estimate of the cavalry strength) cuts down the total effective to 20,500 (p. 388-90). In that estimate, however, he does not, I believe, include the 2340 artillerymen.

* Todleben, p. 384, 387, 388.

CHAP.
II.
Two, by the road which leads from Tchorgoun to Kadiköi.

Colonel Scudery's column was to issue from the Tractir road, across the North Valley, and advance upon the Arabtabia or Redoubt ' Number Three.'

The main body of the cavalry with its attendant batteries was to enter the North Valley, and there form in columns of attack to await Liprandi's next orders.

A battalion of the Ukraine regiment, with a company of riflemen and a battery of field-artillery, was to constitute the reserve.

Finally, General Jabrokritsky, though not under the orders of Liprandi, was to cover the intended attack by descending from the region of Mackenzie's Farm and taking post on the Fedioukine Hills.

Notwithstanding the trust they repose in the direct intervention of Heaven, the Turks know how to eke out their faith by means sufficiently human; and being too warlike a people to be careless of the value of foreknowledge in regard to the designs of the enemy, they see the use of a scout. The officer who had the merit of obtaining, at this time, good, decisive intelligence, was Rustem Pasha, the Turkish Brigadier-General. On the 24th of October, a spy employed by him brought back an account which disclosed Liprandi's designs for the morrow. The man announced that troops to the number of 25,000, and of all arms, were to march upon the plain of Balaclava, and he even prepared his hearers to expect an advance from the direction of Baidar. He was care-

fully examined by Lord Lucan, as well as by Sir Colin
Campbell; and, both Generals coming to the conclu-
sion that this report was well worthy of attention,
'Lord Bingham (his father's aide-de-camp), was sent
by Lord Lucan to Headquarters with a letter from
Sir Colin Campbell conveying the intelligence. Lord
Bingham delivered the letter and the tidings it
conveyed to the Quartermaster-General, but did not
succeed in obtaining an interview with Lord Raglan,
who was then engaged with Canrobert. General
Airey, it is true, interrupted the conference of the two
Commanders, and showed Lord Raglan the letter;
but the answer first elicited was only a message of
acknowledgment sent back in the words, ' Very well!'
Afterwards, Lord Raglan requested that any new
occurrence which might take place should be reported
to him; but no fresh orders resulted from the information thus furnished. The truth is that only
a few days before, Lord Raglan had been induced by
a similar report to send down 1000 men of the 4th
Division, who had to be marched back when it proved
that the enemy was not advancing.* He could ill
afford to exhaust the time and strength of his men in
these marches and countermarches, and he seems to
have come to the conclusion that it would be inexpe-
dient for him to be again despatching reinforcements
to the outer line of defence in the plain of Balaclava,
unless he should learn that the enemy was actually
advancing against it.

CHAP.
II.

The way
in which
the infor-
mation
was dealt
with.

The morn-
ing of the
25th Oct.
Tidings
of the
impending
attack up-
on the
Turkish
redoubts.

* This was on the 21st of October.

CHAPTER III.

CHAP.
III.

25th Oct.
The hour
before
daybreak.

Advance
of Lord
Lucan and
his Staff
in the di-
rection of
Canro-
bert's Hill.

Break of
day. Two
flags seen
flying from
the fort
on Can-
robert's
Hill.

The im-
port of
this.

IN accordance with its daily custom, the English
cavalry on the morning of the 25th of October had
turned out an hour before daybreak; and the men
were standing to their horses when Lord Lucan,
already in the saddle and followed by his Staff,
moved off at a walk towards Canrobert's Hill. Two
of the Divisional Staff—Lord William Paulet, I think,
and Major M'Mahon, who had now, it seems, been
joined by Lord George Paget—were riding some distance in rear of their chief, and had come within
about 300 paces of Canrobert's Hill, when a streak of
pale light in the horizon before them began to disclose the morning. Presently, there was grey enough
to show through the dusk that Canrobert's Hill was
not without its standard; but soon it became almost
clear, and presently afterwards certain, that from
the flag-staff of the work two ensigns were flying.
' Holloa ! ' said one, ' there are two flags flying !
' What does that mean ? ' ' Why, that surely,' said
another,—' that surely is the arranged signal—the
' signal that the enemy is advancing. Are you quite
' sure ? ' The questioner was soon answered; for

scarcely had he spoken when the fort opened fire C H A P.
from one of its 12-pounder guns. The Staff-officers III.
hurried forward to overtake their chief; and Lord Lord
George Paget galloped back at speed to the cavalry George Paget, in
camp, where (in the absence of Lord Cardigan, who the ab-
had the practice of sleeping on board his yacht, and Lord Car-
had not yet come up from Balaclava) he took upon takes up-
himself to mount the Light Brigade. He had hardly to mount
done this when a messenger came in from the front Brigade.
with an order despatched by Lord Lucan (then re- from Lord
connoitring with Sir Colin Campbell in the direction the imme-
of our advanced post) which directed the immediate vance of
advance of the cavalry. the cav-

Thus it seems that the Turks not only obtained the Vigilance
earliest intelligence of the impending attack, but were this occa-
also the first to perceive the advance of the enemy. the Turks.
The elevation of Canrobert's Hill may have aided
their surveys; but without being watchful and sagacious, they could hardly have succeeded in being
beforehand with so keen a soldier as Sir Colin
Campbell.

We watched the sweet slumbers of a Cabinet whilst
assenting to the cogent despatch which enforced this
invasion; but now, in the midst of the campaign, and
at a moment when accounts have come in, which an-
nounce an attack for the morrow in the direction of
the Baidar valley, we may steal before break of day to
the ground where the enemy is expected, and there,
seek our ideal of vigilance in the outlying cavalry
picket.

We shall seek in vain. The English soldier's want

CHAP.
III.

The English soldier's want of vigilance.

of vigilance is so closely allied to some of his greatest qualities (as, for instance, to his pride, and his sullen unwillingness to be put out of his way by mere danger), that our countrymen incline to think of it with indulgence, nay, perhaps, with an unconfessed liking; but if the fault is in some measure natural and characteristic, it has been aggravated apparently by the empty ceremonies of military duty in peace-time; for to go on rehearsing men day after day, and year after year, in the art of giving and taking pretended alarms about nothing, and to carry on these rehearsals by means of formulated sentences, is to do all that perverted industry can towards preventing, instead of securing, the 'bright look-out' of the seaman.

The relation that there is between standing armies and war bears analogy to that which connects endowed churches with religion;* and, in particular, the Anglican arrangements for securing the infant mind against heresy show a curious resemblance to those which are made during peace for preventing surprises in war-time. Whether aiming at the one or the other of these objects, man tries to secure it by formula. Just as through the means of set questions

* I have been justly reminded by Dean Stanley that the practice of arming young creatures with dogma is not at all confined to established churches; and, as now corrected, I agree that, although not furnished by the State, any funds provided for a particular worship in a continuous, chronic way, have a tendency to produce the effect mentioned in the text. It seems that in some of the churches got up by subscription the theology professed by the children is much more bold and violent than that which obtains in our Anglican nurseries. — *Note to 3d Edition.*

and answers, the anxious theologian arms children
against 'false doctrine,' in the trust that, when they
come to riper years, they may know how to treat his
opponents, so also with him who makes rules for the
governance of soldiers in peace-time, the hope, it
seems, is that they may learn to be vigilant against
night surprises by repeatedly saying their catechism.
The common 'challenge' is brief; but, it being fore-
seen that he who is appointed to watch may himself
require watching, the functionaries called 'visiting
'rounds' have been invented whose duty it is to see
that the sentries are at their posts and awake; but
as this task of supervision has itself also lapsed into
form, the result is, that at a military post requiring
great vigilance, there goes on, all night, a reiteration
of set questions and answers, which tends to avert
real watchfulness by suggesting that a mere formal
sign of not being absolutely asleep will sufficiently
answer the purpose. Men trained to 'look out' as
do sailors, are more likely to pierce to the utmost of
what eye and ear can reach, than those who are repeating to one another, and repeating and repeating
all night, set lessons, of which this is one: ' Halt!
' who goes there?' ' Rounds!' ' What rounds?'
' Visiting rounds!' ' Visiting rounds advance! All's
well!' When these words have been reiterated by
the same men a few thousand times, they are as
lulling as the monotone waves that beat and still beat
on the shore. The truth is, that the object of securing
a really keen watchfulness is one which lies out of
the true scope of mechanical arrangements. A man's

CHAP.
III.

wits may be easily deadened, they can hardly be
sharpened, by formula.

The out-
lying
picket.

Far from detecting the earliest signs of an advance
in force, and being at once driven in, our outlying
picket enjoyed its tranquillity to the last, and was
only, indeed, saved from capture, by the ' field officer
' of the day,' who learnt, as he rode, what was passing, and conveyed to the men of the watch—just in
time to secure their escape—that warning of the enemy's approach which they themselves should have given.

The ene-
my's ad-
vance per-
ceived by
Lord
Lucan and
Sir Colin
Campbell.

Lord Lucan and Sir Colin Campbell were together
a good way in advance; and, as day broke, they saw
the enemy's columns of infantry in march—saw them
converging upon the easterly approaches of the
Causeway Heights from the directions of Tchorgoun
and Baidar. It soon became apparent that, whatever
might be his ulterior design, Liprandi's first object
was the seizure of the Turkish defences, beginning

Intelli-
gence sent
off to
Lord
Raglan.

with Canrobert's Hill; and Lord Lucan did not fail
to despatch an aide-de-camp to Headquarters with
intelligence of the impending attack.*

Lord Lu-
can's dis-
position of
the cav-
alry and
horse-
artillery.

Our cavalry was brought forward; and the guns of
Maude's troop of horse-artillery were got into battery
on the right of the Arabtabia or Number Three
Redoubt. The Light Cavalry regiments were placed
in reserve under the southern slopes of the Causeway

Lord
Lucan's
' demon-
'strations'
with his
cavalry.

Heights; and Lord Lucan, then acting in person with
his Heavy Brigade, sought to check the advance of
the enemy by ' demonstrations;' † but—with the full

* Captain Charteris was the officer sent.

† ' Lord Lucan with the Heavy Cavalry moved about, making de-
' monstrations and threatening the enemy.'

approval of Sir Colin Campbell, who indeed seems to
have counselled this policy—he determined to confine himself to threats. His threats failed to deter;
for the Russians pursued their design like men who
had yet found no hindrance; and indeed it seems
probable that the firmness of purpose they soon after
disclosed was in some measure occasioned by the
circumstance of their having detected our cavalry
leader in a determination to threaten without striking.
Since the ground, in most places, was favourable for
the manœuvring of horsemen, with no such obstructions as would prevent them from attempting flank
attacks on the enemy's infantry and artillery, it may
be that a cavalry officer fresh from war-service would
have been able to check Liprandi, and to check him,
again and again, without sustaining grave loss; but
if a man can so wield a body of cavalry as to make
it the means of thus arresting for a time an attack
of infantry and artillery without much committing
his squadrons, he has attained 'to high art' in his
calling; and to expect a peace-service general to'
achieve such a task, is much as though one should
take a house-painter at hazard and bid him portray
a Madonna. There were riding amongst our squadrons men well tried in war—men famed alike for
their valour and their skill as cavalry officers; and
although the perversity of our State authorities
laboured, as it were, to neutralise the unspeakable
value of such experience by putting the men who
possessed it under peace-service generals, yet if
Campbell's command had included that cavalry arm

CHAP.
III.

which formed so large a proportion of the scanty resources, available, at first for defence, it is imaginable that he would have been able to say a few words to some such a man as Morris, which would have had the effect of checking the enemy without bringing grave loss on our squadrons.* Such a result would appear to be the more within reach, when it is remembered that Liprandi's advance was in three columns moving upon ' external lines ' without speedy means of intercommunication, and that Gribbé's column—the one upon which the whole enterprise much depended—comprised only three battalions of infantry.†

The advance of General Gribbé from the direction of Baidar. He seizes Kamara, and establishes a battery, which opens fire at close range on the Redoubt No. L.

The Russians had begun their advance at five o'clock in the morning. Without encountering the least opposition, General Gribbé, moving forward from the direction of the Baidar valley with three battalions, a squadron of horse, and ten pieces of cannon, had been suffered to take possession of the village of Kamara; and when there, he was not only enabled to cover the advance of the assailing forces on their left flank, but also on the high ground above—ground commanding the object of attack—to establish his ten guns in battery, with the purpose of directing their fire, at close range, upon the work crowning Canrobert's Hill.‡

* I refer to Captain Morris (commanding the 17th Lancers) and Lieutenant Alexander Elliot (aide-de-camp to General Scarlett) merely as the two war-service officers of cavalry then in the Crimea whose names first occur to me. They were both of them men who had earned fame in honest war.

† See, in the Appendix, Lord Lucan's view as to this.

‡ This battery included, besides six light field-pieces of the No. 6

THE BATTLE OF BALACLAVA.   53

Nearly at the same time, Semiakine's forces having
advanced from Tchorgoun gained the slopes of the
ridge on the north-east and north of Canrobert's Hill.
With five battalions (besides a separate body of riflemen) and ten guns, General Semiakine in person
prepared to operate against the work on Canrobert's
Hill * ; whilst, on his right, General Levoutsky took
up a like position with three more battalions and ten
guns.† His goal was the Redoubt Number Two.

At the same time Colonel Scudery, who with the
four Odessa battalions, a company of riflemen, three
squadrons of Cossacks, and a field-battery, had advanced from the Tractir bridge, was now moving
upon the Arabtabia.‡

The main body of the cavalry under General Ryjoff,
with its attendant troops of horse-artillery, was already in the North Valley, and supporting the advance
of the columns.

Whilst the Russians were marching upon the
heights which they now occupied, and whilst they
were there establishing their thirty guns in battery,

CHAP.
III.

Advance
of the cen-
tral col-
umn under
General
Semiakine:

Of Levout-
sky's
force:

Of Colonel
Scudery's
column:

Of the
Russian
cavalry,
and the
batteries
it escort-
ed.

The emer-
gency in
which
Lord Lu-
can had to
act.

Light Battery, four guns of heavier calibre belonging to the Position
Battery No. 4 (Liprandi's despatch, October 26, 1854). The three bat-
talions were the 1st, 2d, and 3d battalions of the Dnieper regiment.
The squadron was one belonging to Jeropkine's Lancers.
* With four battalions of the Azoff regiment, one—viz., the 4th—
of the Dnieper battalions, the 2d company of the Rifle battalion,
four heavy guns of the Position Battery No. 4, and six pieces of the
Light Battery No. 6.
† The three Ukraine battalions, four heavy guns of the Position
Battery No. 4, and six guns of the Light Battery No. 7.
‡ On Redoubt 'Number Three.' The riflemen forming part of Scud-
ery's column were of the 4th Rifle battalion, the Cossacks of the 53d
Cossack Regiment, and the battery was No. 7 of the 12th brigade.

C H A P. Lord Lucan, as we see, was present with a superb
   III.   division of cavalry, and this upon fine ground, which,
though hilly, was very free from obstructions; but
except his six light pieces of horse-artillery, he was
wanting in the ordnance arm, and of infantry forces
he had none. Thus, then, by a somewhat rare concurrence of circumstances, there was brought about
an emergency which enforced, and enforced most
cogently, the decision of a question involving more
or less the general usefulness of the cavalry arm.

Some are chary, it seems, of acknowledging a condition of things·in which cavalry can be used for the repression of the ordnance arm. Others fully agreeing
that a body of horse, with its great extent of vulnerable
surface, must beware of coming, or at all events of
remaining, under the fire of artillery, are yet of opinion
that cavalry, after all, is the very arm which, in many
contingencies, can best be exerted against the power
of ordnance. They say that artillery in march, or
engaged in unlimbering, is good prey for horsemen;
that artillery established in battery is assailable by
horsemen at its flanks; and that, in general, where the
country is at all open, a powerful and well-handled
cavalry ought to be able to challenge the dominion of
artillery by harassing it incessantly, by preventing
it from getting into battery, and, failing that, by dis-
quieting its batteries when formed.

His deci-   The decision of Lord Lucan was much governed
sion.   by a sense of the great need there would be for the
aid of our cavalry if the enemy, after carrying all
the outer defences, should come on and attack Bala-

clava ; * but it would also seem that his determina- C H A P.
III.
tion—a determination entirely approved, and even,
I hear, originated by Sir Colin Campbell—involved a
leaning to the first of the two opinions above indicated.

Be this as it may, the result was that, without *The Rus-
being met by any hindrance on the part of our cav- *siaus were*
alry, the Russians were suffered to advance from three *their bat-*
points of the compass and converge upon the chain of *against*
little redoubts which extended from Canrobert's Hill *bert's Hill*
to the Arabtabia. The thousand or twelve hundred *No. 2*
Turks who manned the three works thus assailed saw *Redoubt.*
converging upon them some eleven thousand infantry
and thirty-eight guns. Upon the heights of Kamara,
which overlooked Canrobert's Hill from the east, and
upon the part of the Causeway Heights which overlooked the same work from the north, the enemy placed
thirty guns in battery ; and he now opened fire upon
the work crowning Canrobert's Hill, as also upon the
Fort Number Two. He was answered by the Turks *Fire an-*
with their five 12-pounders ; † and, for a while, by our *by the*
troop of horse-artillery, but apparently with little *(without*
effect. Captain Maude, the officer commanding the *much*
troop, was horribly wounded by a shell which entered *our troop*
the body of his horse and there burst. *artillery.*

Maude's troop had come into action without a due *Captain*
following of waggons ; and, before long, its ammuni- *wounded.*
tion was already so nearly exhausted as to leave but
a small supply for even one gun.

* See Lord Lucan's statement in the Appendix.
† Three on Canrobert's Hill, and a couple on the Number Two
Redoubt.

CHAP.
III.
The troop
of horse-
artillery
sent out of
fire by
Lord
Lucan.

The fort
on Canro-
bert's Hill
silenced
by over-
whelming
fire.

Continued
resistance
of the
Turks.

Disposi-
tions made
by General
Semiakine
for storm-
ing Can-
robert's
Hill.

As soon as Lord Lucan heard this, he ordered that the troop should be withdrawn and kept out of fire until the want could be supplied.*

It was hardly to be expected that under the fire of thirty guns, including eight pieces of heavy calibre, the three 12 - pounders which formed the armament of Canrobert's Hill would long remain undisabled. The fort became silent, and already the hapless battalion which manned it must have undergone heavy slaughter; but notwithstanding this, and although it became now apparent that the hill was to be attacked by largely outnumbering bodies of infantry, the brave Turks were still unconquered. They moved, indeed, from the unsheltered part of the work to the side where more cover was offered; but there they stood fast and awaited the attack of the infantry.†

It was with the five battalions acting under his personal direction that General Semiakine determined to storm Canrobert's Hill. Covered by the fire of the artillery, and by two companies of riflemen, pushed forward in skirmishing order, he advanced rapidly with three battalions of the Azoff regiment, disposed in columns of company, and so ranged in two lines of columns as that the first line was only about 100 paces in advance of the second. In a third line, General Semiakine brought up the 1st battalion of the Azoff regiment and the 4th of the Dnieper battal-

* Ibid. Maude's severe wound was the reason why Lord Lucan instituted no inquiry as to the cause which led to this want of ammunition.
† This sketch may help to illustrate the attack of the eleven bat-

ions, each formed in a 'column of attack.' Advanc- C H A P.
ing in this order, he approached to within about 100 <u>III.</u>
paces of the hill-top, and at once gave the signal for The work
'the assault. Then the two foremost lines of columns, stormed.
led by Colonel Krudener, the commander of the Azoff
regiment, and supported by the two columns of attack,
moved rapidly forward. Encountering no fire of cannon to check them, the foremost of these troops con-
verged from their extended front upon the small object of their attack, swarmed in across the ditch,
swarmed over the feeble parapet, and, standing at
length within the fort, closed at once with the remnant
of the single battalion there bravely awaiting the on- Over-
slaught. The force which thus stormed the work, and whelming
strength
which threw itself upon the remnant of the one Turk- of the
Russians
ish battalion, consisted, as we see, of five battalions; in point of
numbers.

talions, with thirty guns, upon the two little works, No. 1 and No. 2,
which were defended by about 1000 or 1200 Turks with five guns.

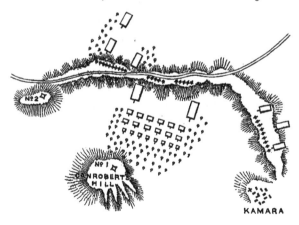

KAMARA

CHAP. but on the side of Kamara, the three other Dnieper
III.   battalions were so operating that Sir Colin Campbell
regarded them as actual partakers in the attack; and,
moreover, Levoutsky's three Ukraine battalions, though ·
not engaged in the storming, were still so placed at
the time as to be aiding the assault by their presence.
Upon the whole, therefore, it may be said that, after
having undergone an overwhelming cross-fire from the
thirty pieces of artillery, which hurled destruction
upon them at ·close range from commanding heights,
the one battalion of Turks which defended this feeble
breastwork, was now pressed by a number of battalions amounting to no less than eleven, and engaged
in close conflict with five.

Close
fighting
between
the Turks
and the
Russians.

It commonly happens in modern warfare that the
dominion of one body of infantry over another is
not found to depend, at the last, upon the physical
strength of man, or the quality of his weapons, but
rather upon faith, or, in other words, upon sense
of power.   In this instance, however, the assailants
and the assailed were both so resolute that, for once,
the actual clash of arms was not to be averted
by opinion.   The many flooded in upon the few,
overwhelming, surrounding, destroying, yet still confronted with heroic desperation, and owing all the
way they could make to the sheer fighting of the
men, who thus closed with their Mussulman foe, and

The fort
at length
carried.

to the weight of the numbers behind them.   With
much slaughter of the devoted Turks—who lost, in
killed only, no less than 170 out of perhaps about
five or six hundred men—the work was carried at

half-past seven o'clock, with its standard and its guns; but it seems that, before moving out, the English artilleryman who had been placed in the ▸redoubt to assist the Turks took care to spike the guns which had armed it. The colour of the Azoff regiment now floated from the summit of Canrobert's Hill.

When the Turks in the three next redoubts saw how it had fared with their brethren on Canrobert's Hill, and perceived that, under the eyes of some 1500 English horse, the work was left to fall into the enemy's hands without a squadron being launched to support it by any attack on the foe, they had what to them would seem reason for thinking ill things of the Christians, and were not without warrant for judging that the English would fail to support them in any endeavour they might make to defend the remaining forts. But whether these Osmanlis reasoned, or whether they simply caught fear, as people catch plague, by contagion, they at all events loosed their hold.* Without waiting for a conflict with the three Ukraine battalions, then already advancing to the assault, or the four Odessa battalions, then also advancing, they at once began to make off, taking with them their quilts and the rest of their simple camp treasures. Coming west with these burthens upon them, they looked more like a tribe in a state of migration than troops engaged in retreat. In their flight they were followed for a while by the fire of

Abandon-
ment by
the Turks
of the
three next
redoubts.

Their
flight un-
der fire of
artillery,
and pur-
sued in

---

* In those redoubts, as in the Number One, the English artilleryman present in each is said to have spiked the guns.

CHAP.
III.

some
places by
Cossacks.

The ene-
my enter-
ing four of
the re-
doubts
and estab-
lishing
himself in
three of
them.

the Russian artillery; and although Lord Lucan sought to cover their retreat with his cavalry, the Cossacks, at some points, pursued, and were able to spear many of the fugitives.* Rustem Pasha had a horse shot under him.

The enemy not only established a portion of his forces on Canrobert's Hill, but likewise in the Number Two Redoubt, as well as in the Arabtabia or Number Three; and he took possession of the seven iron 12-pounder guns with which the three works had been armed. He also, with the Odessa battalions, marched into the Redoubt Number Four; but instead of undertaking to hold the work, he did what he could to raze and dismantle it. He then withdrew, because he deemed the position too far in advance to allow of his undertaking to hold it.

Our cavalry now became exposed to some musketry shots which were successfully directed against it from the positions of the lost redoubts; and, as it was also apparent that our horsemen were in the line of the fire which the gunners along our inner line of defence might soon have occasion to open, Lord Lucan, in accordance with an arrangement to that effect which had been preconcerted with Sir Colin Campbell, withdrew his division to a part of the South Valley which was between the Number Four and the Number Five Redoubts. The position he then took up was across

* Captain Tatham, R.N., the senior naval officer in the harbour of Balaclava, chanced to come up at this time, and although he knew no Turkish, he yet by his peculiarly cheery voice and gesture was able to rally the fugitives who most nearly approached him, and cause them to align with their brethren on the right of the 93d.—*Note to 2d Edition.*

the valley, his squadrons facing eastward. He was so placed as to be able to take in flank any enemy's force which might bend away from the valley and endeavour to pass to the south, with intent to assail Balaclava.

CHAP.
III.

Fresh dis-
position
of our cav-
alry.

Such, then, was the first period of the battle of Balaclava; and it must be acknowledged that the engagement, if it had closed at this time, would have furnished a distressing page for the military history of England. War often demands bitter sacrifices, and may sometimes force men to repress—not only their generous impulses, but—even those appeals of the conscience which a too fiery soldier might treat as the absolute dictates of honour. It may therefore well be that Lord Lucan performed a stern duty, when (with the sanction of Sir Colin Campbell) he determined that our cavalry must be patient of the attack directed against Canrobert's Hill, must endure to see English guns captured, must suffer our allies to be slaughtered without striking a blow to defend them; and the soundness of his conclusion can hardly be determined by the casuists, but rather by those who know something of the conditions in which the power of the cavalry arm (when cavalry chances to be the only available force) can be wisely, and therefore rightly, exerted.*

If our people in general had known the truth, they would have been guilty of unspeakable meanness

* The opinion of our cavalry, so far as I have been able to observe it, tends to sanction Lord Lucan's decision.

CHAP.   when they cast off all blame from themselves, and
III.   laid it upon the Turkish soldiery—upon men who
had been not only entrusted to the honour and friendship of our army, but were actually engaged at a
post of danger in defending the first approaches to
the English port of supply.*

The truth is, however, that the great bulk of our
army (including Lord Raglan himself) had regarded
the work on Canrobert's Hill as a fastness susceptible
of a protracted defence ; and—strange as the statement
may seem—were, for a long time, unacquainted with
the nature of the conflict there sustained by the brave
Turkish soldiery.   Several causes contributed to obscure the truth.   In the first place, the defence of
the work, though carried to extremity, was still of
necessity brief ; for when once the men, numbered
by thousands, had swarmed in over a feeble parapet
on the top of an isolated hillock which was held by
only some 500 or 600 men, the end, of course, could
not be distant ; and although there were numbers of
our cavalry men who had been so posted as to be able
to see that the Turks stood their ground with desperation, and were in close bodily strife with the enemy
before they gave way under his overwhelming numbers, yet to the great bulk of the spectators, whether
English or French, who gazed from the steeps of the

* Lord Lucan was never one of those who thus spoke. He could see
the nature of the conflict on Canrobert's Hill, and I believe he has
always spoken generously of the firmness with which the Turks awaited
the onslaught of overpowering numbers. Sir Colin Campbell was also
a spectator ; and he says in his despatch,—'The Turkish troops in
' No. 1 persisted as long as they could, and then retired.'

Chersonese, no such spectacle was presented. They CHAP. looked from the west; and, the attack being made upon III. the north-eastern acclivity of Canrobert's Hill, they saw nothing of the actual clash that occurred between the brave few and the resolute many. They descried the enemy on the heights of Kamara and on the line of the Woronzoff road, but lost sight of him when from that last position he had descended into the hollow to make his final assault; and soon afterwards, without having been able to make out what had passed in the interval, they saw the Turkish soldiery beginning to stream down from the gorge of the work. Then almost immediately they saw the red fezzes pouring out from the other redoubts, so that what they observed on the whole was a general flight of the Turks. They saw nothing of the fierce though short strife which ended in the slaughter of 170 out of the 500 or 600 men on Canrobert's Hill; and I believe it may be said that the loss sustained by the devoted garrison of this little field-work long remained unknown to the English. Considering that the Turkish soldiery died fighting in defence of the English lines, this may seem very strange and unnatural; but the truth is, that between the soldiers of the Prophet and the men of our Army List there was so great a gulf that it proved much more than broad enough to obstruct the transmission of military statistics. The man temporal who would ask for a 'Morning State,' with its column after column of figures, is baffled, of course, by the man spiritual, who replies, that by the blessing of the Almighty his servants are as the

CHAP.
III.

leaves of the forest; and soon ceases to apply for a list of 'casualties' if he only elicits an answer asserting the goodness of God and an indefinite accession of believers to the promised gardens of Paradise.* Certainly, Lord Raglan remained long unacquainted with the nature of the defence which the Turks had opposed to the enemy on Canrobert's Hill.† It was from ignorance of the bare facts, and not from dishonest or ungenerous motives, that our people threw blame on the Turkish soldiery.

---

* I find in the correspondence between the French and English Headquarters some trace of an attempt on the part of one of the hapless Turkish commanders to have justice done to his people ; but probably the remonstrant did not know how to state a fact in such way as to obtain for it any real access to the European mind, for it does not appear that he succeeded in conveying any clear idea to the mind of General Canrobert.

† This is shown very clearly by the tenor of his correspondence. Any one who ever had means of judging of Lord Raglan's nature must be able to imagine the eagerness with which, upon learning the truth, he would have hastened to redress the wrong done.

CHAPTER IV.

ALL this while, the French and the English Com- CHAP.
manders on the Chersonese had been too distant from $\underbrace{\text{IV.}}$
the scene of the attack against the Turkish redoubts
to be able to sway the result; but they, each of them,
proceeded to make arrangements for ulterior operations.

Upon being apprised of the impending attack, *The spot on which*
Lord Raglan had at once ridden up to that part *Lord Rag-*
of the ridge which best overlooked the scene of *lan placed himself*
the then commencing engagement;* and as soon as *upon being apprised*
his sure, rapid glance had enabled him to apprehend *of the attack.*
the probable scope and purport of his assailant's design, he determined to move down two out of his five *His dis-*
infantry divisions for the defence of Balaclava. The *positions for the*
1st Division, under the Duke of Cambridge, and *succour of Balaclava,*
the 4th Division, under General Cathcart, were ac- *and for securing*
cordingly despatched upon this service. *the forces on the*
Cherso-
† The order to the Duke of Cambridge was in substance *nese against a*
apparently to descend into the south valley by a line some *surprise.*

---

* The spot he occupied was one close to the Col, on the north side
of the road. Thence he witnessed the capture of the work on Canrobert's Hill, and the flight of the Turks from the other redoubts.—
Note to 3d Edition.

† This new interpolation is too long for a 'footnote,' and therefore

CHAP.
IV.
way to the right of the Woronzoff road; and at all events,
Lord Raglan was well satisfied with the way in which
H.R.H. obeyed the command.

With respect to Cathcart, it was otherwise, and a detailed
statement is necessary. On observing the flight of the
Turks, Lord Raglan at once called to him a staff-officer, and
desired him to proceed as quickly as possible to Sir George
Cathcart, and to request him to move his Division immediately to the assistance of Sir Colin Campbell.* The
officer was just starting, when General Airey came up to
him and said, 'Remember you are on no account whatever
' to conduct the 4th Division by the Woronzoff road. He
' said this with marked emphasis.' The officer then galloped
as fast as he could to the 4th Division camp, and found Sir
George Cathcart dressed and seated in his tent. Then
followed this colloquy :—

STAFF-OFFICER.—Lord Raglan requests you, Sir George,
to move your Division immediately to the assistance of the
Turks.

CATHCART.—Quite impossible, sir, for the 4th Division to
move.

STAFF-OFFICER.—My orders were very positive, and the
Russians are advancing upon Balaclava.

stands printed above; but being in a separate type, it cannot of course
be confounded with the "text" of the former editions, which I am still
anxious to leave unaltered. The same remark applies to the interpolation made at p. 219.—*Note to 3d Edition.*

* There was, I think, some ambiguity in this order, for it might
either mean that the 4th Division was to make straight for the immediate
front of Balaclava, or for that part of Sir Colin's ground from which
the Turks had just fled; but the very able staff-officer intrusted with
the mission had no doubt that the first of these objects was the one
meant, and as a circumstance favouring that view it should be borne in
mind that Balaclava was then in danger of an attack from the east as
well as from the north. My impression is, that the second of the two
objects was the one contemplated by Lord Raglan; but even on that
supposition—for recourse to the Woronzoff road was strictly and rightly
prohibited—the route by the Col (which was practicable for artillery)
was probably the best that could be taken by a force marching from
Cathcart's camp.

CATHCART.—I can't help that, sir. It is impossible for
my Division to move, as the greater portion of the men have only just come from the trenches. The best thing you can do is to sit down and take some breakfast with me.

STAFF-OFFICER (after respectfully declining the invitation).—My orders are to request that you will move your Division immediately to the assistance of Sir Colin Campbell. I feel sure every moment is of consequence. Sir Colin Campbell has only the 93d Highlanders with him. I saw the Turks in full flight from the redoubts.

CATHCART.—Well, sir, if you will not sit down in my tent, you may as well go back to Lord Raglan, and tell him that I cannot move my Division.

The staff-officer touched his cap, left the tent, and rode off a few yards, considering how he could best act. After a few moments' consideration, he saw all the terrible consequences that might result from his yielding to Cathcart. His mind was soon made up. He returned to Sir George Cathcart, and at once told him that he (the staff-officer) should not return to Lord Raglan; that he had received orders to come for the 4th Division, and that he should remain till it was ready to move off. He pointed out firmly but respectfully that much valuable time had been lost, and said he still hoped that Sir George would give orders for the Division to fall in. Sir George listened attentively to all the staff-officer urged, and then to his great relief said, 'Very well, sir; I will consult with my staff-officers, and see 'if anything can be done.' Cathcart then went away, and in a short time some bugles sounded, and the Division began to turn out. Under the guidance of the staff-officers (who considered that Kadiköi was the point to make for), the Division marched off to the Col.*

Lord Raglan, however, was not without suspicion that the operations in the plain of Balaclava might be

* Circumstances indicative of Cathcart's state of temper, and in some measure tending to account for it, will be found narrated in Vol. V. of the 'Invasion of the Crimea.'

C H A P.
IV.

a feint, and that the real attack might be made from Sebastopol upon the besieging forces. He took care to make provision for such a contingency; and his oral directions for the purpose were conveyed by Captain Calthorpe, one of his aides-de-camp, to Sir Richard England, the Commander of the 3d Division.

General Canrobert also on the ridge. His dispositions.

General Canrobert, also, upon hearing of the attack galloped up to the ridge overlooking the Balaclava plain; and ultimately, though not all at once, the French Commander moved down to the foot of the heights both Vinoy's and Espinasse's brigades of infantry, and also the two cavalry regiments of the Chasseurs d'Afrique, regiments comprising eight squadrons, and commanded by General d'Allonville.

Apparent difference of opinion between the French and the English Commanders.

There was, however, an evident difference between the opinion which governed the English Commander and the one entertained by Canrobert. Keenly alive, as was natural, to a danger which threatened his only seaport, and hoping besides, I imagine, that the somewhat dimmed prospects of the siege might be cleared by a fight in the plain, Lord Raglan, at this time, had not entertained the idea of surrendering ground to the enemy, and was preparing to recover the heights. General Canrobert, on the other hand, was of course less directly concerned in keeping watch over Balaclava; and having become impressed with a belief that it was the object of the Russians to draw him down from his vantage-ground on the Chersonese, he seems to have resolved that he would baffle the enemy's supposed policy by clinging fast to the upland. Accordingly, it will be seen (if we chance to

speak further of these French infantry reinforce- CHAP.
ments), that though Vinoy's brigade pushed for- ⌣IV.⌣
ward, at one time, to ground near the gorge of
Kadiköi, it was afterwards withdrawn from its advanced position, and ordered to rejoin the other
brigade of the 1st Division close under the steeps of
the Chersonese.

As a means of covering Balaclava, the position The new
taken up by Lord Lucan near the gorge of Kadiköi tion which
is believed to have been very well chosen; but the lan made
Commander-in-Chief, at this time, was indulging the cavalry
expectation of something like a battle to be fought division.
with all arms; and he apparently desired that his
cavalry should not be entangled in combat until the
arrival of the two divisions of foot, then already despatched, should give Lord Lucan an opportunity of
acting in co-operation with our infantry forces. He
accordingly sent down an order which compelled Lord
Lucan, though not without reluctance, nor even, indeed, without anger, to withdraw his horsemen to
ground on the left of the Redoubt Number Six at the
foot of the Chersonese upland.*

When this retrograde movement of our cavalry had Approach-
been completed, the whole of the forces of all arms with centration
which Canrobert and Lord Raglan proposed to engage west of
Liprandi might be regarded as approaching to a state way
of concentration near the westernmost limits of the forces with

* Captain Wetherall was the bearer of the order, which ran thus:
'Cavalry to take ground to the left of second line of redoubts occu-
' pied by Turks;' and the Captain, at Lord Lucan's request, waited to
see the order executed in the way which he judged to be accordant
with Lord Raglan's meaning.

CHAP.
IV.
which the
Allies pro-
posed to
engage
Liprandi.

plain. The ground, however, upon which the Allies were thus gathering lay at distances of not less than a mile from the gorge of Kadiköi; and it not only resulted, from the last disposition of the cavalry, that the small body under Sir Colin Campbell which defended the approach to Balaclava was left for the moment uncovered, but that (by reason of the period required for the transmission of a fresh order, and for

Isolation
of Bala-
clava.

countermarching our squadrons) this state of isolation might continue some time, in despite of all Lord Raglan could do.

Position of
Liprandi's
infantry at
this time.

On the other hand, the position of Liprandi was this: With his victorious infantry and artillery disposed near the captured redoubts, he occupied a slightly curved line, which began at Kamara, and extended thence westward by Canrobert's Hill and the Causeway Heights, till it reached a point somewhat in advance of the Arabtabia.

The Odes-
sa regi-
ment be-
came the
index of
the ene-
my's
changing
resolves.

The four Odessa battalions, posted near this Arabtabia or Number Three Redoubt, marked the limit of the venture which the Russian Commander was assigning to his infantry in the direction of the Allied camps. Indeed we shall see that this Odessa regiment, for the rest of the day, was a faithful and sensitive index of the enemy's intent, mounting guard over the site of the Arabtabia, so long as the Allies were yet distant, falling back when our cavalry seemed going to attack it, and countermarching at once to the old ground when Liprandi saw that the French and the English Commanders were inclined to acquiesce in his conquest.

The Russian cavalry, supported by its attendant batteries, was drawn up across the North Valley, with its left resting on the lowest slopes of the Causeway Heights, and its right on the Fedioukine Hills.

Position of the Russian cavalry.

Nor was Liprandi's little army the only force with which the Allies would now have to cope, for Jabrokritsky, having descended from the Mackenzie Heights, was debouching from the Tractir road, and preparing to take up a position on the slopes of the Fedioukine Hills.

Jabrokritsky's force.

These Russian forces had no pretension to match themselves against the troops which the Allies on the Chersonese could, sooner or later, send down for the relief of Balaclava; but, on the other hand, it was certain that a long time must elapse before the infantry despatched from the upland could be brought into action against the assailants of Balaclava; and the configuration of the ground was such, that every French or English battalion engaged in its descent from the Chersonese could be, all the while, seen by the enemy. Liprandi, therefore, could act at his ease; and it was for no trifling space of time that this privileged security lasted. He perhaps under-reckoned the probable duration of the licence which he thus might enjoy; but the actual result was, that from the seizure of Canrobert's Hill to the moment when the Allies were ready to come into action, there elapsed a period of some three hours.*

All these Russian forces secure for the time against the attack of infantry.

The period of licence thus enjoyed by Liprandi.

* Canrobert's Hill is stated to have been taken at 7.30, and it was half-past ten before the Allies had any of their infantry reinforcements so far in advance as to be ready to undertake an attack.

CHAP. IV.   So, although the moment might come when, by the nearer approach of the Allies marching down from the upland, Liprandi would be reduced to the defensive, or else compelled to retire, yet, for the time, the Russian General was not only secure against the contingency of being attacked by infantry, but also had such prey within reach as might tempt him to become the assailant.

The forces now threatening Balaclava.   The arrival of Jabrokritsky, now debouching from Tractir, entitled Liprandi to consider that troops which had come thus near were a present accession of strength; and, taken altogether, the Russian troops actually under Liprandi, or near enough now to co-operate with him, were a force complete in all arms, and numbering, as we saw, some 25,000 men with 78 guns. Yet (now that our cavalry had been withdrawn to the foot of the Chersonese), the only field force with which Sir Colin Campbell stood ready to oppose all these Russian troops in front of Kadiköi was a single battery of field-pieces, 400 men of the 93d Highlanders, commanded by Colonel Ainslie,* 100 invalids under Colonel Daveney, who had been sent down to Balaclava for embarkation; and, besides, two battalions of Turks, not hitherto carried away by the ebb of the Mussulman people.

Their strength.

The forces that could be forthwith opposed to them.

* Only six companies of the regiment were at first available for this service in front of Kadiköi ; the two remaining companies of the battalion being on duty, under the command of Major Gordon, in the inner line of defence. Major Gordon, however, with the force under his orders, rejoined the main body of the battalion before the moment of its encounter with the Russian cavalry.

Liprandi did not seize the occasion.　He, perhaps, had failed to divine the extreme weakness of the little gathering which undertook to defend the gorge of Kadiköi; but, be that as it may, he attempted no attack with his infantry upon the approaches of Balaclava.　For a long time, he remained in a state of inaction; but at length when his period of licence was approaching its close, he resorted to that singular venture with his cavalry of which we shall now have to speak.

CHAP
IV.

Liprandi's determination to abstain from seizing the occasion.

His plan of trying a venture with his cavalry.

CHAPTER V.

CHAP.
V.

The de-
sign with
which this
was re-
sorted to.

SOME of our countrymen have imagined that this enterprise of Liprandi's cavalry was a real attempt on the part of the enemy to possess himself of Balaclava ; but the Russians declare that the object really contemplated was only that of ruining a park of artillery believed to be near Kadiköi ;* and, judging from the apparently hesitating nature of the movement, as well as from the fact of its having had no support from the infantry, there would seem to be ground for believing that some minor purpose of the kind indicated by the Russians was the one really entertained. The Russian cavalry had been brought into discredit by submitting to be null at the battle of the Alma ; and it seems not unlikely that expiation of former shortcomings may have been one of the objects in view.

The ad-
vance
of the
Russian
cavalry.

Be this as it may, General Ryjoff with the main body of the Russian cavalry, and supported by field-batteries, began to move up the north Valley.†

* Todleben.
† With respect to the numerical strength of this great body of cavalry, see *post*, p. 76. According to General Todleben, it comprised 2300 horsemen, being fourteen squadrons of hussars and nine sotnias of Cossack, p. 387, 393-94.

The 93d Highlanders, now augmented to a strength of about 550 by the accession of the two companies under Gordon, were drawn up in line, two deep, upon that rising ground in front of the village of Kadiköi which was afterwards called the 'Dunrobin' or 'Sutherland' Hillock. Tower of the Coldstream, and Verschoyle,* another young officer of the Guards, chancing to be in Balaclava this morning with some thirty or forty men, had seized the occasion for showing the warlike qualities of energy, high spirit, and prompt judgment; for they gathered their people together, brought them up to the front, ranged them quickly along with the Highlanders, and in this way brought Campbell a small accession of strength to eke out his scant means of defence.† The hundred invalids, under Colonel Daveney, were drawn up on the left of the 93d.‡ On either flank of the scanty body of British infantry thus posted, there stood a battalion of Turks.§ Campbell's means of defence were materially aided by Barker's field-pieces, already in battery upon convenient ground near the hillock, as well as by a portion of the batteries constituting the inner line of defence, and especially, it seems, by

CHAP. V.

Campbell's arrangements for defending the approach by Kadiköi.

* Hamilton, I hear, was one of the officers who took part in this volunteered service.—*Note to 2d Edition.*

† I am indebted solely to Colonel (now Sir Anthony) Sterling's very valuable MS. letters for the knowledge of the service thus rendered.

‡ Campbell's despatch says the invalids were drawn up ' in support ;' but I have reason for thinking that the statement in the text is accurate.

§ This account of the disposition made by Sir Colin Campbell may seem to differ in some minute particulars from his published despatch ; but there are matters on which the testimony of a subordinate officer is more conclusive than the report of his chief.

CHAP.
V.
a battery of two heavy guns under the command of
Lieutenant Wolf of the Royal Artillery.*

Campbell
withdrew
his men to
the foot of
the hil-
lock, and
caused
them to
lie down.
The advance of the Russians soon brought their
artillery to a ground within rage of Campbell's small
force; and, two of the Highlanders, besides some of
the Turks, being wounded by the fire then opened,
Campbell sought to give his men shelter. He therefore moved them back to the foot of the hillock which
their ranks had hitherto crowned, and caused them
there to lie down. Preparing for such en eventuality
as that of the gorge being forced, he despatched
Colonel Sterling to Balaclava with orders to apprise
the commander of the frigate† which lay in the harbour of the pending attack.

Detached
body of
Russian
horse ad-
vancing
towards
the gorge
of Kadi-
köi.
Camp-
bell's sol-
diers again
crown the
hillock.
Meanwhile the Russian cavalry continued to
advance up the North Valley; but four squadrons
detached themselves from the mass, and came shap-
ing their way for the gorge of Kadiköi—the ground
Campbell stood to defend.‡ When these horsemen
were within about a thousand yards of him, Campbell
gave a brisk order to his little body of foot, directing
them at once to advance, and again crown the top of
the hillock. This was done at the instant by the

* If the battery doing this service formed part of the 'inner line of
'defence,' it must have been one manned by the Royal Marine Artillery.
—*Note to 2d Edition.*

† So ordered by Campbell, but the Wasp was a corvette. As to the
ships at this time in the harbour, see Note X. of Appendix.—*Note to
2d Edition.*

‡ According to Todleben, the force must have been vastly more than
400 strong—consisting, he says, of nine squadrons, partly belonging to
the regiment called the 'Saxe-Weimar' Hussars, and partly made up
of Cossacks; but I accept Campbell's estimate of the force, and he puts
it at 400.

Highland battalion and the few score of English sol- C H A P.
diers who had come up to range alongside it. The
troops did not throw themselves into a hollow square
(as is usual in preparing for cavalry), but simply
formed line two deep. On this slender array all was
destined to rest; for the two battalions of Turks
which had hitherto flanked the Queen's troops were
by this time without cohesion. It would seem that
the disintegration of the Mussulman force had begun
at the moment when Campbell withdrew his line
to the foot of the hillock, and was completed, some
few instants later, upon the evident approach of the
Russian cavalry. At all events, these two battalions
of Turks were now dissolved or dissolving. For the
most part, both officers and men turned and fled, Flight of
making straight as they could for the port, and they the Turks.
cried, as they went, Ship! ship! ship!

By this defection in presence of the enemy's ad- Position of
vancing cavalry, Campbell was suddenly shorn of after the
two-thirds of the numerical strength engaged in the Turks.
defending the gorge; and the few hundred British
soldiers who had hitherto constituted but a fraction
of his force were now almost all that remained to
him upon the hillock in front of Kadiköi.* Whilst
he waited the movements of an enemy who was
altogether some 25,000 strong, he could not help
seeing how much was now made to depend upon

* I say *almost*, because there were men among the Turks who manfully stood their ground. It would be a great error to question the
courage of the fugitives. The one bane of the Turkish forces is the
want of officers to whom the men can look up. Without that ingredi-
ent cohesion is apt to fail, however brave men may be.

CHAP. V.

His determination to impart to the 93d the gravity of the occasion.

His words to the men.

Their answer to his appeal.

Continued advance of the four Russian squadrons.

the steadfastness of the few hundred men who remained with him still on the hillock. He had, however, so great a confidence in his Highlanders that he judged he could safely impart to them the gravity of the occasion. He rode down the line, and said : 'Remember there is' no retreat from here, 'men ! You must die where you stand !'* The men cheerily answered his appeal saying, 'Ay, ay, 'Sir Colin ; we'll do that.'†

It was whilst our men were still lying on their faces at the foot of the hillock that the four Russian squadrons began their advance ; and it is said that the mission of this detached force was to try to seize one of the batteries connected with the inner line of defence. The horsemen, it seems, rode on, not expecting a combat with infantry ; when suddenly they saw the slender line of the Highlanders springing up to the top of the hillock. Not unnaturally the Russian horsemen imagined that they were falling into some ambush ;‡ and on the other hand, the men of the 93d, with a wild impetuosity which was characteristic of the battalion as then constituted, showed a mind to rush forward as though undertaking to charge and exterminate cavalry in the open plain ; but in a

Campbell wielding his 93d.

moment Sir Colin was heard crying fiercely, 'Ninety-third ! Ninety-third ! damn all that eagerness !' and the angry voice of the old soldier quickly steadied the line. The Russian squadrons had come within long

* These words were heard by Captain (now Major) Burroughs, the officer then in command of the 6th company of the 93d.

† And these.

‡ Communications from the Russian officers to ours.

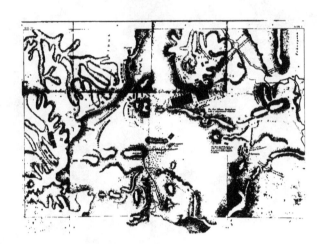

musketry range. The Highlanders and the men alongside them delivered their fire; and although they emptied no saddles, they wounded some horses and men.* The horsemen thus met abandoned at once their advance upon Campbell's front, and wheeled to their left as though undertaking to turn his right flank. Sir Colin turned to his aide-de-camp, and—speaking of the officer who led the Russian squadrons—said, 'Shadwell! that man understands his business.' To meet his assailant's change of direction, Campbell caused the grenadier company of the 93d, under Captain Ross, to bring the left shoulder forward, and show a front towards the north-east.

Stopped at once by this ready manœuvre, and the fire that it brought on their flank, the horsemen wheeled again to their left, and retreated. They retreated together, but not in good order; and the fire of our artillery increased their confusion.

Thus was easily brought to an end the advance of those 400 horsemen who had found themselves, during a moment, in the front of a Highland battalion. Springing out of no foregone design against Campbell's infantry, the attack fell so short that it scarcely gave any example of what might be attempted by horsemen against a body of foot drawn up in line, and two deep. The Queen's troops arrayed on the hillock were able, indeed, to prove their mettle; but the occasion they found was not such a one as is given to infantry by a resolute onslaught of horse. The trial they had to pass through on this morning

* Communications from the Russian officers to ours.

CHAP.
V.

The fire from their line.

Its effect.

The altered movement of the assailing squadrons.

Campbell's counter-manœuvre.

Its effect. Retreat of the horsemen.

Feebleness of the charge undertaken by these Russian squadrons.

The real nature of the trial sustained by the Queen's

CHAP.
V.

troops
formed up
on the
hillock.

of the 25th of October was not one directly resulting
from any kind of sharp combat, but still it was a
trial imposed upon them by the hitherto adverse
tenor of the engagement, and, in that sense, by
stress of battle. Without being at all formidable
in itself, the advance of the four Russian squadrons
marked what might well seem at the moment to
be an ugly, if not desperate crisis in the defence
of the English seaport. Few or none, at the time,
could have had safe grounds for believing that,
before the arrival of succours sent down from the
upland, Liprandi would be all at once stayed in his
career of victory; and in the judgment of those, if
any there were, who suffered themselves to grow
thoughtful, the whole power of our people in the
plain and the port of Balaclava must have seemed to
be in jeopardy; for not only had the enemy over-
mastered the outer line of defence, and triumphantly
broken in through it, but also, having a weight of
numbers which, for the moment, stood as that of an
army to a regiment, he already had made bold to be
driving his cavalry at the very heart of the English
resources, when the Turkish battalions—troops constituting two-thirds of that small and last body of
foot with which Campbell yet sought to withstand his
assailant—dissolved all at once into a horde of fugitives thronging down in despair to the port. If, in
such a condition of things, some few hundreds of infantry men stood shoulder to shoulder in line, confronting the victor upon open ground, and maintaining·
from first to last, their composure, their cheerfulness,
nay, even their soldierly mirth, they proved themselves

by a test which was other than that of sharp combat, but hardly, perhaps, less trying.

And the Highlanders whilst in this joyous mood were not without a subject of merriment; for they saw how the Turks in their flight met a new and terrible foe. There came out from the camp of the Highland regiment a stalwart and angry Scotch wife, with an uplifted stick in her hand; and then, if ever in history, the fortunes of Islam waned low beneath the manifest ascendant of the Cross; for the blows dealt by this Christian woman fell thick on the backs of the Faithful. She believed, it seems, that, besides being guilty of running away, the Turks meant to pillage her camp; and the blows she delivered were not mere expressions of scorn, but actual and fierce punishment. In one instance, she laid hold of a strong-looking, burly Turk, and held him fast until she had beaten him for some time, and seemingly with great fury. She also applied much invective. Notwithstanding all graver claims upon their attention, the men of the 93d were able to witness this incident. It mightily pleased and amused them. It amuses men still to remember that the Osmanlis, flying from danger and yearning after blissful repose, should have chosen a line of retreat where this pitiless dame mounted guard.*

The new foe encountered by the Turks in their flight.

* She was a very powerful woman. In later years—I do not know the origin of the appellation—she used to be known in the regiment by the name of the ' Kokona.'—*End of Note to First Edition.* Mr Henry Stanley has now kindly enabled me to give the meaning of the word. It is a modern Greek word, κοκωνα, signifying ' Lady ' or ' Madam,' and is applied by Turks to Christian ladies. It is the very word by which —in deprecation of her wrath—an assaulted Turk would have been likely to address the lady.—*Note to Second Edition.*

CHAPTER VI.

CHAP. IF a man has to hear that in the open forenoon of
VI.
‿‿‿ an October day a body of Russian horse which numbered itself by thousands could come wandering into
the precincts of the English camp without exciting
early attention on the part of our cavalry people, he
ought to know what was the cause which made such
an incident possible.

Towards the west of the Balaclava plain, the
ground was so undulating, and the view of it here
and there so obstructed by orchards or vineyards, that
although an observer well placed would be able to
descry the advance of any enemy's force long, long
before it could be close at hand, yet the near approach
of even great bodies of troops might be hidden from
the mind of a general who contented himself with the
knowledge that was to be got from low ground. It
may be easily imagined that, in the existing condition
of things, our cavalry generals could not venture to
separate themselves from their troops by even those
slight distances which divided the low ground from
Want of   neighbouring heights; but then also they failed to
arrange-
ments for charge others with the duty of maintaining a watch-

ful look-out from any of the commanding knolls and
ridges which featured the landscape around them;
and from this single omission there well might come
two broods of error—the first brood consisting of
'surprises,' like the one which gave rise to this comment—the other brood comprising those ugly misconstructions which must always be likely to occur where
he who sends orders can survey the whole field, and
he who would try to obey them has only a circum-
scribed view.

The main body of the Russian cavalry, under the
orders of General Ryjoff, moved briskly up the North
Valley, having with it some 32 pieces of field-artillery;
and as yet, the force did not bend southward (as the
four detached squadrons had done), but pushed on
so far up towards the west (without being assailed by
our cavalry), that at length it incurred two shots, both
discharged from the line of batteries which fringed
the edge of the Chersonese. Checked apparently by
this fire, the Russian cavalry, which had previously
seemed to be one immense column, now showed itself to consist of two distinct masses, and during
some moments it seemed disposed to fall back; but
presently, the whole force, acting closely together,
wheeled obliquely aside towards the line of the Woronzoff road, and began to cross over the Causeway
Heights, as though minded to invade the South
Valley, or else, at the least, to survey it. Lord
Cardigan's brigade had just been moved to a position more advanced than before, and it now fronted

CHAP.
VI.

towards the east. Therefore, although the configuration of the ground was such as to keep General
Ryjoff in ignorance of what he had on his flank,
yet, when he thus passed over the heights, he was
moving (obliquely) across the front of our Light
Cavalry.

So far as I have heard, there is no ground at all for
believing that, when the Russian horse thus wheeled
and faced to the south, it had yet had a glimpse of
the foe with which, in hard fight, it was destined to be

Its sudden
discovery
of a great
opportu-
nity.

presently striving ; but as soon as the foremost horsemen of the leading column had moved up to the top
of the ridge, they all at once found that a great occasion was come.

The march
of the
eight
squadrons
of Heavy
Dragoons
which had
been sent
under
Scarlett
towards
the ap-
proaches
of Kadi-
köi.

Long before the flight of the Turkish battalions in
the gorge of Kadiköi, Lord Raglan's sure glance had
enabled him to detect their unstable condition ; and
he had, therefore, sent an order directing that eight
squadrons of Heavy Dragoons should be moved down
to support them. Lord Lucan had entrusted the task
to Brigadier-General Scarlett, the officer who commanded our Heavy Brigade ; and Scarlett was in the
act of executing Lord Raglan's order, when the Russian cavalry, as we have just been seeing, turned
away from the valley and moved up over the summit of the Causeway ridge. Having with him the
5th Dragoon Guards, the Scots Greys, and the Inniskilling Dragoons—regiments numbering altogether
six squadrons—and having, besides, provided that to
make up the 'eight,' two squadrons of the 4th
Dragoon Guards should follow him, Scarlett was

marching along the South Valley, and making his
way towards the east, with the Causeway Heights
on his left.

For the purpose of seeing how these troops were
brought into action, the order of march should be
known. The movement being regarded as a movement within our own lines, and one therefore proceeding through ground in the unchallenged dominion of the
English, was not conducted with the military precautions which would have been otherwise judged necessary, and no horsemen covered the march by moving
along the top of the Causeway ridge. Scarlett did
not apparently entertain an idea that Russian cavalry
could come so high up the North Valley as the 'Num-
'ber Five' Redoubt, and manœuvre on the ground
which it reached, without bringing our Light Cavalry
down on it.* Therefore no special directions were
thought to be needed for this little march—a march

Cause
which in-
duced
Scarlett to
dispense
with pre-
cautions.

* This sketch—which, however, is not offered as a plan indicating
the actual positions of the respective forces—may aid the comprehension of the text.

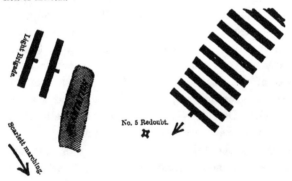

No. 5 Redoubt.

CHAP. through our own camping-ground—and no more
VL   elaborate operation was intended than that of mov-
       ing all the three regiments by the same route in open
The order column of troops.   It chanced, however, that in turn-
of march.
       ing one of the enclosures which obstructed its path,
       the 1st squadron of the Inniskillings took the right-
       hand side of the obstacle, whilst the other squadron
       passed by the left of it; and in this way it resulted
       that the movement went on in two columns, the right
       hand column being led by the 1st squadron of the
       Inniskillings, and closed by the 5th Dragoon Guards;
       whilst the left-hand column was led by the 2d squad-
       ron of the Inniskillings, and closed by the two squad-
       rons of the Scots Greys.   Those three last-named
       squadrons were moving in open column of troops, but
       the right-hand column marched by 'threes.' *

The   At the moment of the sudden discovery which will
ground
which had be presently mentioned, the six squadrons thus led
been
reached   by Scarlett were marching in a direction nearly
by the
2d squad- parallel with the line of the Causeway ridge, at a
ron of the
Inniskil- distance of some seven or eight hundred yards from
lings and
the Greys its summit; and the left-hand column was so shap-
at the
time now   ing its course as to be able to skirt the remains of
in ques-
tion;   the Light Brigade camp, and also the lower fence of a
       vineyard there sloping down southward in the eye of
       the sun.   The camp had been imperfectly struck; but
       some tents were yet standing, and the picket-ropes
       had not been removed.

       * General Scarlett's impression was, that all six squadrons were mov-
       ing upon the same line of march, and in open column of troops; but
       minute inquiry led to the conclusion stated in the text.

General Scarlett with Elliot, his aide-de-camp, was
on the left of the column formed by the 2d squadron
of the Inniskillings and the Scots Greys.   Intent upon
the special duty which had just been assigned to his
squadrons by Lord Raglan's last order, he was keenly
bending his sight in the direction of the Highland
battalion which defended the approaches of Kadiköi,
when Elliot cast a glance towards the ridge on his
left, and saw its top fretted with lances.   Another moment and the sky-line was broken by evident squadrons of horse.   Elliot, young as he was, had yet been
inured to war, and he quickly was able to assure
himself not only that powerful masses of Russian
cavalry were gathered, and gathering, on the ridge,
but that they fronted towards the South Valley and
were looking down almost at right angles upon the
flank of our marching column.   Of course, the aide-
de-camp instantly directed the eyes of his chief to
the summit of the ridge on his 'left.   For a moment,
Scarlett could hardly accept Elliot's conclusion; but
in the next instant he recognised the full purport
of what had happened, and perceived that he was
marching across the front of a great mass of Russian
cavalry, which looked down upon the flank of his
column from a distance of but a few hundred yards,
and might be expected, of course, to charge down
on it.   This, then, was the occasion which fortune
had proffered to the Russian cavalry.

Scarlett's resolve was instantaneous, and his plan
simple.   He meant to form line to his left, and to
charge with all six of his squadrons.   Accordingly

Marginal notes:

CHAP.
VI.

and by
Scarlett.

Sudden
appear-
ance of the
enemy's
cavalry on
the flank
of Scar-
lett's dra-
goons.

Scarlett's
resolve.

CHAP.
VI.

The order he gave.

'Scarlett's 'three 'hundred.'

Ground taken to the right.

The 5th Dragoon Guards.

he faced his horse's head towards the flank of the column, and called out, 'Are you right in front?'* The answer was, 'Yes, sir!' Then Scarlett gave the word of command, 'Left wheel into line!'

The troops nearest to Scarlett were those which formed the left-hand column—that is, the 2d squadron of the Inniskillings, which was in front, and the two squadrons of the Greys which brought up the rear. Those three squadrons were the force which constituted 'Scarlett's three hundred.'

Scarlett conceived at this time that the 5th Dragoon Guards would ' form up in prolongation of his front on the left of the Greys; and, to leave a clear front for the regiment thus supposed to be coming into line, he found it necessary that the ' three hun- ' dred ' should move some way east of the vineyard before commencing their onset. He therefore gave an order to ' take ground to the right.'

The 5th Dragoon Guards had not yet so closely approached as to be ready to align with Scarlett's ' three hundred ; ' and it seems that Elliot, the Brig- adier's aide-de-camp, delivered to the regiment an order which was regarded as directing it to act in support to the Greys.† The position which the 5th Dragoon Guards actually took up was on the left rear of the Greys. On the right of the 5th Dra- goon Guards, but divided from it by a considerable

---

* This was a very apt question ; for, as we shall afterwards see, some portions of the Heavy Brigade were marching 'left in front.'

† I believe General Scarlett has no recollection of having sent this order ; but the proof of the words given in the text seems irresistibly strong.

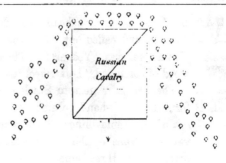

Russian
Cavalry

BATTLE OF BALACLAVA.

PLAN

Shewing the Order in which the Six
Squadrons with Gen.l Scarlett were
marching when the approach of the
Russian Cavalry was first observed.

Site of
Light Cavalry
Camp.

VINEYARD

✱ *General*
Scarlett.

Greys.

2.d Squadron of
Inniskillings.

Marching in open
Column of Troops.

5.th Dragoon Guards
Marching by threes

1.st Squadron of
the Inniskillings
marching by threes.

interval, there stood the 1st squadron of the Inniskillings.

The 4th Dragoon Guards and the Royals were approaching; so altogether, besides the first line, there were seven squadrons which might ultimately take part in the conflict, though not until after the moment when the foremost 'three hundred' would be already engaged.

The embarrassment of determining whether he will direct, or whether he will lead, is one which very commonly besets the mind of a cavalry general who commands several regiments just about to engage in a conflict with powerful adversaries; but it pressed upon Scarlett with a somewhat unusual severity; for he had no time to be delegating authority, or giving effective instructions for the guidance of his supports; and, in one point of view, it might be bold to take it for granted that a general in command of several squadrons could be warranted in leaving a large proportion of them to come into the fight their own way; but then, on the other hand, our troops were young, were new to battle; and, it being determined that a very scant number of them were to be led on —and that, too, uphill—against a vast mass of cavalry which reckoned itself by thousands, there was ground for believing that they might need the example of a general officer, not for the purpose of mere encouragement, but in order to put them above all doubt and question in regard to their true path of duty.

In such a dilemma, shall a man be the Leader or

CHAP. the General? · He cannot be both.   Shall he strive
VI.   to retain the control over all his troops, as does an infantry General sending orders this way and that? Or
rather, for the sake of leading his first line, shall he
abandon for the moment his direct authority over the
rest, and content himself with that primitive act of
generalship which is performed by showing the way?

His deci- The soundness of Scarlett's decision may fairly be
sion.
questioned;* but he chose as chose Lord Uxbridge in
the last of the battles against the great Napoleon; †
nay, he chose as did Murat himself, for when the
great cavalry chief was a king and a commander of
mighty numbers, he still used to charge in person, and
to charge at the head of his squadrons.

Lord Lu-   And now, all at once, by the arrival of his Divi-
can. The
part taken sional General, Scarlett found himself relieved from
by him
after hear- any anxiety occasioned by his decision. It seems
ing of the
advance of that, after having despatched Scarlett and his Heavy
the Rus-
sian cav- Dragoons on the mission assigned to them by the
alry.
Commander-in-Chief, Lord Lucan had been apprised
by one of Lord Raglan's aides-de-camp of the enemy's
advance up the valley with a large body of cavalry;
and that presently, upon having his glance directed

* For the reason adverted to in the preceding paragraph.
† Our cavalry Generals have very commonly adopted this way of performing their duty ; but the decision of Lord Uxbridge (afterwards the
Marquess of Anglesea) is a specially convenient example of the dilemma
referred to in the text ; for on the one hand his personal leadership
of the first line resulted in a charge of surpassing splendour ; but then
also great losses followed, because it was found that practically, his anterior directions to the supports did not seem applicable a few moments
later, and at all events, were not obeyed in a manner accordant with
Lord Uxbridge's design.

to the right quarter, he himself had not only descried CHAP.
VI.
Ryjoff's masses of horse, but had been able to see that
a portion of them was bending southward across the
Causeway ridge. Thereupon, it appears, he had first
given his parting instructions to Lord Cardigan, the
commander of the Light Brigade, and had then ridden off at speed in the track of Scarlett's left column.
When, upon overtaking the squadrons, he found them
moving in column of troops with their left flank towards
the enemy, he believed that this operation (though in
reality, perhaps, it had resulted from Scarlett's second
order to take ground to the right) was a continuance
of the march towards Kadiköi. He therefore conceived that, to save time in what he took to be a
pressing emergency, it was his duty at once, and in
person, to give such directions to the troops as he
judged to be needed, without first apprising General
Scarlett, and conveying the orders through him. Accordingly, therefore, by his personal word of command,
he directed the troops to wheel into line; * and it
seems that he was heard and obeyed by the Greys,
but not by the Inniskillings; for that last regiment
received no orders except those which came from the
lips of General Scarlett. It is evident that, at such
a time, any clashing of the words of command which

* Indeed, if Lord Lucan's impression be accurate, he delivered in
succession the same three orders that were given by Scarlett—*i.e.*,
orders to wheel into line, to take ground to the right, and (for the
second time) to wheel into line. In my judgment, any dispute as to
which of the two generals was the first to give the orders would be too
trivial to deserve public attention; but if there be a military reader
who thinks otherwise, he will probably perceive that the truth can be
deduced from the facts stated in the text.

CHAP.
VI.
proceeded from the two generals might have been dangerous; but in their actual result, Lord Lucan's separate though concurring orders wrought little or no confusion.

Meeting
between
Lord Lu-
can and
General
Scarlett.

Hitherto, the divisional commander and his brigadier had not come in sight of one another; but whilst Scarlett (after having once wheeled, and then taken ground to the right) was again giving orders to wheel a second time, into line, Lord Lucan rode up to him; and, in the face of the enemy's masses of horse then closely impending over them, the General of the division and the General of brigade found moments enough for the exchange of a few rapid

The com-
munica-
tions be-
tween
them.

words. According to General Scarlett's recollection of what passed, he explained why it was that, after first wheeling into line, he had found it necessary to take ground to his right, and received an assurance that his intended attack would be supported by Lord Lucan with other troops.

Lord Lucan, indeed, believes that, in expressing his wish to have the charge executed, he spoke as though giving an order which had originated with himself, and that he said to his Brigadier :— 'General Scarlett, take these four squadrons'—the four squadrons of the Greys and the Inniskillings— 'and at once attack the column of the enemy;'* but if he used words of command where words of mere sanction were what the occasion required, it seems probable that he ended the conversation with a more

* What Lord Lucan took to be 'four' were in reality three squadrons. See *ante*, p. 88.

appropriate phrase, saying simply to Scarlett: — 'Now, then, do as you like.' Whatever were the words interchanged, they at all events proved that Scarlett's determination to lead an immediate charge against the enemy's cavalry had the sanction of his divisional commander.

Of course, it must be well understood that the attack we shall have to speak of took place under Lord Lucan's actual and personal authority. Holding command over the whole division of which the Heavy Dragoons formed a part, he had come up so early as to have ample time for preventing the charge if he had thought fit to do so; and as it happened that, far from preventing, he eagerly sanctioned, the charge, nay, personally helped on the preparations for the measure, and undertook to support it by fresh troops—he made himself in the fullest sense responsible for the operation, and became, in all fairness, entitled to a corresponding share of any merit there was in the design. He either ordered or sanctioned the charge; and the question, 'Who led it?' will not be brought into dispute.

Lord Lucan's part in the attack.

When the operation of wheeling a second time into line had been brought to completion by the Inniskillings and the Greys, our six squadrons ranged thus: In first line there stood the second squadron of the Inniskillings, with the Greys on their left. In second line the first squadron of the Inniskillings was on the right rear of the other Inniskilling squadron; and on its left there was the 5th Dragoon Guards, forming up in left rear of the Greys.

Positions of the six squadrons at the moment anterior to Scarlett's charge.

CHAP.   The whole force thus ranged or ranging was be-
  VI.
———   tween 500 and 600 strong; and the three squadrons
in front which had first to encounter alone the whole
of the enemy's masses, numbered something less than
300.

The num-   By the concurring opinions of Lord Lucan and of
bers of the
Russian   many French officers, including General Canrobert,
cavalry
confront-   and also, I believe, General Morris, the mass of
ing Scar-
lett.   Russian cavalry preparing to descend upon these 300
dragoons was estimated as amounting, at the least, to
3500 men; and (unless it be understood that Jërop-
kine's six squadrons of Lancers were in another part
of the field, or that the horsémen receding from the
fire of the 93d Highlanders had not rejoined the
main body) it would result from even the official
acknowledgment of the Russians that this mass of
horse was some 3000 strong.* Even supposing the
force to have comprised but two-thirds of that number—and I cannot allow myself to state it at more
than about 2000—the column was still one of no
common weight and massiveness. It need hardly be
said that the same numerals which import but a
moderate strength, if applied to foot-soldiers, are
many times more potent when used for the reckoning
of cavalry. Our island people rarely cast their eyes
upon such a spectacle as that of cavalry in mass; and
yet, without having done so, they can hardly conceive

* Strictly, 2900. For the particulars of this force, and for inquiry
as to the question whether the two exceptions suggested by the above
parenthesis should or should not be made, see note in the Appendix.

the sense of weight that is laid upon the mind of a CHAP.

man who looks up the slope of a hill at a distance of VI.

a few hundred yards, and sees there a column of
horse — even if it were but 2000 strong — close
gathered in oblong or square.

And that—so far as concerned its power of man- Deliberate
œuvring—this great body of horse was in a high executed
state of efficiency, it soon gave proof; for when the of the
squadrons had gathered on the summit of the ridge, cavalry.
their leader for some reason determined that he
ought to take ground to his left, and the change was
effected with a briskness and precision which wrung
admiration from some of our best cavalry officers.

So soon as the column had taken all the ground
that was thought to be needed, it fronted once more
to the English. Then presently, at the sound of the Its ad-
trumpet, this huge mass of horsemen, deep-charged down the
with the weight of its thousands, began to descend slope.
. the hillside.

Making straight for the ground where our scanty
three hundred were ranging, and being presently
brought to the trot, it came on at a well-governed
speed, swelling broader and broader each instant, yet
disclosing its depths more and more. In one of its
aspects, the descending of this thicket of horsemen
was like what may be imagined of a sudden yet
natural displacement of the earth's surface; for to
those who gazed from afar the dusky mass they saw
moving showed acreage rather than numbers.

All this while, the string of the 300 red-coats were
forming Scarlett's slender first line in the valley be-

CHAP.
VI.

neath, and they seemed to be playing parade. At the moment I speak of, the troop officers of the Greys were still facing their men; and their drill rules, it seems, had declared that they must continue to do so till the major of the regiment should at length bring them round by giving the order, 'Eyes right!' Not yet would the Greys consent to be disturbed in their ceremonies by the descending column.

It was with seeming confidence that Scarlett sat eyeing the approach of the Russian mass, whilst the three squadrons ranging behind him went composedly on with the work of dressing and re-dressing their front; yet the moment seemed near when, from the great depth of the column and the incline of the ground, the front ranks of the Russians would have less to dread from their foe than from the weight of their own troops behind them; and unless the descent of the column should be presently stayed, even the enemy himself (though by chance his foremost squadrons should falter) might hardly have any choice left but to come sweeping down like a torrent, and overwhelming all mortal resistance.

The Russian cavalry slackening pace, and coming at length to a halt.

But before the moment had come when the enemy, whether liking it or not, would find himself condemned to charge home, he began, as it seemed, to falter. He slackened the pace. He still slackened —his trumpets were sounding—he slackened, and came to a halt.

Surmise as to the cause of the halt.

Our cavalry-men, so far as I know, have failed to hit on any solution of what they regard as a seemingly enormous mistake on the part of General

Ryjoff; and the Russians, not caring to dwell on the story of their conflict with our Heavy Dragoons, have never thrown light on the question. It, however, seems likely that a commander leading down his massed thousands with design to attack may have judged that he was met by a formidable obstacle when he saw extending before him a camp imperfectly struck, where some of the tents were yet standing and where also some horses were picketed.* If such was General Ryjoff's apprehension, he may well have been strengthened in it by observing the deliberately ceremonious preparations of the scanty red squadrons below : because he would be led to infer that their apparent sense of security must be based on knowledge of the ground in their front, and the hindrances with which it was strewed.

Or, again, it may be that, from the first, the enemy had intended to halt at what he judged a fit distance, for the purpose of executing and perfecting the manœuvre which must now be described.

Either whilst the mass was descending, or else as soon as it halted, a partial deployment was effected, which brought the force, taken as a whole, into a state of formation not new to St Petersburg, though but little affected elsewhere. In prolongation of the two front ranks of the column both to the right and to the left, two wings or fore-arms were thrown out, and this in such way that whilst the trunk — if thus one may call it—was a huge weighty mass of great depth, the two limbs which grew out from it were

CHAP. VI.

Deployment effected by the Russians on each flank of their column.

* Sick horses.

C H A P.
VI.

constituted by a formation in line. In this way, the appalling effect of great weight was supposed to be combined with the advantage which belongs to extension of front; and evidently the designer imagined that, by the process of wheeling them, the two deployed 'lines might be made puissant engines for defence or for counter-attack. By inclining them more or less back the arms might be made to cover the flanks of the column; whilst, by folding them inwards, they might be so wielded as to crush all close comers with an easy and pitiless hug. The mass which acted in support had a front commensurate with that of the column it followed, but without any deployment from the flanks. It advanced so exactly on the track of the body in front, and soon showed so strong a tendency to close upon it, that virtually it added its weight to the weight of the great mass it followed, without attempting to aid it by any independent manœuvres. So although, whilst these horsemen were marching, and even during part of the conflict, a space could be seen still existing between the first mass and the second, yet, so far as concerns their bearing upon the fight, the two columns were substantially as one.

Around the serried masses thus formed there circled a number of horsemen in open or skirmishing order.

Scarlett's task.

When the extension of the Russian front had developed itself, Scarlett failed not, of course, to see that, enormously as his thin line of two ranks was overweighted by the vast depth of the column before him, the extent to which he was outflanked both on

his right hand and on his left was hardly less overwhelming; but whether he still expected that the 5th
Dragoon Guards would align with the Greys, or whether
he by this time understood that it would be operating
on their left rear, he at all events looked trustfully to
the help that would be brought him by this his own
regiment as a means of resistance to the forces which
were outflanking him on his left. Towards his right,
however, he equally saw the dark squadrons far, far
overlapping his front; and, for the checking of these,
he knew not that he had even so much as one troop
close at hand, for he supposed at that time that his
first line included the whole of the Inniskillings.
Scarlett, therefore, despatched Major Conolly, his brigade-major, with orders to bring forward one or other
of the two regiments which had not 'marched off with
the rest, and oppose it to the enemy's left.

It seemed evident that, for the English, all rational
hope must depend upon seizing the occasion which
the enemy's halt was now proffering; and to the truth
of this conviction the Divisional General and his Brigadier were both keenly alive. Lord Lucan, indeed,
grew so impatient of delay that he more than once
caused his trumpeter to sound the 'charge;' but Scarlett and all his people were much busied in preparing;
and, so far as I have heard, no attention was awakened by the sound of the divisional trumpet.

Though our people saw clearly enough that at all
hazards, and notwithstanding all disparity of numbers,
the enemy's impending masses must be attacked by
Scarlett's scant force, they still had no right to imagine

that they could achieve victory, or even ward off disaster, by means of the kind which a General of Cavalry
is accustomed to contemplate. When an officer under-
takes a charge of horse, his accustomed hope is, that
he will be able to shatter the array of the foe by the
momentum and impact of his close serried squadrons
led thundering in at a gallop; and, indeed, it is a
main part of his reckoning that the bare dread of the
shock he thus threatens will break down all resistance
beforehand. For Scarlett, there could be no such hope.
The scantiness of his numbers was not of itself a fatal
bar to the prospect of conquering by impact; but he
was so circumstanced as to be obliged to charge uphill
and over ground much impeded in some places by the
picket-ropes and other remains of the camp. Nor
was this the worst. The vast depth of the column
forbade all prospect of shattering it by a blow; for
even though the troopers in front might shrink, and
incline to give way under the shock of a charge, they
would be physically prevented from making a step to
the rear by the massiveness of the squadrons behind
them.

But, however desperate the task of Scarlett's three
hundred dragoons, no one of them seems to have
questioned that it was right to attack; and, the
element of doubt being thus altogether excluded,
they at least had that strength which belongs to
men acting with a resolute purpose.

The great
numbers
of military
Except in the instances of combats under the walls
of besieged fortresses, it can rarely occur that armies,

or large portions of armies, are not only so near and CHAP.
so well placed for the purpose of seeing, but also so VI.
unoccupied with harder tasks as to be able to study spectators
who were
a combat going on under their eyes; and still more witnesses
of the
rare must be the occasions which modern warfare combat.
allows for seeing a conflict rage without looking
through a curtain of smoke; but, besides our Light
Cavalry Brigade which stood near at hand, there had
gathered large numbers of military observers — including French, English, and Turks—who, being at
the edge of the Chersonese upland, were on ground
so inclined as to be comparable to that from which
tiers upon tiers of spectators in a Roman amphitheatre
used to overlook the arena; and the ledges of the
hillside were even indeed of such form as to invite
men to sit whilst they gazed. The means that people Distinctive col-
had of attaining to clear perceptions were largely in- ours of the
uniforms
creased by the difference that there was between the worn by
the Rus-
colour of the Russian and that of the English squadrons. sians and
the Eng-
With the exception of a few troops which showed their lish dragoons.
uniform—the pale-blue pelisse and jacket of a hussar
regiment—all the Russian horsemen, whether hussars,
or lancers, or Cossacks, whether officers or troopers,
were enveloped alike in the murky grey outer-coats
which, by this time, had become familiar to the eye
of the invaders. The grey was of such a hue that,
like the grey of many a lake and river, it gathered
darkness from quantity; and what people on the
Chersonese saw moving down to overwhelm our 'three
hundred,' were two masses having that kind of blackness
which belongs to dense clouds charged with storm.

CHAP.   The English dragoons, on the other hand, were in
VI.   their scarlet uniform, and (with the exception of the
Greys, who had the famed 'bearskins' for their head-
gear) they all wore the helmet. The contrast of
colour between the grey and the red was so strong
that any even slight intermixture of the opposing
combatants could be seen from the Chersonese. So
great had been the desire of the English in those
days, to purchase ease for the soldier at the ex-
pense of display, that several portions of our dragoon accoutrements had been discarded. The plumes
of the helmets had been laid aside, and our men
rode without their shoulder - scales, without the
then ridiculed stock, and, moreover, without their
gauntlets.

The group   Whilst the gazers observed that troop-officers in
of four
horsemen   front of our first line were still facing to the men,
now col-
lected in   still dressing and re-dressing the ranks, they also now
front of
the Greys.   saw that, in front of the centre of the Greys, and at a
distance from it of five or six horses' length, there was
gathered a group of four horsemen. Two of these were
side by side, and a little in front of the others. Of the
two foremost, the one on the left wore the cocked-hat
which indicated the presence of a Staff-officer, and
suggested indeed, at first sight, that the wearer might
be the General who commanded the brigade ; but a
field-glass corrected the error, showing instantly that
the horseman who thus caught the eye from a distance was no more than a young lieutenant—Lieutenant Alexander Elliot, the aide-de-camp of General
Scarlett. But to the right of the young aide-de-camp

there was another horseman, on a thorough-bred bay, standing fully, it seemed, sixteen hands. To judge from his head-gear, this last horseman might seem to be no more than a regimental officer of dragoons—for he wore the same helmet as they did—but an outer-coat of dark blue, thrown on, it seemed, over his uniform, served to show that he must be on the Staff. Because of the bright contrast disclosed between the warm summer hue of his features and a drooping mustache white as snow, it was possible to see from afar that this officer must be General Scarlett. Of the two horsemen who kept themselves a little in rear of the General, the one was his trumpeter, the other his orderly. This last man had attained to high skill as a swordsman, and was a valorous, faithful soldier. If it were not for the general spread of incredulity, it would be acknowledged that he drew his lineage from some mighty giantess of former ages, for he bore the surname of Shegog.

Scarlett's yearning at this moment was for the expected prolongation of his line towards its left, and he compelled himself to give yet some moments for the forming of his 5th Dragoon Guards; but on his right, the one squadron of the Inniskillings (the squadron which he took to be the whole regiment) was both ready and more than ready. Differing in that respect from the rest of the 'three hundred,' the squadron had a clear front, and the sense of this blessing so inflamed it with warlike desire, that during the moments of delay, Scarlett had to be restraining the line by waving it back with his sword.

CHAP. The squadron chafed proudly at the touch of the
VI.   curb, and it seemed that if the General were to
relax his care for an instant, it would bound forward up the hillside, and spring all alone at the
column.

The custom of the service requires that an officer
who has the immediate command of a body of cavalry
engaged in the duty of charging shall be the actual
leader of the onslaught in the strictest sense, riding forward at a distance of at least some few yards in advance
of his squadrons ; but it must not be supposed that
those who originated or sanctioned this practice were
acting in contemplation of any such circumstances as
those which now existed, or that they ever intended to
subject a general officer, or indeed any other human
being, to the peculiar species of personal hazard which
Scarlett had resolved to confront. As tested by its
general operation, the practice is not one which unduly exposes the life of the chief ; for when a strong
body of horse is hurled at full pace towards the foe, it
commonly happens that either the attack or the resistance gives way before the moment of impact ; but in
this rare example of a slow, yet resolute, charge of
three hundred, directed uphill against broad and deep
masses of squadrons which reckoned their strength
by thousands, it seemed nearly certain from the first
that the General leading it must come, and come
almost singly, into actual bodily contact with a host
of adversaries, and remain for a time engulfed in it
because the enemy's front ranks were so barred against
all retreat by the squadrons behind them, that there

could be no hope of putting the body to flight by the CHAP. VI. mere approach of our squadrons.

At this time, the distance between the Russians and General Scarlett is believed to have been about 400 yards.

For the better understanding of what presently followed, it is well to know that when a brigadier is directing a movement which must be executed by only a portion of his force, the notes of the brigade trumpet do not instantly and directly take effect upon the troops ; because the order of the brigadier, in the case supposed, must be repeated by the regimental officers. It will also be useful to remember that squadrons in general are not moved from a halt to a charge by a single word of command. When the process is gone through with full deliberation, the first order is this :—'The line will advance at a walk!' and, the trumpet successively sounding the orders which follow, the force is brought on to its final task through the stages of 'Trot!' 'Gallop!' 'Charge!'*

Scarlett's deviation from the accustomed practice:

Now, Scarlett well knew how much all depended upon striking at the enemy's masses whilst yet they stood halted ;† and so far as concerned his own orders, he was hardly in the humour for travelling through all the anterior stages. He turned to his trumpeter and said at once, ' Sound the charge!'

The order he gave his trumpeter.

* The walk, I believe, is often if not indeed generally omitted ; but the other three stages are de régle.

† According to the impression of Lord Lucan—differing in that respect from those who took part in the execution of the charge—the Russian column by this time had resumed its advance down the hill.

C H A P.
VI.

Scarlett's advance.

His distance from his squadrons.

Whilst the notes were still pealing, and before they could take full effect upon the squadrons behind him, Scarlett moved forward at a trot; and although the impediments of the camping-ground made it necessary for a rider in this the first part of the onset to pick his way with some care, yet the horse Scarlett rode was a horse of such stride and power, that his rate of advance was not slow, even over the obstructed ground; and, as soon as the clear field which was at length gained enabled the leader to get into a gallop, the distance between him and his squadrons was swiftly increased. In a few moments, he was so far in advance of them that Elliot judged it right to call the attention of the chief to the position of his squadrons. Those squadrons were by this time advancing; but the impediments of the camping-ground proved of course more obstructing to the serried ranks of the Greys than to a horseman with only one companion and two attendants. Scarlett could not question that the distance between him and his squadrons had become extravagantly great; but still judging, as he had judged from the first, that it was of vital moment to strike the enemy's column whilst halted, he rather desired to accelerate the Greys than much to retard his own pace. Therefore, still pressing forward, though not quite so swiftly as before, he turned partly round in his saddle, shouted out a 'Come on!' to the Greys, and invoked them with a wave of his sword.

When the squadrons attained to clear ground, they began to reduce the space which divided them from

BATTLE OF
BALACLAVA
The Heavy Cavalry
Charge

THE VINEYARD

The Fourth Dragoon Guards about to attack

The Royals advancing at a Gallop

The first Squadron of the Inniskillings about to attack

Scarlett

Lord Lucan, this position
varied from time to time

2nd Squadron of the Inniskillings
The Greys

The 5th Dragoon Guards
about to attack

Scarlett's three hundred charging

their leader; but it is computed that, at the moment of Scarlett's first contact with the enemy's column, the distance' between him and the squadrons which followed him was still, at the least, fifty yards.

The Brigadier now found himself nearing the front of the column at a point very near its centre, and the spot at which Scarlett thus rode was marked by the presence of a Russian officer who sat erect in his saddle some few paces in front of his people, and confronting the English intruder.

Scarlett by this time was charging up at high speed, and, conjoined with the swiftness thus attained, the weight of a sixteen-hands horse gave his onset a formidable momentum. The Russian officer turned partly round in his saddle, with a gesture which seemed to indicate that he sought to beckon forward his people, and cause them to flood down over the four coming horsemen; but already Scarlett and his aide-de-camp were closing. Moved perhaps by such indication of rank as was to be gathered in one fleeting moment from the sight of a staff-officer's hat, the Russian officer chose Elliot for his adversary, and was going to make his first thrust, when along the other side of him, rushing close past the elbow of his bridle-arm, General Scarlet swept on without hindrance, and drove his way into the column.

It was by digging his charger right in between the two nearest troopers before him that Scarlett wedged himself into the solid mass of the enemy's squadrons. When a man has done an act of this kind, and has lived to speak of it, it is difficult for him to be sure of

The Russian officer in front of the column at the part where Scarlett was about to assail it.

Scarlett sweeping past the bridle-arm of the Russian officer, and driving into the column.

what might be happening close around him, but Scarlett observed that of the adversaries nearest to him,
whom he had not, he knew, gravely wounded, there
were some who dropped off their horses without having been killed or wounded by him ; and it seemed
to him, if he were to judge only from his own eyes,
that they were throwing themselves to the ground of
their own accord.

It was well perhaps, after all, that Scarlett, in leading the charge, was extravagantly ahead of his troops ;
for it seems he was able to drive so far into the column
as to be protected by the very bodies of his adversaries
from the shock which must needs be inflicted by the
Greys and Inniskillings when charging the front of
the column.

General
Scarlett
in the
column.
From the moment when the Brigadier had thus
established himself in the midst of his foes, it resulted,
of course, that his tenure of life was by the sword, and
not by the sword which is a metaphor, but by that
which is actual, and of steel. Scarlett, it seems, had
no pretension to be more than a passably good swordsman, and he had the disadvantage of being near-
sighted ; but he knew how to handle his weapon, and
in circumstances which exposed him to attack from
several at the same time, he had more need of such
unflagging industry of the sword-arm as might keep
the blade flashing here, there, and on all sides in
quickly successive whirls, than of the subtle, the delicate skill which prepares men for combats of two.

Elliot's
encounter
with the
It was partly, perhaps, from the circumstance of
Elliot's approaching him on the side of his sword-arm

that the Russian officer in front of the column chose the aide-de-camp for his antagonist instead of the chief ; but be that as it may, he faced Elliot as he approached and endeavoured to cut him down. Evading or parrying the cut, Elliot drove his sword through the body of the assailant, and the swiftness with which he was galloping up whilst delivering this thrust was so great that the blade darted in to the very hilt; but until the next moment, when Elliot's charger had rushed past, the weapon, though held fast by its owner, still could not be withdrawn. Thence it resulted that the Russian officer was turned round in his saddle by the leverage of the sword which transfixed him. In the next instant, Elliot, still rushing forward with great impetus, drove into the column between the two troopers 'who most nearly confronted him, and then, with a now reeking sword, began cleaving his way through the ranks. Shegog and the trumpeter came crashing in after; so that not only Scarlett himself, but all the three horsemen who constituted his immediate following, were now engulfed in the column.

C H A P.
VI.

Russian officer in front of the column.

The three horsemen riding with Scarlett.

A singular friendship had long subsisted between the Scots Greys and the Inniskilling Dragoons. It dated from the time of that famous brigade in which three cavalry regiments were so brought together as to express by their aggregate title the union of the three kingdoms, yet offer a sample of each ;* but the circumstance of the Greys and the Inniskillings having been

The ancient friendship between the Scots Greys and the Inniskilling Dragoons.

* The 'Union Brigade.' The regiment which in that historic brigade represented England was the 'Royals.'

C H A P. brigaded together in the great days can hardly be
   VI.   treated as alone sufficing to account for the existence and duration of this romantic attachment; for
it so happens that the sentiment which thus bound
together the thistle and the shamrock has never included the rose. The friendship between the Scottish
and the Irish regiment had the ardour of personal
friendship, and a tenacity not liable to be relaxed by
mere death ; for a regiment great in history bears so
far a resemblance to the immortal gods as to be old
in power and glory, yet have always the freshness of
youth. Long intervals of years often passed in which
the Greys and the Inniskillings remained parted by
distance, but whenever it became known that by some
new change of quarters the two regiments would once
more be brought" together, there used to be great
joy and preparation ; and whether the in-marching
regiment might be the Greys or the Inniskillings,
it was sure to be welcomed by the other one with
delight and with lavish attentions.   .

When last the sworn friends were together in what
they might deign to call fighting, they were under the
field-glass of the great Napoleon. Then, as now, the
Greys charged in the first line, and on the left of the
Inniskillings.*   .

The dis-   Of the two comrade regiments, each had its distin-
tinguish-
ing char- guishing characteristics. The Inniskillings, with still
acteristics
of the two some remaining traces in their corps of the old war-
regiments.

---

* It had been intended by Lord Uxbridge that they should act in
support, but circumstances superseded his directions, and caused them to
charge in first line.

like Orange enthusiasm, were eager, fiery, impetuous.* C H A P.
The Scots Greys, with a great power of self-restraint, VI.
were yet liable to be wrought upon by their native
inborn desire for a fight, till it raged like a consuming
passion. From the exceeding tenacity of their nature,
it resulted that the combative impulses, when long
baffled by circumstances, were cumulative in their
effect; and the events of the day—the capture of
British guns under the eyes of our horsemen—the
marching, the countermarching, the marching again,
without ever striking a blow, and finally, the dainty
dressing of ranks under the eyes of the enemy's host—
all these antecedent trials of patience had been heat- The tem-
ing and still heating the furnace by the very barriers Greys at
which kept down the flame. If, with the Inniskillings, this time.
the impetuosity I spoke of was in a great measure
aggregate, that yearning of the Scots for close quarters
was, with many, the passion of the individual man,
and so plain to the eye that the trooper became something other than a component part of a machine—became visibly a power of himself. English officers who
were combative enough in their own way, yet saw with
wonder not unmingled with a feeling like awe that
long-pent-up rage for the fight which was consuming
the men of the Greys.

In the earlier part of the advance now at length Unavoid-
commenced by the three squadrons, there was nothing ness of the
that could much impress the mind of an observer who in its

earlier
moments.

* The proportion of the regiment recruited from Ireland was very
much smaller than it had been in former times, but still the Orange
element, coupled with the force of regimental tradition, was enough to
warrant the statement contained in the text.

CHAP.
VI.
failed to connect it in his mind with the prospect of what was to follow; and a somewhat young critic was heard to condemn the advance by declaring it 'tame.' The truth is—and that we discovered before, whilst tracing the steps of Scarlett—that the Greys had to pick their way as best they could through the impediments of the camp; and although Colonel Dalrymple White with the 2d squadron of the Inniskillings had clear ground before him, he was too good an officer to allow the fiery troops he was leading to break from their alignment with the obstructed regiment on his left.

Progress of the advance.
But when the Greys got clear of the camping-ground, both they and the Inniskilling squadron on their right began to gather pace; and when the whole line had settled into its gallop, there began to take effect that spontaneous change of structure which often attends cavalry charges, for the front rank began to spread out, and from time to time the rear-rank men, as opportunities offered, pushed forward into the openings thus made for them. This change was carried so far that in large portions of the line, if not through its whole extent, the two ranks which had begun the advance were converted by degrees into one. The 'three hundred,' whilst advancing as they did at first in two ranks, were enormously outflanked by the enemy, and it seems that from this circumstance men were instinctively led to give freer scope to the impulses which tended to a prolongation of front.

Involun-tary ex-tension of our line whilst ad-vancing.

There was now but small space between our slender line of 'three hundred' and the dark serried mass

which had received their leader into its depths; and C H A P.
the Russian horsemen—so ill-generalled as to be still
kept at the halt *—began here and there firing their
carbines. Colonel Griffith, commanding the Greys,
was so struck, it seems, by a shot in the head as to
be prevented from continuing to lead on his regiment.

The † two squadron-leaders of the Greys were in
their places; and of these Major Clarke, the leader
of the right squadron, was the senior officer, but he
did not yet know that he had acceded to the temporary command of the regiment,‡ and continued to
lead the right squadron.

Besides § Major Clarke, thus leading the first squadron, and being in command of the regiment,‖ the
officers who now charged with the Greys were these :
—Captain Williams led the 2d squadron; Manley,
Hunter, Buchanan, and Sutherland were the four
troop-leaders of the regiment ; the adjutant was Lieutenant Miller ; the serre-files were Boyd, Nugent, and

CHAP. VI.

The Rus-
sian horse-
men re-
sorting to
firearms.

The offi-
cers who
charged
with the
Greys.

---

* See footnote *ante*, p. 105.

† The words 'Colonel and' should be added after the word 'The'.
See the next footnote.—*Note to 3d Edition.*

‡ This is a mistake, and a very serious one, which I most gladly
rectify ; for Colonel, now General Griffith, led the Greys into the mass
of the Russian cavalry, cut through it, and entered the supporting
column. It was *after* this, and whilst charging back again with men of
the Greys, that he received the pistol-shot in the head which for a while
disabled him. See in the Appendix his letter, and also a statement by
Dr Ramsay Brush, late of the Greys.—*Note to 3d Edition.*

§ The words 'Colonel Griffith and' should here be inserted.—*Note
to 3d Edition.*

‖ He had *not* then acceded to the command of the regiment. Colonel
Griffith (who had not yet received his wound) was both commanding
and leading the regiment. See the three last foot-notes.—*Note to 3d
Edition.*

CHAP. Lenox Prendergast. And to these, though he did not
  VI. then hold the Queen's commission, I add the name of
John Wilson, now a cornet and the acting adjutant of
the regiment, for he took a signal part in the fight.

The offi-   Besides Colonel Dalrymple White, who was pre-
cers who
charged   sent in person with this moiety of his Inniskillings,
with the
2d squad- the officers who charged with this, the 2d squadron of
ron of the the regiment, were Major Manley, the leader of the
Inniskil-
lings.   squadron; Lieutenant Rawlinson, and Lieutenant and
Adjutant Weir.

I believe that after General Scarlett and the three
horsemen with him, who had already engulfed themselves in the dark sloping thicket of squadrons, the
next man who rode into contact with the enemy's

Colonel   horse was Colonel Dalrymple White, the commander
Dalrym-
ple White of the Inniskillings, and then acting in person in
at the
head of   front of his second or left-hand squadron. Straight
the 2d
squadron before him he had a part of the enemy's column so
of the
Inniskil- far from where Scarlett went in as to be altogether
lings.   new ground (if so one may speak of a human
mass), whilst, by casting a glance in the direction
of his right front, he could see how enormously the
enemy was there outflanking him; but he followed
in the spirit with which Scarlett had led, and drove
his way into the column.

Major   Whilst Major Clarke was leading in the right
Clarke.
squadron of the Greys without knowing that he had
acceded to the command of the regiment,* an accident
befell him, which might seem at first sight—and so

---

* He had *not* then acceded to the command of the regiment. See
the four last foot-notes.—*Note to 3d Edition.*

indeed he himself apparently judged it—to be one of
a very trivial kind, but it is evident that in its effect
upon the question of his surviving or being slain it
trebled the chances against him. Without being
vicious, his charger, then known as the 'Sultan,' was
liable to be maddened by the rapture of galloping
squadrons, and it somehow resulted from the frenzy
which seized on the horse that the rider got his
bearskin displaced, and suffered it to fall to the
ground. Well enough might it appear to the
pious simplicity of those Russian troopers who saw
the result, and not the accident which caused it, that
the red-coated officer on the foremost grey horse rode
visibly under the shelter of some Satanic charm,
or else with some spell of the Church holding good,
by the aid of strong faith, against acres upon acres
of swords; for now, when Clarke made the last rush,
and dug 'Sultan' in through their ranks, he entered
among them bare-headed.

The difference that there was in the tempera-
ments of the two comrade regiments showed itself
in the last moments of the onset. The Scots Greys
gave no utterance except to a low, eager, fierce moan
of rapture—the moan of outbursting desire. The
Inniskillings went in with a cheer.

With a rolling prolongation of clangour which resulted from the bends of a line now deformed by its
speed, the 'three hundred' crashed in upon the front
of the column. They crashed in so weightily that
no cavalry, extended in line and halted, could have
withstood the shock if it had been able to shrink and

The charge
of the
three hun-
dred.

CHAP.
VI.
fall back; but whatever might be their inclination, the front-rank men of the Russian column were debarred, as we saw, from all means of breaking away to the rear by the weight of their own serried squadrons sloping up the hillside close behind them; and, it being too late for them to evade the concussion by a lateral flight, they had no choice—it was a cruel trial for cavalry to have to endure at the halt—they had no choice but to await and suffer the onslaught. On the other hand, it was certain that if the Russian hussar being halted should so plant and keep himself counter to his assailant as to be brought into diametric collision with the heavier man and the heavier horse of the Inniskillings or the Greys whilst charging direct at his front, he must and would be overborne. It might, therefore, be imagined that many of the troopers in the front rank of the Russian column would now be perforce overthrown, that numbers of our dragoons would in their turn be brought to the ground by that very obstacle—the obstacle of over-turned horses and horsemen—which their onset seemed about to build up, and that far along the front of the column the field would be encumbered with a heap or bank of prostrated riders and chargers, where Russians would be struggling for extrication intermingled with Inniskillings or Greys. Such a result would apparently have been an evil one for the 'three 'hundred,' because it would have enabled the unshattered masses of the enemy to bring their numbers to bear against such of the redcoats as might still remain in their saddles.

It was not thus, however, that the charge wrought CHAP.
its effect. What had first been done by Scarlett and VI.
the three horsemen with him, what had next been
done by Dalrymple White, and next by the squadron-
leaders and other regimental officers whose place was
in front of their men, that now, after more or less
struggle, the whole of these charging 'three hundred'
were enabled to achieve.

The result of their contact with the enemy was a
phenomenon so much spoken of in the days of the old
war against the French Empire, that it used to be
then described by a peculiar but recognised phrase.
Whether our people spoke with knowledge of fact, or
whether they spoke in their pride, I do not here stay
to question; but in describing the supposed issue of
conflicts in which a mass of Continental soldiery was
assailed by English troops extended in line, it used
to be said of the foreigners that they 'accepted the
'files.' * This meant, it seems, that instead of opposing his body to that of the islander with such rigid
determination as to necessitate a front-to-front clash,
and a front-to-front trial of weight and power, the
foreigner who might be steadfast enough to keep his
place in the foremost rank of the assailed mass would
still be so far yielding as to let the intruder thrust
past him and drive a way into the column.

* It was to infantry, I believe, that the words used to be applied;
but it has been adjudged that they describe with military accuracy the
reception which was given by the Russian column to Scarlett's 'three
'hundred.' Lord Seaton—Colonel Colborne of the illustrious 52d
Regiment—was one of those who handed down the phrase to a later
generation.

118   THE BATTLE OF BALACLAVA.

C H A P.   Whatever was the foundation for this superb faith,
   VI.   the phrase, as above interpreted, represents with a
singular exactness what the front rank of the Russian
column now did. These horsemen could not fall back
under the impact of the charge; and, on the other
hand, they did not so plant themselves as to be each
of them a directly opposing hindrance to an assailant.
They found and took a third course. They 'accepted
'the files.' Here, there, and almost everywhere along
the assailed part of the column, the troopers who stood
in front rank so sidled and shrank that they suffered
the Grey or the Inniskillinger to tear in between them
with the licence accorded to a cannon-ball which is
seen to be coming, and must not be obstructed, but
shunned. So, although, by their charge, these few horsemen could deliver no blow of such weight as to shake
the depths of a column extending far up the hillside,
they more or less shivered or sundered the front rank
of the mass, and then, by dint of sheer wedge-work
and fighting, they opened and cut their way in. It
was in the nature of things that at some parts of the
line the hindrance should be greater than at others ;*
but, speaking in general terms, it can be said that,
as Scarlett had led, so his first line righteously followed; and that, within a brief space from the moment
of the first crash, the 'three hundred,' after more or
less strife, were received into the enemy's column.

* Such hindrances must have chiefly occurred at spots where a few of
our troopers may have chanced to be clumped together for some moments. Amidst all the stores of information on which I rely, I find no
proof that any of our people were detained on the outside of the column
by stress of combat.

Lord Raglan was so rich in experience of the great CHAP. VI. times, and so gifted with the somewhat rare power of swiftly apprehending a combat, that he instantly saw the full purport, and even divined the sure issue, of what our dragoons were doing; but it was not without some dismay on the part of other English beholders, that Scarlett and his 'three hundred' were thus seen to bury themselves in the enemy's masses. And with every moment, the few thus engulfed in the many seemed nearer and nearer to extinction. For awhile, indeed, the Inniskillinger and the Grey — the one by his burnished helmet, the other by the hue of his charger, and both by the red of their uniforms — could be so followed by the eye of the spectator as to be easily seen commingling with the dark-mantled masses around them; but the more the interfusion increased, the greater became the seeming oppressiveness of the disproportion between the few and the many; and soon this effect so increased, that if a man gazed from the heights of the Chersonese without the aid of a field-glass, he could hardly ward off a belief that the hundreds had been swamped in the thousands.

Yet all this while General Scarlett and the 'three 'hundred' horsemen who had followed him into the column were not in such desperate condition as to be helplessly perishing in this thicket of lances and swords. If, indeed, they had faltered and hovered with uncertain step in the front of the great Russian column till it might please General Ryjoff to sound 'the trot,' they must have been crushed or dispersed

CHAP. by the descending weight of his masses; but our
VI. horsemen, by first charging home and then forcing
their way into the heart of the column, had gained
for themselves a strange kind of safety (or rather
of comparative safety), in the very density of the
squadrons which encompassed them.   It is true that
every man had to fight for his life, and that too with
an industry which must not be suffered to flag; but
still he fought under conditions which were not so overwhelmingly unfair as they seemed to be at first sight.

Scarlett's men, as we know, were 'heavy dragoons,'
whilst the Russians were either hussars or troops
of other denominations, ranging under the head of
'light cavalry;' but in the fight now about to be
waged this difference was of less importance than
might be imagined. The weight of our men and the
weight of their horses had served them well in the
charge; and even in the closely-locked combat of
few against many to which they had now committed
themselves, the red-coated troopers were likely to be
advantaged by their greater height from the ground
and the longer reach of their sword-arms; but in
point of defensive accoutrements they were less protected than the light cavalry were with whom they
had to contend.   Except the helmets worn by the
one squadron of the Inniskillings, the 'three hundred'.
had no sort of covering or accoutrement contrived for
defence.*   They were without their shoulder-scales,

* The bearskins of the Greys gave no doubt great protection, but can
hardly be said to have been contrived for the purpose.

and even without their gauntlets. The Russians, on C H A P. VI. the other hand (with the exception of a very small proportion of them who wore and disclosed their pale-blue hussar jackets), were all encased in what was (for the purpose of this peculiar combat) a not inefficient suit of armour; for the thick, coarse, long grey outer-coat which they wore gave excellent protection against the cuts of an Englishman's sabre, and was not altoge-ther incapable of even defeating a thrust;* whilst the shako was of such strength and quality as to be more effectual than a helmet against the edge of the sword.†

In such skill as is gained by the sword exercise, there was not perhaps much disparity between the combatants; but the practice of our service up to that time had failed to provide the troopers with those expedients of fence which he would be needing when assailed in the direction of his bridle-arm; and this of course was a somewhat imperilling defect for a horseman who had to combat in a crowd of enemies, and was liable to be attacked on all sides.

Though reckoned by thousands, and having for the moment no heavier task than that of overwhelming or shaking off somewhat less than three hundred assailants, the Russians were prevented from exerting the strength of their column by the very grossness of its numbers, formed up as they were on a limited

* The edges of our men's sabres seemed to rebound from the loose thick grey cloth, and sometimes—I know one instance especially—the point of a sword thrust hard at a Russian thus clothed was bent back by the resistance it encountered.

† One day the Vicomte de Noë and an English officer undertook to test the strength of a Russian shako; and the Vicomte declares that they were actually unable to cleave it with a hatchet.

CHAP. space, and wedged into one compact mass. Still no
VI.   one among the 'three hundred,' whether fighting in
knots with others, or fighting all alone in the crowd,
could fail to be under such actual stress of simultaneous assailants as to have to confide in his single
right arm for all means of defence against numbers;
and, upon the whole, it would seem that the mere
physical conditions of the fight were largely in favour
of the Russians; but in regard to the temper of the
combatants, there were circumstances which tended
to animate the few and to depress the many. Under
conditions most trying to cavalry, the Russians
evinced a degree of steadfastness not unworthy of a
nation which was famous for the valour of its infantry; but kept as they had been at a halt, and condemned (in violation of the principles which govern
the use of cavalry) to be passively awaiting the
attack, it was impossible for them to be comparable
in ardour, self-trust, and moral ascendant to horsemen exalted and impassioned by the rapture of the
charge, and now in their towering pride riding this
way and that with fierce shouts through the patient
long-suffering mass.

In some parts of the column the combatants were
so closely locked as to be almost unable, for awhile,
to give the least movement to their chargers; and
wherever the red-coated horseman thus found himself inwedged and surrounded by assailants, it was
only by the swift-circling 'moulinet,' by an almost
ceaseless play of his sabre whirling round and round
overhead, and by seizing now and then an occasion

for a thrust or a cut, that he was able to keep himself
among the living; but the horse, it seems, during these stationary fights, instinctively sought and found shelter for his head by bending it down, and leaving free scope for the sabres to circle and clash overhead. At other places—for the most part perhaps in those lanes of space which were constituted by the usual ' intervals' and 'distances' intersecting the mass— there was so much more freedom of movement that groups of as many as ten or twelve Russians who had fallen out of their ranks would be here and there seen devoting themselves to a common purpose by confederating themselves, as it were, against particular foes, and endeavouring to overwhelm the knot of two or three Greys or Inniskillingers which they deemed to be the most in their power. Where this occurred, the two or three redcoats, more or less separated from each other, would be seen striving to force their way through the masses before them, and attended on their flanks and in their rear by a band of assailants, who did not, most commonly, succeed in overpowering the tall horsemen, but persisted nevertheless in hanging upon them. Our troopers, thus encompassed, strove hard, as may well be supposed, to cut down the foes within reach; but in general the sabre seemed almost to rebound like a cudgel from the thick grey outer-coat of the Russian horseman; and upon the whole, there was resulting as yet but little carnage from this singular example of a fight between a heavy column of halted cavalry and the knots of the taller horsemen who were riving in deeper and deeper.

CHAP. VI.

With but few exceptions, the Scots Greys were of the race which the name of their regiment imports; and, from a conjuncture of circumstances which must needs be of rare occurrence in modern times, the descendants of the Covenanters had come upon an hour when troopers could once more be striving in that kind of close fight which marked the period of our religious wars—in that kind of close fight which withdraws the individual soldier from his fractional state of existence, and exalts him into a self-depending power. A Scots Grey, in the middle of our own century, might have no enraging cause to inflame him; but he was of the blood of those who are warriors by temperament, and not because of mere reasons. And he, too, had read his Bible. Men who saw the Scots Grey in this close fight of Scarlett's, travel out of humanity's range to find beings with which to compare him. His long-pent-up fire, as they say, had so burst forth as to turn him into a demon of warlike wrath; but it must not be inferred from such speech that he was under the power of that 'blood frenzy' of which we shall afterwards see an example; and the truth can be satisfied by acknowledging that, as his fathers before him had ever been accustomed to rage in battle, so he too, in this later time, was seized and governed by the passion of fight. When numbers upon numbers of docile obedient Russians crowded round a Scot of this quality, and beset him on all sides, it did not of necessity result that they had the ascendant. Whilst his right arm was busy with the labour of sword against swords, he could so use his bridle-hand as to be fastening its grip upon the long-coated men of a milder race, and tearing them out of their saddles.

Engaged in this ceaseless toil of fighting for life, as well as for victory, the Greys and the Inniskillingers were hardly so self-conscious as to be afterwards able to speak at all surely of the degree of confidence with which they maintained this singular combat of the few against many ; but of those who observed from a distance, there was one who more swiftly and more surely than others could apprehend the features of a still pending conflict. Almost from the first, Lord Raglan perceived that our horsemen, though scant in numbers, and acting singly or in small knots, still showed signs of having dominion over the mass they had chosen to invade.* Whether the cause of this ascendant be traced to the greater height and longer reach of our horsemen, to the unspeakable advantage of being the assailants, to the inborn pride and warlike temperament of our men, or finally, to all these causes united, the actual result was that the redcoats, few as they were, seemed to ride through the crowd like sure tyrants. The demeanour of the Russian horsemen was not unlike what might have been expected. Gazing down as they did from a slope, even those who were not in the foremost ranks could see the exceeding scantiness of the force which had made bold to attack them, and accordingly they seemed to remain steady and free from alarms of the kind which seize upon

* The conflict, Lord Raglan wrote, ' was never for a moment doubt-
' ful.'—Public Despatch.

CHAP. masses; but still the individual trooper who chanced
 VI.   to be so placed in the column as to have to undergo
the assaults of one of the Scots Greys or Inniskilling
dragoons, seemed to own himself personally over-
matched, and to meet the encounter almost hopelessly,
like a brave man oppressed by the strong. Without
apparently doubting—for there was no sign of panic
—that overwhelming numbers must secure the general result, he yet found that, for the moment, those
mere numbers could not give him the protection
he needed, and he would so rein his charger, and
so plant himself in his saddle, and so set his features, as to have the air of standing at bay. Of the
objects surrounding our people whilst engaged in
this closely locked fight, none stamped themselves
more vividly on' their minds than those numberless
cages of clenched teeth which met them wherever
they looked.

From the time when the ' three hundred ' had fairly
closed with the enemy, there was but little recourse
to carbine or pistol; and the movement of the horses
within the column being necessarily slight, and on
thick herbage, there resulted little sound from their
tramp. The clash of sabres overhead had become so
steady and ceaseless, and its sound so commingled
with the jangle of cavalry accoutrements proceeding
from thousands of horsemen, that upon the whole it
was but little expressive of the numberless separate
conflicts in which each man was holding to life with
the strength of his own right arm.

In regard to the use men made of their voices, there

was a marked difference between our people and the
Russian horsemen. The islanders hurled out, whilst
they fought, those blasts of malediction, by which
many of our people in the act of hard striving are
accustomed to evoke their full strength; whilst the
Russians in general fought without using articulate
words. Nor, instead, did they utter any truculent,
theological yells of the kind which, some few days
later, were destined to be heard on the battle-field.
They had not, as yet, been sanctified. It was not till
the 4th of November that the army of the Czar under-
went that fell act of consecration which whetted his
people for the morrow, and prepared those strange
shrieks of doctrinal hate which were heard on the
ridges of Inkerman. But although abstaining from
articulate speech and from fierce' yells, the grey-
mantled horseman in general was not therefore mute.
He sometimes evolved, whilst he fought, a deep,
gurgling, long-drawn sound, close akin to an inchoate
roar; or else—and this last was the predominant
utterance—a sustained and continuous 'zizz,' of the
kind that is made with clenched teeth; and to the
ears of those who were themselves engaged in the
fight, the aggregate of the sounds coming thus
from the mouths of the Russians was like that of
some factory in busy England, where numberless
wheels hum and buzz. And meanwhile, from those
masses of Russian horsemen who stood ranged in
such parts of the column as to be unable to engage
in bodily combat, there rose a low murmur of that
indefinite kind which attests the presence of a crowd

CHAP. without disclosing its humour. As heard on the
VI. edge of the Chersonese, a mile and a half towards
the west, the collective roar which ascended from
this thicket of intermixed combatants had the unity
of sound which belongs to the moan of a distant
sea.

If this struggle bore closer resemblance to the
fights of earlier ages than to those of modern times,
it had also the characteristic of being less destructive
than might be imagined to life and limb. General
Scarlett's old Eton experience of what used to be there
called a 'rooge' was perhaps of more worth to him than
many a year of toil in the barrack-yard or the exercise-
ground. Close wedged from the first in an enemy's
column, and on all sides hemmed in by the Russians,
he was neither killed nor maimed, for the sabre which
stove in his helmet was stopped before reaching his
skull, and the only five wounds he received were, each
of them, so slight as to be for the time altogether un-
heeded. By some chance, or possibly as a consequence
of wearing a head-gear which announced the presence
of a Staff-officer, Lieutenant Elliot, the aide-de-camp
of the Brigadier, was beset with great determination
by numbers gathering round him on all sides; and
although his skill as a swordsman and the more
than common length of his blade enabled him for a
while to ward off the attacks of his many assailants, they at length closed about him so resolutely
that it seemed hardly possible for a single horseman
thus encompassed by numbers to defend himself many
more moments; but at this very time, as it happened,

his charger interposed in the combat.* The horse had C H A P.
VI. become so angered by the pressure of the Russian troop-horses closing in upon his flanks and quarters, that, determining to resent these discourtesies, he began to lash out with his heels, and this so viciously as not only to ward off attacks from the rear, but even in that direction to clear a space. There were four or five Russians, however, who resolutely addressed themselves to the task of extinguishing Elliot; and at a moment when he had somewhat overreached himself in returning the thrust of a Russian trooper—a man with blue-looking nose and a savage, glittering eye—he received a point in the forehead from his hideous adversary. At the same time, another of his assailants divided his face at the centre by a deep-slashing wound, whilst a third dealt a blow on the head which cut through his cocked-hat, and then by the sabre of yet a fourth assailant he was so heavily struck in the part of the skull behind the ear that, irrespectively of the mere wound inflicted by the edge of the weapon, his brain felt the weight of the blow.† There followed a period of unconsciousness, or rather, perhaps, we should call it, a period erased from the memory, for Elliot remained in his saddle, and it is hard to say how he could have been saved if the effect of the blow had been so dis-

* If it had depended upon Elliot himself, I should never have heard of the circumstances here mentioned. He was an entire stranger to me, and it is to others that I owe the great advantage of having been brought into communication with him.

† The wound which divided his face was so well sown up that it has not much marred his good looks.

C H A P. abling as to prevent him from using his sword-arm.
VI. It is true he was much hacked, having received
altogether in this fight no less than fourteen sabre-
cuts, but he lived nevertheless,—nay lived, I observe,
to be returned as 'slightly wounded,' and to find that
his name, though most warmly and persistently recommended by Scarlett, was kept out of the public
despatches.*

Of course, the incursion of the Brigadier and the

---

* This resulted from a decision of Lord Lucan's. Lord Lucan conceived it to be his duty to suppress Scarlett's despatch recommending
Elliot's services for official recognition, and to name only one of the
cavalry aides-de-camp as amongst those who had 'entitled themselves
' to the notice of the Commander of the Forces ;' but—and now comes
what to the uninitiated must seem almost incredible—the aide-de-camp
whom Lord Lucan honoured with this distinction in exclusion of Elliot
and in defiance of Scarlett's despatch, was an officer (Lord Lucan's first
aide-de-camp) who, as it happened, had not had an opportunity of being
in any one of the cavalry charges. When I first became acquainted
with this monstrous inversion, I believed that I could not do otherwise
than ascribe it to Lord Lucan, and I resolved to comment upon his
decision in the way which so gross a misfeasance would deserve if it
were the act of a free agent. I suspend my determination in this respect,
because further inquiry has led me to apprehend that, if Lord Lucan
had named the right man instead of the wrong one, he would have been
regarded as outraging the custom of the service beyond all the measure
of what any one not holding supreme command could be expected to
attempt. Supposing that be so, Lord Lucan, of course, cannot fairly
be charged with more blame than other men of equal authority who
continue a vicious practice without protesting against it ; but if he, on
this ground, is to be absolved, what is to be said of an army system
which compels such a falsification ? Well, what in such case would
have to be said is this : that the military reputation of England is at
the mercy of a Trade-Union, which compels people placed in authority
to enforce its rules for the repression of excellence by official inversions
of fact.

It may be worth while to add that Elliot could not be named for the
Victoria Cross because what he did was no more, after all, than his duty.
See in the Appendix papers relative to the exclusion of Elliot's name.

three horsemen with him had more of the character of a 'forlorn hope' than could belong to the enterprise of the squadrons which followed him into the column ; but, upon the whole, these combats of Scarlett's and his aide-de-camp were more or less samples of that war of the one against several which each of the 'three hundred' waged.

This close bodily fighting put so great and so ceaseless a strain upon the attention and the bodily power of the combatants, that, with some, it suspended to an extraordinary degree all care about self. Thus Clarke, for example, who had led on his squadron bare-headed, was so deeply cut on the skull by the edge of a sabre as to be startling to the eyes of others by the copious channel of blood which coursed down his head and neck ; yet he himself, all the while, did not know he had received any wound. And along with this ennobling interruption of man's usual care after self, there was often a fanciful waywardness in his choice of the objects to which he inclined attention. Colonel Dalrymple White, for example, after riding alone, as we saw, into an untouched part of the column at the head of his second squadron, had received such a heavy sabre-cut on his helmet as cleaved down home to the skull ; and although he remained altogether unconscious of the incident thus occurring to himself, he found his attention attracted and even interested by an object which did not concern him. He saw a fair-haired Russian lad of seventeen, enwrapped like the rest in the coarse heavy over-coat which was common to officers and men ; and what seems to have

CHAP. interested him,—for he looked with the eyes of a man
VI. who cares much for questions of race—was the power-
lessness of a levelling costume to disguise the true
breed, and the certainty with which, as he thought, he
could detect gentle blood under the common grey cloth
of a trooper. 'He looked,' says Colonel White,—'he
looked like an Eton boy.' The boy fought with great
bravery; but it was well if he had no mother, for
before the fight ended he fell, his youthful head
cloven in two.

Though each man amongst the 'three hundred' was
guided, of course, in his path by the exigencies of the
particular combats in which he engaged, and though
many besides were so locked in the column from time
to time as to be able to make little progress, yet, upon
the whole, the tendency of the assailants was to work
their way counter to the ranks of the enemy's squadrons, and by degrees both Greys and Manley's squadron of Inniskillings pressed further and further in, till
at length, it would seem, there were some who attained
to the very rear of the column.* These did not, however, emerge into the open ground in rear of the column
(where a line of Cossacks stood ranged in open order),
but preferred to keep back and remain fighting within
the column, taking, each of them, such direction as
best consisted with the exigencies of personal combat.
Now it happened that, by this time, the Russians
—though not perhaps even imagining the idea of

* This rests rather upon the observation of men who gazed from
above than upon the distinct assertion of combatants who had penetrated thus far.

retreat—had still so much followed their inclination C H A P.
to be hanging upon the flanks and the quarters of
every Scots Grey whilst advancing, that very many
of them now faced towards their rear, and from
this cause apparently it resulted that in seeking, as he
naturally would, to be front to front with those who
were most keenly besetting him, many a Scots Grey
who had cut his road through from the front to the
rear of the column, now found himself busied in once
more riving the column, but riving it in the opposite
direction. Whatever the cause, it is certain that
there set in, as it were, a back eddy, and that the
Greys for the most part were now cleaving the mass
of their foes by a movement in the direction of the
Russian front.* There was a change, however, in the
demeanour of the Greys, for whereas in the earlier
moments of the fight they had seemed to be altogether intent upon slaughter, they now wore the
more careless aspect of men who had proved their*
ascendant.

But although in reality this back current of the
Greys formed an actual continuation of their attack,
it was still, in the literal sense of the term, a retrograde movement; and towards the proper left of the
column where Manley's squadron of the Inniskillings
was fighting, men could more or less see the direction
in which the Greys moved, without perceiving the

* *I. e.*, towards the English rear. It was whilst thus 'charging back'
with his men that Colonel Darby Griffith received the wound which
for the time disabled him, and caused Dr Brush to take him for a while
out of action. See foot-notes (*ante*, p. 113, *et seq.*), and the letters of
General Griffith and Dr Brush in the Appendix.—*Note to 3d Edition.*

C H A P. circumstances which governed their course. The sight
  VI.
────── of a number of the Greys in apparent retreat was
not the only cause which now tended to overcast
hope.

The great Russian column was proving that, notwithstanding the mismanagement which had exposed
it whilst halted to the almost insulting attack of three
squadrons, it still was of too firm a quality to be all
at once disintegrated and brought to ruin by the
incursion of the small groups of the redcoats who
were riving it in opposite directions ; and it now began
to seem likely that in this conflict of three hundred
against a column numbered by thousands, mere time
might govern the issue by lessening every minute the
relative power of the few. At this juncture also the
huge and dense Russian mass began to enforce a sense
of the power that there is, after all, in the mere weight
of numbers ; for—without by this movement appearing to disclose any weakness—the column now swayed
to and fro, and swayed so mightily as to make a man
own himself helpless against the bodily weight of a
crowd which could rock him one way or the other
against all the strength of his will.

So although the 'three hundred' still toiled at
their work of close fighting with a strength of resolve
which knew no abatement, there yet were some of
their numbers — and that, perhaps, amongst those
most gifted with warlike instinct—who hardly now
suffered themselves to imagine that the enterprise of
the three squadrons which had forced their way into
the heart of this column (without having brought it

to ruin by the shock of their uphill charge) could be wrought, after all, into a victory by dint of mere personal combats with vastly outnumbering horse- men.

Whilst this was the state of the fight as it seemed to men locked in close strife, there were, all at once, heard British cheers sounding in from outside of the column, sounding in from one quarter first, but then almost instantly from another, and close fol- lowed by a new kind of uproar. Presently, from the south-east, there sounded the shout of a squadron which Inniskilling men knew how to recognise, and with it a crash—a crash prolonged for some moments —in the direction of the Russian left front. Then, and from the same quarter, there broke out the roar of fresh tumult which was unlike the din of the fight going on in the midst of the column, and had rather the sound of such combat as might be waged by armed horsemen when not closely locked. The column, which every moment had been more and more heavily swaying, now heaved itself up the hill- side, and this time without being commensurately lifted back, as before, by the reaction of the moving power.

But the time has now come for observing the manœuvres of those two deployed Russian wings which, on the right hand as well as the left, pro- longed the front ranks of the column.

At the time when Scarlett's 'three hundred,' after closing upon the front of the column, had hardly The man- œuvres of the two

CHAP.   done more than begin their labour of man-to-man
VI.   fighting, the commander of the Russian cavalry made
Russian bold to undertake one of those new manœuvres for
wings.   which the peculiar structure of his winged column
         is supposed to have been specially fashioned. Re-
         membering, it would seem, the teachings of St Peters-
         burg, he resolved to surround the three squadrons
         which were charging through the front of his column,
         and enfold them in the hug of the bear. Therefore
         on the right hand and on the left, the wings or fore-
         arms which grew out from the huge massive trunk
         began to wheel each of them inwards.

         There was many an English spectator who watched
         this phase of the combat with a singular awe, and
         long remembered the pang that he felt when he lost
         sight of Scarlett's 'three hundred.' To such a one
         the dark-mantled squadrons overcasting his sight of
         the redcoats were as seas where a ship has gone
         down, were as earth closing over a grave. One of
         the ablest of our Light Cavalry officers has striven to
         record the feelings with which he looked down on
         this part of the fight:—'How can such a handful
         ' resist much more make way through such a legion ?
         ' Their huge flanks overlap them, and almost hide
         ' them from our view. They are surrounded, and
         ' must be annihilated. One can hardly breathe !'

The cir-   Yet if any observer thus trembling for the fate of
cumstan-
ces under Scarlett's 'three hundred,' had had his gaze less
which
they were closely rivetted to one spot, he would have seen that,
attempt-
ed.   however desperate might be the condition of this
         small body of horsemen, now seemingly lost in gross

numbers, there was no fresh ground for alarm in this
singular manœuvre of the Russian cavalry. General Scarlett had attacked the great column with so small a proportion of his brigade, that, when the 'three ' hundred' had engulfed themselves in the column, there still remained four distinct bodies of Heavy Dragoons (consisting altogether of seven squadrons), which, sooner or later, the English might bring to bear upon all the fresh exigencies of the combat; and it is plain that to some, nay, to most, of these seven squadrons, the enemy's in-wheeling flanks were offering no common occasion. On the other hand, the Russians, notwithstanding their great numerical strength, had so committed themselves to the plan of acting in mass as to be virtually without 'supports;' for although, as we saw, there was a part of the force which at first had been placed some way in rear of the main body, the distance was shortened in the course of the advance down the slope; and after the halt of the main column, the supporting force so closed down upon it as virtually to destroy the separation between the two bodies, and to merge them in one cumbrous mass.

The seven squadrons of which we just spoke constituted the forces now preparing to act in support, which Lord Lucan, by his personal directions, might still endeavour to wield. He was on the ground from which the Greys had advanced when beginning their attack. Already he had despatched an order directing Colonel Hodge to charge with the 4th Dragoon

Lord
Lucan.

His order
to the 4th
Dragoon
Guards.

C H A P. Guards,* and he states that by voice and by gesture—
VI.   for at the moment he had no aide-de-camp at hand—

His alleg-
ed direc-
tion to
another
regiment.

he tried to enforce the instant advance of a regiment on his left rear ; but he adds that nevertheless that regiment remained obstinately halted.† Lord Lucan did not give any other directions to the squadrons constituting his second line. Becoming apparently

* And unless Lord Lucan's memory deceives him, the order was to charge the enemy's column *on its right flank.* I should have so stated it in the text, if it were not that the officer (not Colonel Hodge) who *received* the order describes it as merely this :—' Lord Lucan desires ' him ' (Colonel Hodge) ' to charge at once with the 4th Dragoon Guards.' I think, however, that Lord Lucan's impression of what he said is pro- bably quite accurate ; and, indeed, it would seem that his version of the order which he *gave* may be reconciled with this account of the terms in which it was *delivered,* because, as we shall see, the position which had been already taken up by the regiment made it obvious without words that the column, if attacked by the 4th Dragoon Guards, must be attacked in flank. See *post,* page 140.

† With equal confidence he declares that the regiment thus appealed to was the 1st Dragoons, the regiment we call the Royals. The state- ments submitted to my consideration oblige me to believe him mistaken ; but he was the commander of the division to which the Royals belonged, and he manfully gave effect to his impression by acts of a decisive kind—by acts of which one, at the least, was public. These are circumstances which make it right for me to acknowledge beforehand that what I shall by-and-by say of the final advance of the Royals is unsanctioned by Lord Lucan's de- spatch, and diametrically opposed to the impression which his mind has received. With the exception of the Greys, there was nothing in the uniforms of our Heavy Dragoon regiments, as worn on this day, which would enable a spectator at a distance of many paces to distinguish one from another. I at first felt embarrassed by the prospect of being compelled by evidence to reject the firm persuasion of the Divisional General, who was present in person and an actor in the scene ; but I ultimately ascertained that he was mistaken in regard to the identity of the force which stood on his right after Scarlett's final advance, and that the correction of this error would so dislocate his account of what he saw in the direction of his left rear as to remove a main part of the difficulty that I had felt.

impatient to push on to the front, he ultimately rode
up by our right to the (proper) left flank of the Russian column.

We knew that from the first, three squadrons * of
the Heavy Brigade had been preparing to second the
onslaught of Scarlett's 'three hundred;' but at the
moment of Scarlett's attack two more of his regiments
were approaching the scene of the fight; and in
speaking successively, as I am now going to do, of
some movements or attacks which were executed by
the 4th Dragoon Guards, by the Royals, by the 5th
Dragoon Guards, and by Captain Hunt's squadron
of the Inniskillings, I pass simply, for the present,
from our left to our right, without intending to represent that these nearly simultaneous operations took
place, one after another, in that very order of time
which would correspond with the order of narration.

The order
in which
some of the
operations
of our sup-
ports are
about to
be re-
corded.

The 4th Dragoon Guards had not yet established
itself on the ground pointed out by Lord Raglan's
first order, when Colonel Hodge, its commander, became aware of the enemy's advance, and knew that
his corps was to follow the squadrons which had
already marched with Scarlett. He at once moved
off in open column of troops, and the subsequent
exigencies of the combat give an interest to the fact
that he marched 'left in front.'

Besides Lieutenant-Colonel Hodge, its commander,
the officers of this regiment were Major Forrest, Cap-

* Hunt's squadron of the Inniskillings and the two squadrons of
the 5th Dragoon Guards.

CHAP.
VI.

tain Forster, Captain M'Creagh, Captain Webb, Captain Robertson, and four * subalterns; namely, M'Donnel, Fisher, Muttlebury, and Deane.

Whilst the regiment was clearing the south of the vineyard, it all at once came in sight of the vast dusky column of Russian cavalry now streaked by the incursions of the redcoats. Indeed, those who looked from beneath were so favoured by the slope of the ground on which the column stood ranged, that from where he now rode with the 1st squadron of the 4th Dragoon Guards, Captain Forster was able to see General Scarlett—he could distinguish him by the blue frock-coat and the glittering helmet—still fighting in the midst of the column, and some way in front of his men.

The men of the 4th Dragoon Guards had been advancing with their swords in their scabbards;† but at sight of a combat going on, though they still were divided from it by a distance of some hundreds of yards, the men instinctively drew. In exact accordance with the design of Lord Lucan, Colonel Hodge at once determined to attack the column in flank.‡ As soon as he had cleared the south of the vineyard he changed direction; and, despite the close presence of the enemy, he boldly continued to advance in what

* This should be *five*, and the name of Brigstocke, the acting adjutant, should be inserted at the head of the list of subalterns—*Note to 3d Edition.*

† Colonel Hodge, I believe, had a theory that the practice of marching with drawn swords was only fitted for peace-time.

‡ I do not say *in obedience to* the order, because I cannot undertake to say that it had yet been received.

may be called marching order; for, still keeping his CHAP.
regiment in open column of troops, he began to move up VI.
the hillside by the somewhat narrow space that there
was between the easternmost fence of the vineyard
and the (proper) right flank of the column. He said
to Captain Forster, who commanded his right squadron, 'Forster, I am going on with the left squadron.
'As soon as your squadron gets clear of the vineyard,
'front, form, and charge.' Hodge went on in person
with his left squadron; and soon, both that and Forster's squadron were wheeled and formed up with
their front towards the enemy's right flank. The
operation by which the whole regiment thus fronted
to its right with each squadron at once in its place,
was made easy and quick by the circumstance that it
had been moving 'left in front.'

The enemy made a hasty endeavour to cover the
flank thus threatened by an evolution from the rear
of his masses; but the troops which he moved for the
purpose were too late to complete their manœuvre,
and Colonel Hodge had the satisfaction of seeing that
although Russian horsemen engaged in this attempt
were interposing themselves between him and the flank
of the column, they might be struck in the midst of
their effort by the charge of his 4th Dragoon Guards.

In the days of his boyhood when Hodge steered
the 'Victory,' there used to be a terse order which
readily came to his lips as often as the boat crossed
the river; and now when he had come to be so
favoured by Fortune as to find himself at the head of
his regiment with no more than a convenient reach

CHAP.
VI.

of fair galloping ground between him and the flank
of the enemy's column, the remainder of the business
before him was exactly of such kind as to be expressed by his old Eton word of command. What
yet had to be done could be compassed in the syllables of :—' Hard all across.' *

For bringing under one view the several positions
from which the Russian column was destined to be
assailed by our supports, it was convenient to begin
with the regiment on our extreme left; but it must be
understood that these movements of the 4th Dragoon
Guards took place at a time somewhat later than that
which might appear to be assigned to them by the
order they have in the narrative.

The
Royals.

The Royals had received no order to leave their
position under the steeps of the Chersonese ; † but
from the ground where the regiment stood posted, the
preparations for the then ·impending fight could be
easily seen ; and apparently it was assumed that the
fact of the regiment being left without orders must
have sprung from mistake. At all events, the
Royals moved rapidly off towards the scene of the
combat.

In its approach to the scene of the fight, this regiment was coming on past the south of the vineyard

---

* The direction given by the steerer to the crew of an Eton longboat
when about to cross the river.

† The brigade comprised *ten* squadrons, whilst Lord Raglan's order
for the movement towards Kadiköi extended to only *eight*. This difference, I take it, was the cause of the Royals having been left without
orders ; but the emergency created by the sudden appearance of the
Russian cavalry was regarded as a full warrant for the movement.

when Scarlett's 'three hundred,' having already de-livered their charge, and being part buried in the column, the right wing of the enemy was all at once seen by the Royals to be folding inwards, as though it would envelop the Greys. The sight of the enemy's cavalry deliberately wheeling in upon the rear of a British regiment, kindled so vehement a zeal in the hearts of the Royals, and so eager a desire to press instantly forward to the rescue, that there was no ceremonious preparation for a charge. A voice cried out, ' By God, the Greys are cut off! ' Gallop! gallop!' Then there broke from the Royals a cheer. Their trumpets sounded the gallop, and without for a moment halting, but endeavouring to ' form line on the move,' the regiment sprang hastily forward. Indeed, the movement of the first or right squadron was so rapid that the left squadron could not perfectly come up with it, and the regiment made its attack in short echelon of squadrons. In this order, but with its ranks imperfectly formed, the regiment advanced at a gallop against the right flank and rear of the in-wheeling line. In spite of this onset, the Russian wing continued its wheeling movement so long as to become defenceless on its extreme right. At the near approach of the Royals, that outer part of the wheeling line which was the most immediately exposed to its assailants broke off from the rest; and then the horsemen who had composed it were either flying or involved in confusion, or else—for several of the Russian hussars made bold to do thus —were valorously advancing and making their way

CHAP. round the flank of the advancing English; but mean-
VI. while, by all this confusion, the inner or left remnant
of the Russian wing was so far covered from the attack, and even, it would seem, from the sight of the
Royals, that it went on with the execution of the
orders received, and continued to wheel inwards.

The English regiment carried on its attack to a
point at which it was just brought into contact with
the broken extremity of the enemy's deployed line;
and a few sabre-cuts were exchanged; * but farther
than this the Royals did not push their advantage;
for the discomfiture of a part of the wing did not
visibly involve the great column; and considering
the disordered state of the regiment, Colonel Yorke
judged it prudent to rally his men before they were
thrown into contact with a huge mass of troops still
preserving their thickest formation. Accordingly, and
at a time when only a few of its pursuing troopers
had as yet ridden in amongst the retreating horsemen, the regiment was halted and ordered to re-form.

Besides Colonel Yorke, who commanded the regiment,
the officers present with the Royals at the time of its re-
forming were Major Wardlaw,† Captain Elmsall, Cap-

* Of the Royals I understand two were there wounded, of whom one
was Sergeant Pattenden.

† Major Wardlaw (now Colonel Wardlaw, the officer now commanding
the regiment), though suffering from illness, had found strength enough
to enable him to be with the regiment in the earlier part of the day, but
afterwards his sickness increasing, he had been forced to go back to
camp. Afterwards, whilst sitting or lying down outside his tent-door,
he saw our Heavy Dragoons with the enemy in their front, and then
instantly mounting his charger (which he had caused to be kept saddled
with a view to such a contingency), he found means to reach the scene
of conflict at the time when the regiment was re-forming.

tain George Campbell, Captain Stocks; and the following subalterns—namely, Pepys, Charlton, Basset, Glyn,
Coney, George* Robertson, Hartopp, and Sandeman.

An exploit performed at this time was observed
with some interest by numbers of the Light Brigade
men, then gazing down at the fight. Troop-sergeant-
major Norris of the Royals, having been separated by
a mischance from his regiment, was a little in rear of
it, and hastening to overtake his comrades, when he
found himself beset on open ground by four Russian
hussars, who must have ridden past the flank of our
people. Norris, however, though having to act alone
against four, found means to kill one of his assailants,
to drive off the rest, and to capture the charger of the
slain man.

Farther towards our right, and so placed as to
be in support to the Greys, though somewhat outflanking their left, there stood the 5th Dragoon
Guards. It was commanded by Captain Desart Bur-
ton; and the rest of the officers then acting with the
corps were Captain Newport Campbell, Captain Inglis,
Lieutenant Halford, Lieutenant Swinfen, Lieutenant
Temple Godman (the adjutant of the regiment),
Cornet Montgomery, Cornet Neville, Cornet Ferguson,
and Cornet Hampton. The regiment had at length
been formed up in line; but its two squadrons were
in inverted order, the first being on the left, and the
second on the right. For a moment there seemed to
be a question whether it might not be prudent to

* This name should have been written *Gilbert* Robertson.—*Note to
Second Edition.*

K

CHAP. transpose the squadrons into their respective places,
VI. but the pressure of time was too cogent to allow of
long ceremony; and, without first correcting its order
of formation, the regiment moved forward. It had
to pass over ground much obstructed by remnants of
the Light Brigade camp; Captain Campbell's charger,
for instance, was overthrown by a picket-rope which
crossed his line of advance; and I believe that, though
Neville owed his mortal wound to the lance of a Cossack, he had first been brought to the ground by one
of these camp obstructions.

At this time, the inner, and still unbroken part of the
enemy's right wing had already wheeled in over an
arc represented by an angle of nearly sixty degrees;
and, strange as the statement may seem, there still is
sound proof of the fact that the obedient Muscovite
troopers continued thus to wheel inwards till they had
come to be obliquely in front of the column, and with
their backs towards our 5th Dragoon Guards. It is
true that amongst these wondrously submissive horsemen there were some who so far fronted as to find
means of hastily using their carbines against our people; but it seems to be established that a portion, at
least, of the in-wheeling line did really suffer itself to
be charged in rear by the 5th Dragoon Guards. It
could not but be that many of the Russians would be
cut down or unhorsed when the English regiment
charged in, as it did, amongst troopers thus rendered
defenceless by the nature of their own manœuvre;
but, on the other hand, very many were protected
from the edge of the sword—nay even, indeed, from its

point—by the thickness of their long, ample coats; and, upon the whole, there were numbers of horsemen, some English, some Russian, who thronged up against that part of the column where the Scots Greys were eddying back ; so that Russians belonging to the column, and Russians belonging to the right wing, and men of the Scots Greys and men of the 5th Dragoon Guards, were here forced and crowded together in one indiscriminate melley.* Nor were these the only components of the crowd. Men of the same brigade, but having tasks assigned them elsewhere, broke away from their duties in camp, and—some of them on invalid chargers—found means to gallop up into the fight. Amongst these, two regimental butchers, each busy with his sword, were conspicuous because of their shirt-sleeves. Moreover, there could be seen here and there a man of the Light Brigade, who, for sake of the strife, had stolen away from his regiment, and was mingled with the rest of the combatants.

And, at the part of the column thus assailed by the 5th Dragoon Guards, there was a change in the bearing of the combatants—a change brought about, it would seem, by exceeding weariness of the sword-arm, but in part too by another cause. After three or four minutes of a new experience, it proved that a

---

* In strictness, perhaps, this word should be spelt 'mesley,' or 'masly' (not 'medley,' a word from another root), but I follow the mode which obtains in ' pell-mell.' The word is so familiar to Englishmen of different classes of life, and so well derived from old French, that there is no reason for allowing it to be supplanted by any such mincing substitute as 'mêlée.'

C H A P.
VI.

man could grow accustomed, as it were, to the condition of being in a throng of assailants, and take
his revel of battle in a spirit as fond as at the beginning, yet by this time less anxious, less fierce, less
diligent. Those truculent Scots, who had cut their
way in without speaking, were now, whilst they fought,
hurrahing. The din of sheer fighting had swelled into
the roar of a tumult.

Alexander Miller, the acting Adjutant of the Greys,
was famous in his regiment for the mighty volume of
sound which he drove through the air when he gave

Efforts made to rally the Greys.

the word of command.* Over all the clangour of
arms, and all the multitudinous uproar, his single
voice got dominion. It thundered out, ' Rally ! '
Then, still louder, it thundered, ' The Greys ! ' †

The Adjutant, as it chanced, was so mounted that
his vast, superb form rose high over the men of even
his own regiment, and rose higher still over the throng
of the Russians. Seized at once by the mighty sound,
and turning to whence it came, numbers of the Scots
saw their towering Adjutant with his reeking sword
high in the air, and again they heard him cry, ' Rally ! '
—again hurl his voice at ' The Greys ! '

He did not speak in mere vehemence, like one who,
although he cry ' Rally ! ' means only a war-cry or
cheer. He spoke as an officer delivering the word of

* I dare not speak of the distance at which, as I learn, his voice could
make itself heard, but I may so far venture as to say that the distance
was such as to be computed by the mile.

† It seems that, even when this regiment is addressed in the vocative
case, it is customary to retain the definite article, and address it as
' The Greys.'

command. But to rally?—the Greys to rally? It well might seem a desperate task to attempt what CHAP. VI.
troops call a 'rally' in the midst of the enemy's
thickset squadrons, but the greater height of the Scots
Greys and their chargers as compared with the invaded mass, made it possible for the taller horsemen,
now seeing one of their officers, and hearing his
word of command, to begin to act together. And, the
notion of using the lessons of the barrack-yard in the
midst of the Russian host was carried yet further.
When troop-officers are forming and dressing a line
they, of course, front towards their men; and since it
was difficult for a man in the melley to know which
might be the front, and which might be the rear, there
was the more need of guidance. The Adjutant deliberately fronted down the slope in the direction by which
the Russians had advanced, and threw into his closing
monosyllable the giant strength of his voice when he
shouted, ' Face—me !' By many of the men of his
regiment he was seen. By many more he was heard.
And now, also, on the right of the Adjutant, the young
Cornet Prendergast, raised high above the ground by
the great height of his charger, and on the other side
Clarke, the leader of the 1st squadron—Clarke still
rode bare-headed and streaming with blood—could
be seen with their swords in the air, undertaking to
rally the Greys. Men under this guidance tried to
gather together the best way they could in a throng;
and, by facing towards the Adjutant (as the thunder
of his voice had enjoined), they began to show the
rudiments of a front.

CHAP.
VI.

The order given by Scarlett to Major Conolly.

When Scarlett despatched his Brigade-Major, with orders to bring up some troops which might more or less confront the vastly outflanking strength of the enemy's left, he supposed that Major Conolly would have to execute this order by riding back in search of the 4th Dragoon Guards or the Royals; and it was not without pain that he thought himself compelled thus to exile a gifted cavalry officer from the fight during several critical minutes.   Major Conolly, how-ever, found means to see the object of the order attained without losing his share of the combat; for, glancing in that direction opposite to the Russian left in which it was judged to be of vital need to have an English force posted, he saw, and saw with great joy, that one of the red squadrons was already there. Quickly reaching the force, he found that it was the 1st squadron of the Inniskillings, commanded by Cap-tain Hunt, who, however, was under the orders of Major Shute, the field-officer then present with this part of the regiment.   Conolly was instantly sure that, under the direction of these officers, the squadron would be so wielded as to do all that was possible to-wards the execution of Scarlett's wish, and he at once determined to act with it in the approaching fight.

Hunt's squadron of the Inniskillings.

The offi-cers pre-sent with the squad-ron.

With the exception of its leader, no captain was present with this squadron, and only one subaltern—namely, Lieutenant Wheatcroft, who commanded one of the troops.   The other troop was commanded by a non-commissioned officer—that is, by the troop ser-geant-major.*

* I have now ascertained that the name of this non-commissioned

Major Shute was an officer of a high order of ability, and Captain Hunt, the squadron-leader, had not only prowess of that quiet and resolute kind which most inspires trust and devotion, but had also that priceless qualification for the wielding of cavalry which is gained by experience of war.

At the moment of the surprise, as we know, this squadron of the Inniskillings had been farther advanced on the road towards Kadiköi than any other of Scarlett's troops ; and it resulted that the position of the squadron at the time when the ' three hundred' had wheeled into line, was in the direction of Scarlett's right rear. The squadron was so placed as to be fronting, not full, but obliquely towards the enemy's left flank.

When the Russian left wing had not only disclosed the intent to wheel inwards, but even had effected good progress in the execution of the manœuvre, Major Shute ordered Hunt to charge it.

Free from the camp impediments which had obstructed Scarlett's 'three hundred,' and afterwards the 5th Dragoon Guards, the interval which divided this squadron of the Inniskillings from the enemy was all good galloping ground, and Hunt moving forward at the head of his squadron, and then rapidly increasing, and still increasing, its swiftness, attained, before the moment of impact, to a full charging pace. The roar of the fight going on was calculated to overlay other sounds, and the thick, stiff elastic herbage which

officer was Sergeant-Major Shiel. He received seven wounds, and three of those wounds were severe ones.

CHAP.
VI.
clothed the soil, was well enough fitted to muffle to
the utmost the tramp of horses ; but even after giving
full weight to these circumstances, it is scarce possible to hear of what happened without more or less
of astonishment.

The troops of the Russian left wing had not only
continued their in-wheeling movement, but had carried
the manœuvre so far that, at the moment of the impact, they had their backs turned towards the squadron
which charged them. Piercing their line like an arrow,
Captain Hunt shot through it, and was followed in
the next instant by the squadron behind him, which
came crashing on upon the rear of the wheeling horsemen, consigning some to slaughter, and driving in the
rest of them, a helpless, unresisting throng, upon the
front of the column. So swift and so weighty had
been the charge that, if so one may say, it welded men
into a mass. Of the tightness with which horsemen
were locked in the melley, some idea may be formed
if I say that, when Conolly found his arms laden and
weighed down by the dead body of a Russian trooper
which had fallen across them, he was for some time
prevented from casting off his unwelcome burthen by
the density and close pressure of the throng which encompassed him on all sides. But although in this
melley, a horseman, of his own will, could not alter
his relative place, yet that throng, of which he had
come to be for the moment an almost passive component, was not altogether motionless. It heaved ;
and, this time, as has been already learnt—for we
come once again to a moment before spoken of—the

swaying of the mass which before had been to and
fro, was perceptibly in the up-hill direction—in the
direction that had been given it (as some imagined)
by the impact of Captain Hunt's charge, and the
weight of the fugitive troops driven in upon the
front of the column. It would seem, therefore—for
otherwise the swaying of the mass in an up-hill direction could hardly have gone on so continuously—
that already the pressure of the squadrons which
formed the centre and rear of the column must have
been loosening.

CHAP.
VI.

And this might well be; for in another quarter,
the attack of the 4th Dragoon Guards was now taking effect. Captain Forster, with the right squadron
of the regiment, had already charged into the melley
which was gathered on the right flank of the column;
whilst farther up the hillside, but acting in the same
direction against the enemy's right flank, Colonel
Hodge, having charged in person at the head of the
left squadron of his regiment, and having burst his
way into the column, was driving fast through it
from flank to flank—driving through it without losing
men—and so faithfully working out the old precept
of 'hard all across!' as to be already on the point of
emerging from the mass of the Russian cavalry at a
spot opposite to the one by which he had entered it.

The 4th
Dragoon
Guards.

Seeing that the column through which Hodge thus
rended his way had been pierced and riven from the
first by Scarlett's 'three hundred,' that already it
had been brought to such a condition as to allow of
the 4th Dragoon Guards cutting through it without

getting harmed, and that both its huge wings had
been shattered and driven in confusedly upon its
front and flanks by the Royals, by the 5th Dragoon
Guards, and finally by Hunt's Squadron of the
Inniskillings, it would be rash to assign to the
attack of any one corps the change which now
supervened ; but, whatever the cause, that resistance
to all rearward movement which had long been exerted by the enemy's deep - serried squadrons now
began to relax. Less and less obstructed, and less
closely locked than before, the melley or throng that
had been jammed into a closely locked mass by the
last charge of the Inniskillings continued to heave
slowly upwards against the slope of the hill. Presently the Russians who had hitherto maintained
their array caused or suffered their horses to back
a little. The movement was slight, but close followed by surer signs. The ranks visibly loosened.
In the next instant, the whole column was breaking.
In the next, all the horsemen composing it had dispersed into one immense herd, and—still hanging
together as closely as they could without hindrance
to their flight—were galloping up the hillside and
retreating by the way they had come.

The break-
ing of the
column.

Retreat of
the whole
body.

Nearly at the moment when the column began to
break, General Scarlett had at length cut his way
through it. He had entered it, as we know, at the
centre of its front, and at the head of the Greys. The
part of the column from which he emerged was its left
flank ; and those of his people whom he then had the
nearest to him were men of the Inniskilling Dragoons.

We saw that even during the fight, and whilst still involved in the throng, the Scots Greys had endeavoured to rally; and some way to their left, but in the same alignment, the Royals (having numbers of men of other regiments intermixed with their squadrons) were still re-forming their ranks; but no other part of our Heavy Brigade had even attempted as yet to recover its state of formation; and as it was inferred that the enemy might have some force on the other slope of the ridge which would be ready to act in support, our officers were more eager to rally their scattered troopers than to encourage pursuit. Indeed almost at the instant of emerging from the depths of the column—he came out of it panting and vehement as though fresh from violent bodily effort*—Colonel Hodge had laid his commands on the two first trumpeters he could see, and caused them to sound the rally.

Notwithstanding this desire to effect a rally at once, many of our dragoons pursued the retreating enemy for some distance, but not with their strength in such a state of coherence as to be able to make the victory signal by extensive destruction or capture of prisoners; and being happily under good control, they were checked and brought to a halt before coming under the fire which awaited them from the slopes of the Fedioukine Hills.

The troop of horse-artillery which accompanied the Light Brigade had by this time some pieces in

* Lord Lucan, who, as we saw, had ridden up by the (proper) left flank of the Russian column, saw Hodge in the act of coming out from it. He also saw General Scarlett emerge.

C H A P. battery which discharged a few shots at the retreating
VI.   horsemen ; * and under the special directions of Sir
Colin Campbell, a like fire was directed against them
from two of Barker's guns.

Results of   It seems that in this singular combat our Heavy
the fight
between   Dragoons had 78 killed and wounded—the Russians
the Rus-
sian cav- a much larger number ; † but it is not by counting
alry and
Scarlett's the mere losses on either side that this cavalry fight
Brigade,   can be judged. On the one hand, our troopers had
so great an advantage from their longer, more commanding reach, and, on the other, the Russians were
so well protected by their shakoes and their heavy
grey coats, that the carnage resulting from the actual
fight bore no proportion to the scale, the closeness,
and the obstinacy of the conflict ; but also, for want
of the mere slaughtering and capturing power that
can be exerted in pursuit by squadrons which are
not in a state of dispersion, the English dragoons
were prevented from conveying to the world any
adequate notion of the victory they had gained.
When they had been rallied and re-formed, they not
only disclosed no abounding exultation, but even
evinced a sense of disappointment which bordered

* The battery of position, No. 4, under the orders of Lieutenant, now
Major H. B. Roberts, of the R. M. Artillery, also delivered fire with
effect upon the retreating horsemen.—*Note to Second Edition.*
† I have no sufficient means of giving the losses which the Russians
sustained in this fight. I can say, however, that (according to General
de Todleben) the whole loss which the Russians sustained in the battle
was 550, and that, according to Liprandi, their loss in infantry was
comparatively small, their loss in cavalry, heavy. I may add, that their
loss in cavalry, whatever it was, must have resulted almost entirely
from their fight with our Heavy Dragoons.

on anger. The men found that at the close of what CHAP. VI. had seemed to them a life-and-death struggle, the enemy had at last been enabled to gallop off without sustaining grave loss, and their inference was that they had been fighting almost in vain. They were mistaken. Without having wrought a great slaughter or captured a host of prisoners, they had gained so great an ascendant that of all the vast body which is known to have been opposed to them there was hardly one squadron which afterwards proved willing to keep its ground upon the approach of English cavalry.

But if the men of our Heavy Brigade were themselves ill content on account of the seeming barrenness of their victory; it was otherwise with the spectators who had witnessed the fight—who had seen the few wrestling with the many ánd finally gaining the day. The admiration with which the French had watched the fight was expressed by them with a generous enthusiasm. 'It was truly magnificent'—so spoke a French general officer who had witnessed the fight—'it was truly magnificent; and to me who ' could see the enormous numbers opposed to you, the ' whole valley being filled with Russian cavalry, the ' victory of the Heavy Brigade was the most glorious ' thing I ever saw.' * The moment the Russian column was seen to be broken, our dragoons were greeted from afar by a cheer from the 93d Highlanders; and before the Brigade had completed its rally, Sir Colin

The admiration excited by the exploit of Scarlett's Brigade.

* Colonel (now General) Beatson was the officer to whom the French General—I cannot at this moment give his name—addressed the above words.

CHAP. Campbell galloped up.   When he had come close to
VI.   the Greys, he uncovered and spoke to the regiment.
'Greys! gallant Greys!' he said, according to one of
the versions, 'I am sixty-one years old, and if I were
'young again I should be proud to be in your ranks.'
Afterwards, accosting Lord Lucan, he declared to him
that the oldest officer could not have done better.
The French sent to Lord Lucan their tribute of enthu-

The con-
gratula-
tion ad-
dressed to
General
Scarlett
by Lord
Raglan.

siastic admiration; and an aide-de-camp came down
from Lord Raglan with two gracious syllables for
Scarlett conveyed in the message, 'Well done!'

Supposing that General Ryjoff was properly obeyed,
it would seem that he became chargeable with several grave errors, and in particular,—

Comments
upon the
fight.

1st, For massing his squadrons in such a way as to
be virtually fighting without any force detached from
his first line—in other words, without any 'sup-
'ports.'

2d, For his halt.

3d, For attempting and continuing the wheeling
movement of his deployed wings in the face of the
English 'supports.'

Anterior to the actual bodily fighting, there was a
phase of the engagment which seems to be deserving
of remembrance.   I speak of the moments when the
Russian column of horse, with all its vast weight,
was moving down the hillside against Scarlett's few
horsemen, then suddenly caught in their march, and
hastening under great stress of time to prepare a
front for the enemy.   The admirable composure then

evinced by our people of all ranks must have been CHAP.
seen by the enemy, and perhaps may have governed VI.
the issue, by inducing him to come to a halt.

A commander of horse, in general, is accustomed
to seek his victory by gathering a great momentum,
and directing the force of his onset against some
object more or less fragile—as, for example, against a
body of infantry drawn up in a hollow square; but
these were not the conditions under which Scarlett
had to attack; and accordingly, his feat has hardly
supplied a good instance of what men commonly
mean when they speak of a cavalry charge. On the
contrary, the physical impossibility of overthrowing
the enemy by the mere shock of a cavalry charge was
the very circumstance which gave to this fight its
peculiar splendour. When Scarlett rode straight at
the centre of a hanging thicket of sabres and lances
which not only outflanked him enormously on his
right hand as well as his left, but confronted him too
with the blackness of squadrons upon squadrons in
mass, he did not of course imagine that by any mere
impact of his too scanty line he could shake the
depths of a column extending far up the hillside;
but he thought he might cleave his way in, and he
knew that his people would follow him. He survived
the enterprise, and even proved to the world that
close fighting under the conditions which he accepted
might be a task less desperate than it seemed; but
his hopefulness, if hopefulness he had when he drove
his horse into the column, could hardly have been

C H A P. warranted, at the time, by the then known teachings
VI. of human experience.*

The time
occupied
by the
fight.

By the judgment of Lord Lucan—not tested, however, by the hand of the watch—it has been computed that from the moment when General Scarlett commenced his charge, to the one when the Russian mass broke, the time was about eight minutes.

In order that the Allies should be able to reap from this fight of our Heavy Brigade any fruits at all proportioned to its brilliancy, it was necessary that they should have had on the ground some fresh and unbroken squadrons which would pursue the retreating mass, and convert its defeat into ruin, or at least into grievous disaster. Were no such squadrons at hand ?

* What is the closest historical parallel that can be found for the charge of Scarlett's three hundred ?

CHAPTER VII.

WHILST this combat of Scarlett's was raging, people witnessed, hard by, a more tranquil scene, and one which indeed was so free from all the tumult of battle as to offer a kind of repose to eyes wearied with gazing at strife. Overlooking the flank of the Russian cavalry in its struggle with Scarlett's brigade, and at a distance from the combatants which has been computed at 400, or 500 yards, there stood ranged in two lines, a body of near 700 men. They all of them bore arms; they all wore military uniforms; and each man was either mounted, or else had his charger beside him. They were troops of the same nation as Scarlett's combating regiments. In truth, they were nothing less than the famous Light Brigade of the English; but, strange to say, these superb horsemen were engaged for the time as spectators, maintaining a rigid neutrality in the war which they saw going on between Russia and our Heavy Dragoons.

Of the impatience with which our Light Cavalry chafed when they found themselves withheld from the fight, some idea perhaps may be formed by any one who

The Light Brigade at the time of Scarlett's engagement.

Its neutrality.

Impatience of the brigade;

CHAP.
VII.
recalls to his mind the far-famed exploit they were
destined to be performing at a later hour of the same
day. It was not without a grating sense of the contrast that, whilst thus condemned to inaction, they
saw Scarlett hotly engaged; and although the commander of the Light Brigade, in giving vent to his
mortification, used one of those cavalry forms of
speech which express approval or endearment in
words of imprecation, it is not for that the less
true that the sentiment which really blended with
his natural vexation was one of admiring and gener-

and of
Lord
Cardigan.
ous envy. Lord Cardigan was himself the public
informant who adduced in a court of justice this
picturesque proof of his feelings—' We were specta-
' tors,' says one of his witnesses, ' of that encounter; and
' those who heard and saw Lord Cardigan during the
' time that was going on, will not easily forget the cha-
' grin and disappointment he evinced when riding up
' and down our line. He constantly repeated, " Damn
' " those Heavies, they have the laugh of us this day." '

The sur-
prise with
which the
neutrality
of the
Light
Brigade
was ob-
served.
As may well be supposed, this abstention of our
Light Cavalry was observed by the Russians with
surprise and thankfulness, by the Headquarters Staff
of the English with surprise and vexation, by the
French with surprise and curiosity. If Canrobert and
those of his people who looked down upon the plain of
Balaclava grew warm and enthusiastic in their admiration of Scarlett's exploit, they were all the more ready
with questions, surmises, and reasonings when they saw
that, during the fight thus maintained by one of our
two cavalry brigades against a largely outnumbering

force, the other brigade remained motionless—nay, even in part dismounted. The impressions of the French in regard to the English lie deposited for the most part in layers or strata, disclosing the periods of the several formations; and if the nature of the comments which were uttered could be inferred from known habits of thought and of speech, it might be found that the theory put forward by any French officer as serving to account for the phenomenon was adopted in general by his comrades of the same age, and repudiated by such of them as were either much older or much younger; but whether, with their grey-headed colonel, the more aged officers of a regiment made sure that the Count of Cardigan was a great feudal chief, with a brigade composed of his serfs and retainers, who, for some cause or other, had taken dire umbrage, and resolved, like Achilles, that his myrmidons should be withheld from the fight; or whether, on the authority of the major—less aged, though equally confident—they held that the feudal system in England had been recently mitigated, and that the true solution of the enigma was to be found in the law of ‘Le Box’—the law making it criminal for an Englishman to interrupt a good fight, and enjoining that singular formation which Albion called ‘a ring;’—whatever, in short, might be the variety of special theories which these French observers adopted, there was one proposition at least in which all would be sure to agree. All, all would take part in the chorus which asserted that the English were a heap of ‘originals.’

Yet, amongst the French officers thus striving to

CHAP. solve the enigma, one at least was inclined to trace
VII. the neutrality of our Light Brigade to a cause of miscarriage which, far from being exclusively English,
has often condemned the great cavalry forces of the
Continent to the imputation of losing opportunities.
No less clearly than any of his comrades the Vicomte
de Nöé perceived the strange error which had been
committed; but he traced it to a want of that initiative power which enables a general of cavalry to seize
his occasion.*

The cause   When we turn from the surmises of the French to our
which pal-
sied the   English sources of knowledge, and there seek to find
Light
Brigade at out the spell which palsied Lord Cardigan's squadrons,
the time of
Scarlett's we learn that the brigade was kept where it stood by
engage-
ment.   the interpretation which its chief had been putting upon
Lord Lucan's parting instructions. The Brigadier
had been left in the position he occupied with directions to defend it against any attack; but other
words accompanied this direction; and upon the whole,
after giving to the terms of the order, as gathered by
him at the time, the best construction which his unaided judgment would furnish, Lord Cardigan hap-
lessly came to the conclusion that it was his duty to
abstain from attacking the enemy in flank whilst our
Heavy Dragoons were attacking him in front, and to

---

* 'Repulsed with loss,' says the Vicomte, 'it [the Russian cavalry]
' regained the heights, where it might have been annihilated if the
' English Light Cavalry, under the orders of Lord Cardigan, had
' charged it during its retreat. There was the occasion, there should
' have been exercised the initiative of the cavalry general, and later in
' the day it was made apparent that bravery is no sufficient substitute
' for initiative.'

PLATE 4.

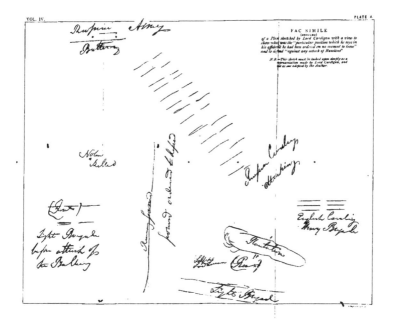

FAC SIMILE
(REDUCED)
*of a Plan sketched by Lord Cardigan with a view to
shew what was the "particular position which he says in
his official he had been ordered on no account to leave"
and to defend "against any attack of Russians"*

*N.B.—This sketch must be looked upon simply as a
representation made by Lord Cardigan, and
not as one adopted by the Author.*

suffer the Russian cavalry to retreat from before him CHAP. VII. —nay, almost, one may say, to retreat across his front —without undertaking to pursue it.*

Lord Lucan, of course, did not mean that his Light Cavalry should meet a conjuncture like the one which actually occurred by remaining in a state of inaction ; but how far the mistake may have derived a seeming warrant from any obscurity or from any misleading tendency in his instruction, that, of course, is a question dependent on the words that were used.† If no

---

* See the accompanying sketch-plan representing Lord Cardigan's idea of the respective positions of the Russian cavalry and of the two English brigades. The plate is upon a reduced scale, but is, in other respects, a facsimile of the drawing which Lord Cardigan prepared for me. The special purpose for which he prepared the drawing was to show what the position was which he considered that he had to defend.

† Lord Cardigan's statement is : 'I had been ordered into a parti-
' cular position by Lieutenant-General the Earl of Lucan, my superior
' officer, with orders on no account to leave it, and to defend it against
' any attack of Russians. They did not, however, approach the position.'—Affidavit of Lord Cardigan. Lord Lucan's version of the order
he gave is this—'I am going to leave you. Well, you'll remember that
' you are placed here by Lord Raglan himself for the defence of this
' position. My instructions to you are to attack anything and every-
' thing that shall come within reach of you, but you will be careful of
' columns or squares of infantry.' Lord Lucan, I believe, considers that
when the Russian cavalry advanced up the North Valley to within a
few hundred yards of Lord Cardigan, when they moved (obliquely) across
Lord Cardigan's front, and proceeded under his eyes to attack English
regiments, they did 'approach the position,' nay did actually invade it,
thereby bringing about the exact contingency under which Lord Cardigan (according to his own version of the instructions) was ordered to
defend the position 'against any attack of Russians.' On the other
hand, it may be thought that even according to Lord Lucan's version
of his own words, they were such as, in the judgment of a peace-service
man like Lord Cardigan, might not unnaturally appear to have a
fettering tendency. Such phrases as '*placed here*,' and '*defence of this
' position*,' followed by the instruction to attack whatever might '*come
' within reach*,' were plainly dangerous. I know not on what ground

CHAP. such palliation shall be established, it must be judged
VII. that Lord Cardigan's abstention resulted from an
honest failure of judgment, from an undue confidence
in himself, and from an imperfect acquaintance with
the business of war, but also from strong sense of
duty—from that same sense of duty, remember, which
was destined to be his guide in the hour then coming,
and to carry him down the North Valley on a venture-
some, nay desperate service.   Still, the miscarriage of
Lord Cardigan's endeavour to construe the order aright
did actually result in the spectacle which we have
just been witnessing ; and, it being apparent that the
inaction to which he imagined himself condemned
was calculated to be gravely injurious to the public
service, it seems useful to inquire whether the mishap
was one of those incidents of war which carry no
lesson, or whether, on the contrary, it can be traced
to a malpractice on the part of the Home Government
which might be avoided in future wars.

The kind
of experi-
ence which
has a ten-
dency to
prevent
men from
putting
sensible
construc-
tions on
orders.

        The task of endeavouring to put a right construc-
tion upon orders given in war, and especially in battle,
is often an anxious and difficult one, yet so enormously important that the honour, nay, the fate of
a nation, may depend upon the way in which it is
discharged.   Now, it would seem that there is one
kind of experience which, if long continued, has a

Lord Lucan thought that Lord Raglan placed the cavalry where he did
in order to charge it with the defence of this position.   I have always
understood that Lord Raglan's object in bringing in his cavalry under
the steeps of the Chersonese was—not to defend any position, but—to
have it in hand, and prevent it from becoming perniciously entangled
in combats.

peculiar tendency to disqualify an officer for the duty
of putting sensible constructions upon orders concerning the business of war. The experience I speak of is that which is possessed by an officer who has served many years in a standing army without having had the fortune to go through a campaign. Such a man, during his whole military life, has been perpetually dealing with fixed conditions and petty occurrences which are mostly of a kind that can be, in a measure, provided for beforehand by even that limited forecast which the rules of an office imply; and as soon as his training has taken its effect to the utmost, he may be said to represent the true opposite of what a commander should be who has to encounter emergencies. So long as soldierly duties are confined to mere preparation and rehearsal, they can be effectively performed by the industrious formalist; but in war all is changed. There, the enemy interposes, and interposes so roughly that the military clock-work of peacetime is ruthlessly shattered. As a guide for construing momentous orders delivered in the hour of battle to a general of the peace-service training, the experience of the barrack-yard becomes a snare. His new theatre of action is so strange, so vast, and so dim—for he now has to meet the unknown—that unless he can rise with the occasion, throwing open his mind and changing his old stock of ideas, he becomes dangerous to his country—becomes dangerous, of course, in proportion to the extent of the command with which he has been entrusted. Supposing the natural capacity equal, there is no stirring missionary,

no good electioneerer, no revered master of hounds, who might not be more likely to prove himself equal to the unforeseen emergencies of a campaign than the general officer who is a veteran in the military profession, and, at the same time, a novice in war. If indeed a general who has hitherto had no experience of war is still in so early a period of his life as to have unimpaired the natural flexibility of youth, he may quickly adapt his mind to the new exigency; but when a State gives high command to an officer who is not only encased with military experience all acquired in peace-time, but is also advanced in years, it fulfils at least two of the conditions which are the most likely to bring about misconstructions of even the plainest orders: and if to these precautions the Government adds that of taking care that the selected General shall be a man of a narrow disposition and a narrow mind—a man cleaving to technicalities and regulations with a morbid love of uniformity—then, indeed, it exhausts a large proportion of the expedients which can be used for insuring miscarriage.

England, ruling as she does over various and widespread dependencies, is so often forced into warlike operations of more or less magnitude, as to be free from the predicament of having at her command no war-tried officers. Therefore, when, with such means at her disposal, she still trusts important commands to her peace-service officers, she has not the plea of necessity. She acts in sheer wantonness. She needs, as it were, a strong swimmer, and hastens to take a man who never has happened to bathe. She wants a skilful ship's captain to maintain her strength on the ocean, and for this purpose chooses a bargeman who has plied thirty years on canals.

As a warning instance of miscarriage resulting from this evil practice, Lord Cardigan's mistake has great worth; because it was so obviously occasioned both by his experience, and by his want of experience —by the abundant military experience which had gathered upon him in peace-time, and by the want of that other experience which men gain in war. Many an officer long versed in peace-service might have made an equivalent mistake; but, on the other hand, it is probable that in such a conjuncture as that in which Lord Cardigan found himself, no man who ever had wielded a squadron in the field would have thought himself condemned to inaction.

The example was made the more signal by an Incident making the error more signal; incident which occurred at the time. Whilst Lord Cardigan sat in his saddle, expressing, under cavalry forms of speech, his envy of the Heavy Dragoons, and adhering to that hapless construction of Lord Lucan's order, which condemned him, as he thought, to a state of neutrality, he had at his side an officer, comparatively young, and with only the rank of a captain, who still was well able to give him that guidance which, by reason of his want of experience in war, he grievously, though unconsciously, needed. Captain Morris, commanding the 17th Lancers, one by bringing into public contrast the qualifications of Lord Car- of the regiments of the Light Brigade, and then in his thirty-fourth year, was a man richly gifted with the natural qualities which tend to make a leader of cavalry, but strengthened also by intellectual cultivation well applied to the business of arms, and clothed, above all, with that priceless experience which soldiers acquire in war. After having first armed himself with a portion at least of the education which Cambridge bestows, he had served with glory in India. In 1843 he had been present at the battle of Maharajpore. In 1846 he fought at the battle of Buddiwal. At the battle of Aliwal in the same year he was wounded whilst charging with his regiment into a mass of Sikh infantry. He was in the battle of Sobraon; he crossed the Sutlej, and entered Lahore with the army. When opportunities of gaining warlike experience were no longer open to him, he returned to the labour of military study, and carried away from Sandhurst ample evidences of his proficiency in higher departments of military learning. Captain Morris was one of those who might have been wisely entrusted with an extended command of cavalry. Few could be more competent to point out to Lord Cardigan the error he was committing—to show him in two words how to construe Lord Lucan's order, and to explain to him that when cavalry has to hold a ' position,' it is not, for that reason, forced to abstain from resisting the enemy.*

Perceiving with vivid distinctness the precious opportunity which the fortune of war was offering,

* I say ' resisting,' because the advance of the Russian cavalry was an actual invasion of the English position—nay, even of the very camping-ground of the Light Brigade.

Morris eagerly prayed that the Light Cavalry might advance upon the enemy's column of horse; or, if that could not be conceded, then that he at least, with his regiment, might be suffered to undertake an attack. That he imparted his desire to Lord Cardigan, and that Lord Cardigan rebuffed him, I cannot doubt; * but for the present purpose—for the purpose, namely, of illustrating the mischief of entrusting high command to a veteran of the peace-service unversed in war—the sworn statement of Lord Cardigan is sufficiently instructive. After speaking of Captain Morris's alleged interposition, he goes on to say that 'Captain Morris never gave any advice, or ' made any proposal of the sort;' that 'it was not ' his duty to do so;' and that he 'did not commit ' such an irregularity.'

When the Oxford undergraduate stopped short of presuming to snatch his fellow-student from a watery

CHAP.
VII.

* I do not forget (as will presently be seen) that Lord Cardigan has denied this ; but my proofs are ample : and indeed Lord Cardigan, though he places the incident at a moment when it had become too late to act with effect, has himself acknowledged to me that Captain Morris sought to push forward with his regiment, and that he (Lord Cardigan) stopped the attempt. Both with respect to the fact itself and the time of its occurrence, Captain (afterwards Colonel) Morris has been explicit. In a letter addressed by him to the Horse Guards he wrote thus :—' Having read . . . . a letter from Major Calthorpe, in which ' he throws between Lord Cardigan and myself the settlement of the ' question as to whether I asked Lord Cardigan, on the 25th of Oc- ' tober 1854, to attack the Russian cavalry in flank at the time they ' were engaged with the Heavy Brigade, and which Lord Cardigan ' most positively denies, I wish to declare most positively that I did ' ask Lord Cardigan to attack the enemy at the time and in the ' manner above mentioned.' See also the conclusive testimony contained in the second affidavit of the Honourable Godfrey Charles Morgan filed in the suit of Cardigan v. Calthorpe.

CHAP.
VII.
grave, on the theory that it was indecorous for one
lad to rescue another without having first been presented to him, the objection was perhaps overstrained,
but, at all events, it proceeded from the formalist who
stood on the bank, and not from the one in the river.
Here, more wonderfully—for Morris was willing,
nay offered, to rescue Lord Cardigan from his error—
it was the drowning man who, on grounds of a stiff
etiquette, protested against being saved.

If Lord Cardigan's idea of an 'irregularity' was
upheld by the sanction of the Horse Guards, it must
be acknowledged that our Home dispensers of military power had performed their task with a rare
completeness. They found a man who was of an
age, and endowed with natural qualities, highly
favourable to effective command, who had had rich
experience in the business of war, who had earned
for himself a large share of glory in combats and
pitched battles. Him they placed under a General
fifty-seven years old, who, without any warlike experience, still sincerely presumed himself competent
to the exigencies of high command in the field; and
then they crowned their work by causing or allowing
the army to understand that it would be an 'irregu-
'larity' for the man who had learnt war on the Sutlej to tender his opportune counsel to the one who
had come from Hyde Park.

A brigade of light cavalry drawn up in two lines on
good turf, and employed in the occupation of gazing
upon a fight sustained against a great stress of numbers by their comrades the Heavy Dragoons; the man

of the Sutlej entreating that the brigade might ad- CHAP.
vance to the rescue, but rebuffed and overruled by VII.
the higher authority of the man from the banks of
the Serpentine who sits erect in his saddle, and is
fitfully 'damning the Heavies' instead of taking part
in their fight—these might seem to be the creatures
of the brain evoked perhaps for some drama of the
grossly humorous sort; but because of the sheer truth,
their place is historic; and if comedy seems to result,
it is comedy prepared in Whitehall.   It is comedy
too of that kind which sometimes teaches and warns.
By the will of our military authorities at home, the
man versed in war was placed under the man versed
in quarrels.   Lord Cárdigan had been charged to
command; Captain Morris had to obey.   The exag-
gerations men look for in satire were forestalled and
outdone by the Horse Guards.

In its actual bearing upon events, the neutrality of
the Light Cavalry proved less hurtful than at first it
seemed likely to be; because Scarlett's dragoons, after
all, found means to achieve their victory without
help from the other brigade.   If Scarlett's 'three
'hundred' had been overwhelmed and destroyed, both
the terms of Lord Lucan's instruction and the inaction maintained by Lord Cardigan would have been
cruelly judged.   As it was, the miscarriage, however
pernicious in its other consequences, did at least bring
glory upon our arms, because it withheld from Scarlett's dragoons that support which must have dimmed
their victory by making it more easy of attainment.
It is true that if the Light Brigade, although abstain-

CHAP.
VII.

Lord Lu-
can's mes-
sage of
reproof to
Lord Car-
digan.

ing from the thick of the fight, had been suffered at the right moment to advance in pursuit, it might possibly have effected captures by a swift and skilled use of the moments during which such a work was practicable; but any force pursuing the enemy beyond a short distance must have very soon come under fire from the guns on the Fedioukine Hills.

Lord Lucan, as may well be supposed, was bitterly vexed by the inaction of his Light Brigade, and at the close of the combat he sent one of his aides-de-camp with a message which enjoined Lord Cardigan in future, whenever his Divisional General might be attacking in front, to lose no opportunity of making a flank attack. The message added, that Lord Lucan would always be ready to give a like support to Lord Cardigan.*

I have traced the fault up to its sources. If ever there were to be uttered a taunt which should impute the inaction of Lord Cardigan to any cause worse than mistake, this short, cogent answer would follow, ' He led the "Light Cavalry charge." ' †

---

* It is right to say that Lord Cardigan has questioned this, but to add, that proof which I must regard as conclusive is in my possession.

† There is a curiously strong chain of testimony which goes to show, that at or towards the close of the Heavy Cavalry fight, the Light Brigade was moved down into the South Valley, and brought into the rear of the ground from which our Heavy Dragoons had made their attack; but counter-testimony of a very cogent kind opposes itself to this conclusion. The decision of the question, although it might have a personal bearing of some interest, is not important in any other point of view.

CHAPTER VIII.

FROM the easternmost ledges of the Chersonese, the chiefs of the two Allied armies, together with great numbers of their people, had been keenly looking down, as we learned, upon the combat of Scarlett's dragoons; but the bulk of these spectators—first anxious and afterwards enraptured—were content to regard the encounter as a trial of cavalry prowess resulting in proportionate glory; and, so far as I know, Lord Raglan was the only officer in the field whose swift instinct informed him at the moment of the way in which this isolated engagement of horsemen might be brought to bear upon the issue of the battle. Years after that day, when in times of peace and amity the narratives, the maps and the plans of the once warring nations were collated and studied, it at last became easy enough for the French and the English to understand the extent of the change which had been wrought in the enemy's position by the victory of our heavy dragoons; but it was given to Lord Raglan to perceive all this at the time.

The defeat of the Russian cavalry carried with it, of course, the retreat of the powerful artillery which the

CHAP.
VIII.

Lord Raglan's instantaneous perception of the new phase into which the battle had passed.

The change that was

CHAP.
VIII.

wrought
in the posi-
tion of the
Russians
by the de-
feat of
their cav-
alry. horse had escorted; and not only was the English
camp and its vicinity now free from even the sight of
an assailing force, but all that part of the North Valley
which divided the Fedioukine Heights from the line
of the Turkish redoubts was left without troops. The
change wrought by Scarlett's dragoons was therefore
such, that whereas the Russians, half an hour before,
had had a miniature battle array which enabled them
for the moment to take the offensive and penetrate
even home to the English cavalry camp, they were
now all at once reduced to what one may call two
weak columns—two weak columns having the whole
breadth of the North Valley between them, no longer
connected with one another except by their rear, and
each of them so placed as to be impotently protruding its small narrow head in the face of the divisions
coming down from the Chersonese, and debouching
in strength upon the plain. An array which before
might have been likened to the closed fist of the
pugilist, was changed, all at once, to a hand with the
two centre fingers retracted and the other two fingers
protruding.* Lord Raglan perceived that in the compass of those brilliant minutes which had been used
to such purpose by Scarlett's dragoons, they had done
the main part of his appointed task by almost win-
ning a battle for him without the aid of a single foot-
soldier or horseman sent down from the main Allied
camp. What he instantly sought to do was, to seize
on the victory which this cavalry fight seemed to open
to him by proceeding at once to the recapture of the
Causeway Heights.

* The diagram on the next page may aid the elucidation.

The arrangements for the recovery of the heights C H A P. had been made, as we saw, long ago, several hours' be- VIII. fore the occurrence which had now so much lightened the task ; and, if the requisite marches of our infantry divisions had attained completion, Sir George Cath-, cart, at the head of the 4th Division, would have been ready to advance against the Arabtabia* Redoubt by the line of the Causeway ridge; whilst H.R.H. the Duke of Cambridge with the 1st Division would have supported the attack by moving along the South Valley. The Duke of Cambridge, it would seem, had lost no time in obeying the order, and was as far in

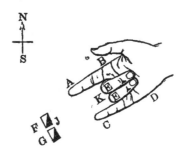

A B—Jabrokritsky's infantry and artillery disposed on the slopes of the Fediou- kine Hills.
C D—Liprandi's infantry and artillery posted along the line of the captured . Turkish redoubts, where the English guns remained.
C—The position of the Odessa regiment.
E E—The defeated Russian cavalry, with a Cossack battery in front of them.
F—Lord Cardigan's Light Cavalry Brigade.
G—General Scarlett's Heavy Cavalry Brigade.
H—The direction by which French and English reinforcements were ap- proaching.
J K—The North Valley.

* The redoubt also called Number Three.

CHAP. advance towards his assigned place as Lord Raglan
VIII. expected him to be;* but Cathcart unhappily [had
failed to march by the route prescribed to him, and]
was not yet on his appointed ground.† Lord Raglan
long before had been expressing his astonishment at
not seeing Cathcart's battalions in march, and had
sent messenger after messenger to endeavour to find
where he was, and to learn the cause of his delay. It
is true that, before the moment we speak of, Cathcart's
Division had at length made its appearance, but it
still had a good way to march before it could commence the intended attack.

‡ And unfortunately the order directing Cathcart to attack
was by him left unexecuted. When Cathcart had reached
the Col, General Airey rode up to him, and said, 'Sir George
' Cathcart, Lord Raglan wishes you to advance immedi-
' ately and recapture the redoubts.' The order was given
very plainly, and Airey, after having delivered it, turned to
the staff-officer who had carried Lord Raglan's original orders
to Cathcart, and said : ' You are acquainted with the position
' of each redoubt, remain with Sir George Cathcart and show
' him where they are.'

After passing the empty redoubts, No. 6 and No. 5, and
leaving some troops in each of them, Sir George marched on
to the No. 4 redoubt, which was also unoccupied ; but there

* He moved his infantry by a route not far south of the Woronzoff
Road, but his artillery descended by the Col.—*Note to 3d Edition.*

† The words placed within brackets should have been omitted. It
is only, I believe, too certain that the non-appearance of Cathcart at the
time expected was caused under the circumstances stated *ante,* p. 65 *et
seq.* See also the statement above given, and the one added at p. 219 *et
seq.—Note to 3d Edition.*

‡ The foot-note *ante* p. 65 applies to this interpolation as well as to
the one there occurring.

he came to a halt, deploying his infantry in two lines, and C H A P. causing it to lie down, at the same time directing his artil-   VIII. lery to open fire upon the Arabtabia. The artillery officers soon pointed out that the range was too great to allow of any useful firing, and then, under Cathcart's direction, his rifle battalion went skirmishing towards the Arabtabia, but this was the utmost that Cathcart did towards obeying the order which had enjoined him to recapture the redoubts.

Lord Raglan's vexation was great, for he felt all the evil of any delay in seizing the advantage which the fortune of war was offering.

Being in this strait, and judging also, with what Circum-stances we now know to have been a true foresight, that under which the weak chain of Russian infantry columns which Lord Raglan stretched towards him endwise along the line of the determin-ed to ap-redoubts would prove somewhat soft to the touch, he peal to his determined, as he was entitled to do, to make an cavalry. appeal to his cavalry. He did not do this appa-rently because the cavalry arm was the one which he would most willingly have selected for his purpose if he had any freedom of choice, but because his in-fantry reinforcements were not yet far enough in advance, and the time was too precious to be lost. Be that as it may, he despatched· to Lord Lucan a written instruction which in the subsequent contro-versies was generally called 'the third order.' It ran thus : 'Cavalry to advance and take advantage of any The third ' opportunity to recover the heights. They will be order. ' supported by the infantry which have been ordered ' [to] advance on two fronts.'* Whilst directing that

* It seems that in the original order the word 'to' was omitted— that there was what looked like a full stop after the word 'ordered'—

C H A P.   actual attacks against the enemy on the heights should
VIII.   be made to depend upon opportunity, this order, it
should be observed, was peremptory and unconditional
in requiring that our cavalry should advance; and
since it came, not from a distant commander, but from
one who looked down upon the whole field, and had
before his eyes all the requisite ingredients of a positive resolve, it is difficult to see how the words could
become open to misconstruction.

Lord Lu-   Lord Lucan, however, so read the order as to con-
can's con-   ceive it his duty to do no more for the moment than
struction
of it.   mount his cavalry, move the Light Brigade to another
position hard by across the North Valley, and cause his
Heavy Dragoons to remain on the slope of the rise there
awaiting the infantry, which, to use his own language,
'had not yet arrived.' Having made these dispositions, Lord Lucan kept his cavalry halted during a
period which he has computed at from thirty to forty
minutes.* If it be asked why, when ordered to advance, he kept his cavalry halted during a period of

and that the word 'advance' was written with a capital A; but the copy
which Lord Lucan afterwards furnished to Lord Raglan was as given in
the text, and I therefore imagine that, notwithstanding the clerical errors
above mentioned, the order at the time must have been read aright by
Lord Lucan. The question seems to be unimportant, for the order is
not made at all less cogent by reading it with its clerical errors uncorrected. I should not have adverted to the matter if it were not that
Lord Lucan—I do not see why—laid stress upon it in his speech addressed to the House of Lords. The copy in my possession is in the
handwriting of Lord Lucan himself, and was furnished by him to Lord
Raglan. Therefore, *for the purpose of proving the tenor of the instruction really conveyed to the mind of Lord Lucan*, the copy is evidently
more authentic than the original.

* By computations upon another basis this period is extended to fifty
or fifty-five minutes.

from thirty to forty minutes, the answer is that he
reasoned. By choosing his way of proceeding—not because it was enjoined in terms, but—because he imagined it to be 'the only way that could [have] been 'rationally intended,' he effected an actual inversion of Lord Raglan's order, and persuaded himself that, instead of the cavalry advancing (as directed) with the prospect of being supported by the infantry, it was the infantry that ought first to advance, the cavalry acting only in support.* The avoidance of delay, as we saw, was the very object which the English Commander had in view when he resolved to appeal to his squadrons. In the mind of Lord Raglan, the length of the ground which still had to be traversed by his infantry was a reason for appealing to the cavalry arm ; whilst, on the other hand, Lord Lucan judged that that same length of ground was a reason for delaying his advance ; so that the very exigency which caused Lord Raglan to desire the immediate aid of the cavalry was the one which induced Lord Lucan to withhold it.

From the height which he had occupied during the whole morning, and with the officers of his Staff around him, Lord Raglan watched for the moment when his cavalry, in obedience to the orders he had despatched,

---

* Lord Lucan's own account of the way in which he attempted to construe this order, and of the mental process by which he attained his conclusion, is as follows: 'Lord Lucan having taken up the position ' clearly directed was prepared to carry out the remainder of his in- ' structions by endeavouring to effect the only object, and in the only ' way that could rationally [have] been intended—viz., to give all the ' support possible to the infantry in the recapture of the redoubts, and ' subsequently to cut off all their defenders.'

CHAP.
VIII.

The impatience and anger amongst men of the Headquarter Staff.

would begin its advance, and he watched with the expectation—an expectation which we now know to have been well founded—that the movement would cause the enemy to abandon his already relaxing hold, and give up the captured redoubts. He watched in vain. His cavalry did not move forward. From the way in which he saw the Russians withdrawing their cavalry and their artillery, but also from the general aspect of the field, he knew that the minutes then passing were minutes of depression to the enemy, and therefore of opportunity for the English. It may well be imagined that at such a time the delayed compliance with his order was provoking; and if his words and his features betrayed mere vexation, or, at all events, well-governed anger, the more youthful men of his Staff were not, I imagine, so careful as to suppress their murmurs of impatience and indignation.

In this temper the Headquarter Staff were gazing upon the field, when some of them who had been pointing their field-glasses along the line of the Causeway ridge perceived all at once, as they thought, that the enemy was bringing forward some teams of artillery horses, with the lasso tackle attached to them;* and they did not doubt—what otherwise seemed very probable—that the enemy, who was evidently preparing to retreat, must be seeking to carry off with him as trophies the English guns taken from the Turks.

---

* I do not myself doubt the accuracy of the impression thus formed, though, in the absence of proof from Russian sources, I have avoided the language of positive assertion.

It seems probable that, before this, Lord Raglan's CHAP.
patience must have almost come to its end, and that, VIII.
without any new motive, he would have presently
despatched a reminding and accelerating message to
Lord Lucan; but the announcement of the artillery-
teams coming up to carry off English guns may well
have determined his choice of the moment for taking
the step, and it gave him an opportunity—which, even
in a moment of anger, his kind and generous nature
would incline him to seize—an opportunity of softening the communication he had to make to the commander of his cavalry; for evidently the pressure
which was to be applied to Lord Lucan, would be
relieved in some measure of its inculpatory aspect,
by basing the necessity for instant action upon a new
fact. Accordingly, Lord Raglan determined to repeat
with increased urgency his hitherto disobeyed order
for the advance of the cavalry, and to give to its commander a fresh motive for despatch, by pressing upon
him the special object of endeavouring to prevent the
enemy from carrying off the guns. This determination
he expressed in terms intimating that the Quartermaster-General, who was close at his side, should give
immediate effect to it. With a pencil, and a slip of The
paper rested upon his sabretash, General Airey quick- 'fourth
ly embodied in a written order the instruction thus order.'
given him; but before Lord Raglan allowed the paper
to go, he dictated some additional words which Airey
at once inserted. The paper when thus completed
became what men have called 'the fourth order.' *

* The terms of the order will be given in a later page.

CHAP.   It was supposed that Major* Calthorpe (an officer of
VIII.   the cavalry, and one of Lord Raglan's aides-de-camp),
who chanced to stand ready and expectant, would be
charged with the mission; but Lord Raglan called
for Captain Nolan (the aide-de-camp of the Quartermaster-General), and specially desired that the order
should be entrusted to him.

Captain   Nolan was no common man. Surrounded as he
Nolan.   was at Headquarters by men of the world whose pleasant society must have been apparently well calculated
to moderate a too wild devotion to one idea, he yet
was an enthusiast—an enthusiast unchilled and un-
shaken. His faith was that miracles of war could be
wrought by squadrons of horse, that the limits of
what could fairly be asked of the cavalry had been
wrongly assigned; and that—if only it could be properly constituted and properly led—the cavalry, after
all, was the arm which should govern the issue of battles. Then, adding to this creed an unbounded trust
in the warlike quality of our troopers, he went on to
conclude that the dominion of England in the world
could best be assured by the sabre. He knew that
where the question of cavalry excellence could be narrowed to a question of cavalry fighting, the English
horsemen had been used to maintain their ascendant.
The great day of Blenheim, he knew, was won in the
main by our cavalry. With a single brigade of our
cavalry at Salamanca, Le Marchant had cut through
a French army. Nolan imagined that nothing but
perverse mismanagement and evil choice of men pre-

* This should be *Captain* Calthorpe.—*Note to 3d Edition.*

vented England from having what he held to be her C H A P.
own—from having an ascendant among nations rest- VIII.
ing mainly, or at all events largely, upon the prowess
of her squadrons. Because this faith was glowing
within him, Nolan had sorrowed and chafed at the
unobtrusive part taken by our cavalry in the earlier
days of the invasion. His journal, going down to the
12th of October, lies open before me. It teems with
impatience of the comparative inaction to which our
cavalry had been condemned ; and discloses a belief—
a belief based apparently, in part, upon somewhat
wild processes of reason—that the commander of our
cavalry was the man upon whom blame should rest.
Nolan must have been solaced, one may suppose, nay,
enraptured, by the feat of our Heavy Dragoons ; but,
on the other hand, he could not but be tortured by
having to witness the inaction to which the Light
Brigade stood condemned, whilst their comrades were
fighting, and for this (if he knew not that the commander of our cavalry was present elsewhere) he probably blamed Lord Lucan. Besides, at the moment we
speak of, an occasion had been offering itself to the
cavalry, and Lord Raglan, as we know, had been ordering it to advance without being yet obeyed. Upon
the whole, therefore, it is easy to understand that
Nolan must have been burning with anger and zeal.

This was the officer to whom, by Lord Raglan's
direction, General Airey delivered the order. Without having had their observance quickened, at the
time, by any foreboding sentiments, men still remember how swiftly the messenger sped on his errand.

CHAP.
VIII.
That acclivity of some seven or eight hundred feet, which divided our Headquarter Staff from the plain of Balaclava below, was of just such a degree of steepness that, whilst no rider of merely ordinary experience and boldness would like to go down it at a high rate of speed, and whilst few of those going slowly would refrain from somewhat easing the abruptness of the path by a more or less zigzag descent, the ground still was not so precipitous as to defy the rapid purpose of a horseman who had accustomed himself, in such things, to approach the extreme of what is possible. The special skill gained by such trials, with the boldness needed for using it, Nolan had in full measure; and he was armed with cogent words for the man whom he had brought himself to condemn as the obstructor of cavalry enterprise. Straight, swift, and intent—descending, as it were, on sure prey—he swooped angering down into the plain where Lord Lucan and his squadrons were posted.

CHAPTER IX.

ALTHOUGH a period of some thirty, forty, or fifty minutes had since elapsed, the position of the Russian army was still nearly the same that it had been when Lord Lucan received his third order.* Jabrokritsky, with some 8 battalions, 4 squadrons, and 14 guns, was established on the slopes of the Fedioukine Hills; and Liprandi, with his infantry and field-artillery still lingering upon the sites of the captured redoubts, continued to protrude so far west along the chain of the Causeway Heights as to have one of his regiments—the regiment of Odessa—drawn up near the Arabtabia Redoubt;† but the whole of his defeated cavalry had been withdrawn to a position so far down the North Valley as to be within a mile of the aqueduct, and about a mile and a half from the ground where Lord Lucan was posted. Drawn up across the North Valley, far in rear of the foremost Russian battalions, this large but discomfited body of horse connected Liprandi's corps-army with the troops

CHAP.
IX.

The position of the Russian army at the time when Nolan reached Lord Lucan.

* The order directing him to advance, and take advantage of any opportunity to recover the Causeway Heights. The words of the order are given at p. 179.
† The Number Three Redoubt.

CHAP.
IX.

of General Jabrokritsky, but connected it only by the rear—connected it in such way that these forces together were the three sides of an oblong, and could be likened, as we saw, to the hand of a man with the two centre fingers held back and the other two fingers extended.* The Odessa regiment formed the tip of that lesser finger which represents the extension of Liprandi's column along the chain of the Causeway Heights. Except at their rear, the two columns thus protruding were divided the one from the other by the whole breadth of the North Valley; and without straying into surmise, it can be stated that they were, each of them, in a condition to be more or less completely rolled up by an attack of cavalry, or even— without waiting for actual collision—by the mere sight of squadrons approaching.†

Close in advance of the discomfited Russian cavalry, and, like them, fronting up the North Valley, some twelve pieces of the Don Cossack ordnance were in battery.‡

At a later moment the smoke from this battery served to screen the horsemen behind it from the sight of the English; but at the time now spoken of, this great body of Russian cavalry, though a mile and a

---

* See the diagram *ante*, p. 177.

† For proof of this—proof by actual experiment—both as regards the column posted along the line of the Causeway Heights, and as regards the other column—the one on the Fedioukine Hills—see later pages narrating the retreat of the Odessa battalions and (subsequently) of the forces on the Fedioukine Hills which were put to flight by D'Allonville.

‡ Eight pieces (*i. e.*, one battery), according to Russian official accounts; but oral testimony shows that the real number of these guns was twelve—*i. e.*, a battery and a half.

half off, could be descried by one standing on the
ground where Lord Cardigán was posted. From the effect of distance and close massing, the dusky, grey columns looked black.

Besides the main body of the Russian cavalry which thus stood drawn up in rear of the Cossack guns, Liprandi now had at his disposal six squadrons of lancers under the command of Colonel Jeropkine;* and these horsemen, divided into two bodies of three squadrons each, were so posted—the one in a fold of the Fedioukine Hills, and the other in a ravine on the side of the Causeway Heights—as to be able to fall upon either flank of any Allied troops which, in pressing Liprandi's retreat, might pursue it far down the North Valley.

The subsequent course of events' made it needless for Liprandi to say, in his public despatch, that after the combat with Scarlett's dragoons he had determined to retreat; but I regard it as certain that, at the time now spoken of, he harboured no idea of defending the Causeway Heights against any real attack. So far as concerned his liability to be assailed by infantry, he was able to prepare his retreat with a great deliberation; for the march of the Allied battalions, creeping down from the Chersonese, was so open to the view of an adversary in the valley below, as to show him how long it must be before they could come into action; but it was otherwise in regard to any attack undertaken by our division of cavalry; and if the tenor of the instructions given to good troops

Intentions of Liprandi at this period of the action.

* A force called the 'combined lancers.'

CHAP.
IX.

could be safely inferred from their actual movements, it might be treated as certain that the Odessa battalions had orders to fall back upon the near approach of our squadrons.

Lord Raglan's perfect apprehension of the state of the battle.

Such seems to have been the position and attitude of the forces now confronting Lord Lucan, and such the condition of things that Lord Raglan had sought to deal with by the order which Nolan was bringing. Lord Raglan, as we know, had the advantage of seeing all from high, commanding ground; but nothing less than his peculiar and instinctive faculty for the reading of a battle-field could have enabled him at the instant to grasp the whole import of what to others was a dim, complex scene, devoid of expression, and to send down an order so closely adapted to the exigency as the one which he had despatched. To strike at the nearest of the Russians that could be found on the Causeway Heights—or, in other words, at those Odessa battalions which stood ranged in front of the Arabtabia—this plainly was the task which (by reason of there being no infantry division yet present on the ground) invited the enterprise of our squadrons; and this also, we shall see, was the task which the order now coming enjoined.

Two points in the enemy's position available for attack.

We shall see that the French, when so minded, could direct an attack with their cavalry upon the head of the Russian detachment now holding the Fedioukine Hills—an attack somewhat similar in its nature to the one which Lord Raglan desired to have made against the tip of Liprandi's position on the Causeway Heights. In truth, there were two ranges of heights, each affording to the cavalry of the Allies so good a point for attack, that the one was decisively chosen—though chosen in vain—by Lord Raglan, and the other by General Morris, the Commander of the French cavalry division.*

CHAP.
IX.

But between the two ranges, thus each of them inviting attack, there unhappily lay a smooth valley, which offered itself to those horsemen who might either be weary of life, or compelled by a sense of duty to go down and commit self-destruction.

The valley that lay between them.

Our Heavy Dragoons were on one of the slopes of the Causeway ridge, not far from the scene of their late victory. Lord Cardigan's brigade stood, drawn up in two lines, and so placed as to be fronting straight down the North Valley.

Position of our cavalry at this time.

Lord Lucan was sitting in the saddle in front of his troops, and between the two brigades, when Nolan came speeding from the Commander-in-Chief, and made haste to deliver the paper with which we saw him entrusted. By pursuing a theory that he seems to have formed in regard to the real authorship of directions from the English Headquarters, Lord Lucan had taught himself to mistake the channel for the source, and to imagine that General Airey must be often the originator of orders which, in fact, he was only transmitting. For this reason, and as tending, perhaps, to account in some measure for the way in which the

Arrival of Nolan with the 'fourth order.'

* See again the diagram *ante*, p. 177, and the plan facing p. 188, taking care to understand that the *first* position of the Odessa regiment and of the batteries near it is the one applicable to this part of the narrative.

C H A P. order was about to act upon the mind or the temper
IX.   of the general to whom it was addressed, it is worth
while to remember two circumstances which would
have been otherwise unimportant. The bearer of the
order, as it chanced, was the aide-de-camp of General
Airey, and its words were in General Airey's handwriting.

The   The order ran thus : ' Lord Raglan wishes the
'fourth
'order.'   ' cavalry to advance rapidly to the front, and try to
' prevent the enemy carrying away the guns. Troop
' of horse-artillery may accompany. French cavalry
' is on your left. Immediate.

(Signed)   ' R. AIREY.'

Whether taken alone, or as a command reinforcing
the one before sent, this order has really no word in
it which is either obscure or misleading. By assigning
' the guns ' as the object, Lord Raglan most pointedly
fixed the line of the Turkish redoubts as the direction
in which to advance ; and it must not be said that
the expression left room in the mind of Lord Lucan
for a doubt as to what guns were meant. He well
knew that the guns indicated by the ' fourth order '
were the English guns taken in the forts — in the
forts crowning those very ' heights ' which, more than
half an hour before, he had been ordered to retake
if he could ; * and no one, indeed, had more poignant

---

* In the controversies arising out of the Light Cavalry charge, it
was sometimes argued that there was a doubt as to what were ' the
' guns ' to which the fourth order pointed ; and that circumstance makes
it convenient to say and to prove, once for all, that Lord Lucan at the
time knew very well what ' the guns ' were. In his despatch addressed
to Lord Raglan, on the 27th of October 1854—the day next but one

reason than Lord Lucan for knowing what the guns
were ; because he was the commander of the force
which—rightly, perhaps, but not, of course, without
mortification—had had to stand by and be witness
whilst Liprandi effected the capture.

If collated with the third order, the written words
brought down by Nolan seem to come with accumu-
lated weight and decisiveness. By the third order,
the commander of our cavalry had been directed to
advance, and take any opportunity of recovering the
heights—those heights, be it remembered, where the
enemy was posted with the seven English guns he
had captured; and now, by this fourth order, Lord
Lucan—being requested to advance rapidly to the
front, and try to prevent the enemy from carrying
away the guns,—was, for the second time, told that he
must operate against the Russians on the Causeway
Heights, and was furnished with a new and special
motive for energy and despatch. Construed singly,
the fourth order looks clear as day ; read along with
the former direction it looks equally clear, but even
more cogent; for, when so considered, it appears to
visit Lord Lucan with something like an expression of
impatience and displeasure for having allowed more
than half an hour to pass after the receipt of the
third order without trying to recover the ' heights.'

I am not without means of explaining how it be-

after the battle—he writes : ' The Heavy Brigade having now joined
' the Light Brigade, the division took up a position with a view of sup-
' porting an attack upon the heights ; when, being instructed to make a
' rapid advance to our front *to prevent the enemy carrying the guns lost*
' *by the Turkish troops in the morning,* I ordered,' &c.

CHAP.
IX.

came possible for Lord Lucan to raise a controversy upon the subject, but the circumstance which opened to him that opportunity was one occurring after the battle; * and the question we now have to treat is the meaning of the few written words which Nolan delivered. After applying to those simple words all such knowledge as I have of the relevant facts, I remain unable to learn how Lord Lucan could read the fourth order without seeing that it directed him to attempt an advance against the head of Liprandi's column—against the head of the column then, occupying those same Causeway Heights where the English guns had been taken. That the order thus interpreted was one which Lord Raglan had most perfectly adapted to the exigency of the hour, we shall by-and-by see valid proof.

Lord Lucan's reception of the order.

Lord Lucan, however, had no sooner read this order, than there was awakened in his mind that spirit of hostile criticism which so marred his usefulness as a subordinate. He proceeded to sit in judgment upon the command of his chief, and at once, without mercy, condemned it. His own account declares that he 'read the order with much con- 'sideration '—'perhaps consternation,' he says, 'would 'be the better word—at once seeing its impracti- 'cability for any useful purpose whatever, and the 'consequent great unnecessary risk and loss to be 'incurred.' The formation of this strangely decisive opinion upon the merits of an order sent him by his Commander-in-Chief, was rendered the more inap-

* This will be shown in a later page.

propriate by the fact, that the Commander who sent C H A P.
IX. the order had the whole field of battle before him, whilst the critic who undertook to condemn it was so placed (upon the lower ground) that to him neither enemy nor guns were in sight;* nor must it be forgotten that this condemnation of the order was based upon its written words, unalloyed by any oral addition, and stands earlier in point of time than that outbreak of Nolan's which was afterwards alleged as a warrant for the course pursued by Lord Lucan.

But, unhappily, Lord Lucan did not content himself with a silent condemnation of the order. With the bearer of the note for his listener, he suffered himself to run out against the order of his chief. Conceiving (erroneously) that he rightly understood the nature of the enterprise which Lord Raglan's written words had enjoined, he urged the uselessness of such an attack, and the dangers attending it.† *The altercation between Lord Lucan and Nolan.*

By this language apparently Lord Lucan challenged the messenger to encounter him in wordy dispute, and to defend, if he could, the order of the Commander-in-Chief.

Nolan was a man who had gathered in Continental service the habit of such extreme and such rigid deference to any general officer, that his comrades imagined him to be the very last man who in that point would ever prove wanting; but perhaps that

---

* 'Neither enemy nor guns being in sight.'—Speech of Lord Lucan in the House of Lords.

† 'After carefully reading the order, I urged the uselessness of such ' an attack, and the dangers attending it.'—Lord Lucan's speech in House of Lords.

CHAP. very reverence for the military hierarchy which had
IX.   hitherto rendered him so superlatively respectful to
general officers, may have made him the more liable
to be shocked by the reception which Lord Lucan
was giving to the order of the Commander-in-Chief.
Up to this moment, however, Nolan was not so un-
governably indignant as to be guilty of more than
imparting an authoritative tone to the words in which
he answered Lord Lucan's denunciation of the order.
' Lord Raglan's orders,' he said, ' are, that the cavalry
' should attack immediately.'

Then quickly, and in a tone of impatience, caused,
it seems, by what he imagined to be the absurdity of
the attack thus enjoined, Lord Lucan said to Nolan,
' Attack, sir ! attack what ?   What guns, sir ? '*

This angry, impatient question was destined to put
an end to all prospect of eliciting from Nolan any
quiet explanation of the mission with which he came
charged, or any of that priceless information in regard
to the enemy's position which, coming as he did from
high ground, the aide-de-camp was well able to give.
To use the homely, nay feminine, language which
describes the action of the emotional forces, Lord
Lucan's words set Nolan going. Throwing his head
back, and pointing with his hand in a direction
which Lord Lucan says confidently was towards
the left-front corner of the valley, the aide-de-camp
replied, ' There, my lord, is your enemy ; there are

---

* I here follow Lord Lucan's written narrative. According to his
speech in the House of Lords, his words were, ' Where and what to
' do ? '

'your guns.'* Lord Lucan declares that these words CHAP. were addressed to him in a 'most disrespectful but ‾‾IX.‾‾ 'significant manner;'† and, even without too much relying upon gesture or cadence of voice, it is easy to see that the apostrophe thus uttered by Nolan was almost in the nature of an indignant rebuke—an indignant rebuke inflicted by a captain upon a lieutenant-general in front of his troops.

Just men will therefore acknowledge that this outbreak of Nolan's was only too well fitted to enrage a general officer, and, by enraging him, to disturb his judgment; but, apart from the effect they might produce upon the temper of Lord Lucan, the gestures and the words of the aide-de-camp cannot fairly be wrought into the kind of importance which was afterwards assigned to them in controversy. The tenor of the apostrophe as recorded by Lord Lucan himself shows plainly enough that, by pointing generally to the direction in which the enemy might be found, Nolan's gestures and words were meant to convey a taunt, not to give topographical guidance; and this is made the more evident by taking care to remember that, when the words passed between the Lieutenant-General and the Aide-de-camp, they were neither of them on ground from which any Russians could be seen; for a messenger, who was so blindly placed at the moment as not to have a glimpse of the

* Lord Lucan's written narrative and speech. As to this answer of Nolan's both those accounts agree; but the speech, in saying how Nolan pointed, says, 'to the further end of the valley.'
† Ibid.

CHAP.
IX.
enemy, could hardly have so trusted to his own and his hearer's recollection of the local bearings as to think of attempting to designate a particular object of attack by pointing to its supposed position.

The haze that was at one time engendered by controversy carried on with imperfect materials is yet further cleared off by observing the angle of difference between the route of the Causeway Heights, which Lord Raglan had enjoined, and the fatal way down the North Valley. Vast and terrible as was the contrast in point of consequences between taking the right way and taking the wrong one, the divergence of the one route from the other at the spot where Nolan made the gesture is represented by an angle of little more than twenty degrees. How is it possible that, where the difference of direction between the two routes at the point of departure had so moderate a width, and where also there was no sight of a Russian battalion or squadron to guide the eye or the hand, the aide-de-camp could have even seemed to forbid the one route or to enjoin the other, by the way in which—burning with anger—he tauntingly pointed to the 'enemy'?

Nolan was one of the last men in the whole army who would have been capable of sending our squadrons down the North Valley instead of to the line of the heights; for, besides that he had come fresh from the high ground which commanded a full view of the enemy's position, and had just been gathering the true purpose of the orders from the lips of Lord Raglan himself, it so happens that he had a special and even personal interest in the recapture of the heights and the guns, because he had maintained, and maintained for a time, against the judgment of some of our Engineers, that the construction of redoubts on the line of the Causeway Heights was an expedient measure. With the overstrained notions he had of what squadrons of horse might achieve, he cannot have failed to ascribe the loss of a position thus specially valued by him to the general officer whom he long had regarded as the obstructor of all cavalry enterprise, and it may well be imagined that he came down exulting in the terms of an order which was framed for compelling Lord Lucan to try to recover the guns. The notion of his having intended to divert our cavalry from the Causeway Heights and send it down the North Valley seems altogether untenable.

If Nolan had been the bearer of a mere verbal order, then, indeed, this outbreak of his might have been in a high degree embarrassing. It might have forced Lord Lucan to consider whether he should send for further instructions, or whether he should instantly gallop up to a ground from which he could have such a survey of the enemy as to know where to attempt an attack; or, finally, it might have put him to the task of endeavouring to winnow the communication addressed to him, by calming the over-excited aide-de-camp, and bringing him to say, if he could, how much of the words he had uttered were words really entrusted to him as a message by the Commander-in-Chief. But Lord Raglan, as we saw, had provided that his directions should be set down on paper; and

CHAP.
IX.

after Nolan's outbreak, it became more than ever the
duty of Lord Lucan to bend his mind faithfully to
the written words of the order, examining as well as
he could the condition of things to which it applied,
and not forgetting that he had, all the while, in his
hands another order, hitherto unexecuted, which enjoined him to advance and try to recover those same
heights on which the guns spoken of in the 'fourth
' order' had been placed and lost by the Turks.

Lord Lucan has since spoken and written as if his
choice lay between the plan of sending the Light
Cavalry down the North Valley, and the plan of not
advancing at all; but the truth is, that neither in the
' third order,' nor in the 'fourth order,' nor, lastly, in
the taunting injunctions of the aide-de-camp, was there
left any room to set up a doubt upon the question
whether our squadrons should or should not advance;
for by all these three channels alike there had come
down strong mandates enjoining our cavalry to move
forward and endeavour something against the enemy.
I repeat that the fullest, the most generous, allowance
ought to be made for the anger and consequent dis-
turbance of mental faculty which Nolan's outbreak
was but too well fitted to occasion; but it is not for
that, the less true that a steady perusal at this time of
Lord Raglan's written instructions by a cavalry commander of sound judgment, who was also unruffled in
temper, and acquainted with the state of the field,
must have led to an immediate advance of our squadrons—to an immediate advance of our squadrons, not,
of course, down the fatal North Valley, but against the

line of the Causeway Heights, where the English guns
had been lost.

How Lord Lucan should have dealt with an aide-
de-camp who had made bold to apostrophise him in
the way we have seen, that is a question which
soldiers, with their traditional canons, will best determine. Since the messenger came fresh from a spot
where he had been hearing the directions of the Commander-in-Chief, and looking down with full command of view upon the position of an enemy invisible
from the low ground, he could not but be fraught
with knowledge of almost immeasurable worth ; and
apparently the immediate interests of the public
service required that an effort should be made to
undo the mischief which had been caused by provoking his indignation, and endeavouring to bring
him back to such a degree of composure as to allow
of his imparting what, only a few minutes before, he
had been hearing and seeing. On the other hand,
the due maintenance of military subordination is, of
course, transcendently important ; and it has been
judged, as I learn, by men held to be of authority in
such matters, that after the utterance by Nolan of
his last taunting words, Lieutenant-General Lord
Lucan should have put the captain under arrest. The
course least susceptible of a rational defence was that
of treating Captain Nolan's indignant apostrophe as a
word of command from Headquarters, and regarding
the scornful gesture which accompanied his words as
a really topographical indication.

This last course, however, as I understand him, is

CHAP.
IX.

Lord Lucan's determination.

the one which Lord Lucan took; for, as soon as he had heard the taunting words, and marked the insulting gesture, he determined to govern his action, not exclusively by the written instructions which he held in his hand, but in part by the angry and apparently rhetorical apostrophe of the excited Captain. Nay, in spite of the two written orders, one pointing to the 'heights,' and the other to the 'guns' on those heights, as the object of the enterprise, he determined to follow what he judged to be the direction of Nolan's out-pointed arm as a guiding indication of the quarter in which the attack should be made.

Dividing the Causeway Heights (where Lord Raglan desired to attack) from the line of the Fedioukine Hills (where D'Allonville was destined to charge), there opened, as we saw, that North Valley where riders seeking their death—without themselves being able to strike in attack or defence for the first full mile of their road—might nevertheless run the gauntlet between two prepared lines of fire, having always before them for a goal—which some of the survivors might touch—the front of a Russian battery, and the whole strength of Ryjoff's squadrons.* Towards this valley, as we saw, Lord Lucan thought Nolan was pointing when he uttered his taunting apostrophe.

So Lord Lucan now proceeded to obey what he judged to be the meaning of the 'fourth order,' as illustrated by the aide-de-camp's words and gesture.

* This statement is not too extensive; for Jeropkine's Lancers were not under General Ryjoff, the officer commanding the bulk of the Russian cavalry.

Believing that it had really become his duty to send a force down the North Valley, he selected Lord Cardigan and the Light Brigade as the man and the men who must first be offered up in obedience to the supposed commands of Lord Raglan. At a trot and alone, he rode off to the ground in front of the 13th Light Dragoons, where Lord Cardigan sat in his saddle.

CHAP.
IX.

Lord Lucan now personally imparted his resolve to Lord Cardigan. There is some difference between the impressions that were formed of this interview by Lord Lucan on the one hand and Lord Cardigan on the other; Lord Lucan believing that with the 'fourth order' in his hand he imparted its contents, or at all events the main tenor of it, to Lord Cardigan, and directed him 'to advance,' without in terms enjoining an 'attack;' whilst Lord Cardigan's statement is that he was ordered 'to attack 'the Russians in the valley about three-quarters of 'a mile distant with the 13th Light Dragoons and 'the 17th Lancers.' *

Lord Lucan's order to Lord Cardigan.

Lord Lucan's idea as to the way in which this direction of his ought to have been executed is as follows :—He says : 'After giving † to Lord Cardi-

* Private memorandum in Lord Cardigan's handwriting, and by him forwarded to Lord Raglan 27th October 1854. I prefer this to Lord Cardigan's subsequent account, as being earlier—within two days of the battle—and being also a statement deliberately prepared for the Commander of the Forces. The 'three-fourths of a mile' was, of course, estimate only, and it applied to an extent of ground which was really more than a mile and a quarter. The two regiments which he mentions as those with which he had attacked were the troops constituting his first line.

† He does not mean that he handed the paper to Lord Cardigan, but

CHAP.
IX.
'gan the order brought to me from Colonel* Airey
'by Captain Nolan I urged his Lordship to advance
'steadily, and to keep his men well in hand.† My
'idea was that he was to use his discretion and act
'as circumstances might show themselves; my opin-
'ion is that keeping his four squadrons under perfect
'control he should have halted them so soon as he
'found that there was no useful object to be gained,
'but great risk to be incurred; it was clearly his
'duty to have handled his brigade as I did the
'Heavy Brigade, and so saved them from much use-
'less and unnecessary loss.'

Lord Cardigan did not so understand the task
which was devolving upon him. From the way in
which his brigade was fronting at the time, he considered that an indefinite order to advance was an
order to advance down the valley against the far distant guns and black masses of cavalry which were
seen to be drawn up across it; and whatever were
the words really used, Lord Cardigan certainly understood that without assailing either of the enemy's two
protruded columns he was ordered to run the gauntlet
between them for a distance of more than a mile,
with the purpose of then charging the battery which
crossed the lower end of the valley, and charging it
moreover in front.

that he either read it over to him, or gave him the tenor of it. According to Lord Cardigan, no such communication took place.

* He means General Airey.

† The way in which Lord Lucan handled the Heavy Brigade in the
North Valley will be seen in a later page.

Understanding that he was thus instructed, Lord CHAP.
Cardigan judged it right to point out the true import ───
of an order to advance down the valley. So, on
hearing the words of his Divisional General, he
brought down his sword in salute, and answered,
' Certainly, Sir; but allow me to point out to you
' that the Russians have a battery in the valley in
' our front, and batteries and riflemen on each flank.'*
Lord Lucan, after first expressing his concurrence in
what he gathered to be the tenor of Lord Cardigan's
observation, went on to intimate—he shrugged his
shoulders whilst speaking—' that there was no choice
' but to obey.'†

Then, without further question or parley, Lord
Cardigan tacitly signified his respectful submission to
orders, and began that great act of military obedience
which is enshrined in the memory of his fellow-
countrymen. He turned quietly to his people and
said : ' The brigade will advance ! '

Before the two Generals parted, Lord Lucan
announced to Lord Cardigan his determination to
narrow the front of the Brigade by withdrawing the
11th Hussars from the first line, and causing it to act
in support. Unless Lord Lucan's memory deceives
him, he also enjoined Lord Cardigan ' to advance

* Lord Lucan's belief is that Lord Cardigan's warning pointed only
to the forces on the Fedioukine Hills, and not to those in front or those
on the right flank.

† He said, according to Lord Lucan, ' I know it, but Lord Raglan
' will have it. We have no choice but to obey.' According to Lord
Cardigan, Lord Lucan said, ' I cannot help that ; it is Lord Raglan's
' positive orders that the Light Brigade attacks immediately.'

CHAP.
IX.

'very steadily and quietly,' and to 'keep his men 'well in hand.'*

It has been judged, that although the observation ventured by Lord Cardigan in answer to Lord Lucan's first words of instruction had somewhat the character of a remonstrance, it still was amply warranted by the occasion; and this, as I gather, was the opinion entertained by the Commander-in-Chief. When Lord Raglan gave the tenor of the remonstrance in a private letter addressed to the Duke of Newcastle, he prefaced the statement by saying that Lord Cardigan was 'as 'brave as a lion.'† Indeed, it would seem that from the moment in which he learnt the nature 'of the task imposed upon him to the one when he bowed to authority and composedly accepted his martyrdom, Lord Cardigan's demeanour was faultless.

* I have not ventured to put the statement in an absolutely positive form, because Lord Cardigan, I believe, has no recollection of having received this direction.

† Letter dated the 28th of October 1854. See this letter in the Appendix.

CHAPTER X.

I.

As altered by Lord Lucan at the moment of direct- CHAP.
ing the advance, the disposition of the Light Brigade X.
was as follows:—The 13th Light Dragoons, com- Disposi-
tions for
manded by Captain Oldham, and the 17th Lancers, the ad-
vance
commanded by Captain Morris, were to form the of the
cavalry
first line; the 11th Hussars, commânded by Colonel down the
North
Douglas, was ordered to follow in support;* and the Valley.
third line was composed of the 4th Light Dragoons
under Lord George Paget, and the 8th Hussars, or
rather, one may say, the main portion of it, under
Colonel Shewell.† Lord Cardigan, as commander of
the whole brigade, had to place himself at the head of
the first line. The second line, consisting of only one

* Before the change thus ordered by Lord Lucan the three first-
named regiments had been all in first line. I speak of the change
actually *effected*, and not of the one *contemplated* by Lord Lucan. He
meant to have placed the 4th Light Dragoons in the same alignment as
the 11th Hussars; but his orders to that last purpose were never communicated to the 4th Light Dragoons. The order for the 11th Hussar
to drop back and act in support was given by Lord Lucan in person to
Colonel Douglas.

† A troop of the 8th Hussars, commanded by Captain Chetwynd, had
been abstracted from the regiment to act as escort to the Commander of
the Forces, and was at the Headquarters camp.

CHAP. regiment, was commanded by Douglas, its colonel;
X.   and the two regiments comprising the third line were
in charge of Lord George Paget. Each of these regiments stood extended in line two deep. The Light
Cavalry was to be supported by Scarlett's victorious
brigade; and with two of Scarlett's regiments—that
is, the Greys and the Royals brought forward in
advance of the other regiments of Heavy Dragoons—
Lord Lucan determined to be present in person. We
shall have to learn by-and-by that there occurred a
conjuncture—and that too at a cardinal time—when
the link which connected the two brigades was hap-
lessly suffered to break; but nevertheless it should
be understood that the advance of not only our Light
Cavalry but also our Heavy Dragoons was meant to
form one operation. We shall find that both of the
brigades (though not in anything like the same degree) were exposed to the trials and the losses which
the nature of the onslaught involved.*

Lord Car-   Lord Cardigan placed himself quite alone at a
digan and
his Staff. distance of about two horses' lengths in advance of
his Staff, and some five horses' lengths in advance of
the centre of his first line.

When once a body of cavalry has been launched
upon a course which is to end in attack, it has to dispense for awhile with reliance upon full, explicit orders

---

* The above observation seems to be rendered necessary by the not
unnatural tendency to concentrate attention upon that part of the
operation which was performed by the Light Brigade. Besides the
casualties in the Divisional Staff which accompanied the Greys and the
Royals, these regiments, as we shall see, sustained no inconsiderable
losses whilst engaged in the duty of supporting the Light Brigade.

PLATE 5.

BATTLE OF BALACLAVA.

The Light Cavalry Charge.

EXPLANATION.

So from which a Field Battery has been withdrawn, thus .°°°°°

Upon the advance of the Light Brigade the "Odessa" Battalions and Ryzoff's Field Battery were withdrawn from the neighbourhood of the Ambush. The Battalions formed squares in expectation of being attacked by Cavalry, and the Battery took up fresh positions as indicated.

In passing down the valley under fire from the front and from both flanks the Light Brigade had already sustained enormous losses, but its remains led by Lord Cardigan are now charging into the front of the twelve Gun Battery which covered the lower end of the Valley. The small portion of the 17th Lancers which outflanks the Battery is led against the Russian Cavalry by Captain Morris.

The Heavy Dragoons under Scarlett are advancing in support. Lord Lucan in person is advancing down the Valley between his two Brigades.

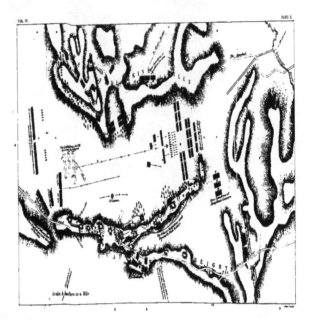

Scale, 6 inches to a Mile.

conveyed by word of mouth; and although there may C H A P.
come the time when the trumpet shall be sounding ⌣X.⌣
' the gallop,' and when afterwards it shall be sounding
' the charge,' yet, upon the whole, the troops of the
first line obtain guidance mainly by carefully watching the leader who rides at the head of the force; and,
the empire of words being thus superseded for the
time by the signalling, if so one may call it, which is
effected by the pace and the position of a single horseman, it seems right, by a kind of analogy, that one
who would listen to the story of a cavalry onslaught
extending along a great distance should be able—as
well as, may be in the mind's eye—to see and distinguish the leader. There is the more reason for this,
since it happens that in the course of the controversies
springing out of the Light Cavalry charge there arose
a question of mistaken identity which has an important bearing upon Lord Cardigan's military reputation.

Lord Cardigan had so good a stature that, although
somewhat long in the fork, he yet sat rather tall in
the saddle, and notwithstanding his fifty-seven years,
he had a figure which retained the slenderness of youth.
His countenance, highly bred and of the aquiline cast,
had not been without such humble share as a mere
brother might be expected to have of that beauty
which once made famous the ancient name of Bru-
denell. Far from disclosing the real faults of his character, the features of the man rather tended to con-
firm the first popular impression that was created by
the tidings of the Light Cavalry charge, and to indicate
a nature which might have in it something of chival-

VOL. IV.   O

CHAP. rous, nay even Quixotic exaltation. His blue, frank-
X.
looking, genial eyes revealed none of the narrowness
of disposition which I have thought myself obliged to
ascribe to him. As might be supposed, he had an
excellent cavalry seat, and was erect—but also stiff—
in the saddle. He wore the uniform of his old regiment, the 11th Hussars ; but instead of dangling loose
from the shoulders, his pelisse—richly burthened in
front with gold lace—was worn closely put on like a
coat, and did not at all break or mitigate the rigid
outline of his figure.* The charger he rode was a
thorough-bred chestnut, with marks of a kind visible
from afar, which in controversy it may be well to
remember. On the near side before, as well as on
the near side behind, the horse had one white leg.†
In the small group which represented the Brigade-
Staff, Lieutenant Maxse, assistant aide-de-camp, and
Sir George Wombwell, extra aide-de-camp to Lord
Cardigan, were, it seems, the only officers present.‡

* In the Crimea at this time the Hussar regiments wore the pelisse
in the same way as Lord Cardigan.

† Under the off hind fetlock, also, the horse—he still survives, or did
a few months ago (1868)—has a stain of white, but so small as not to be
visible from a distance. As far as could be seen by any one on the
field of battle not coming close to the horse, he had no white stains on
his legs, except one high 'white stocking' before and another high
'white stocking' behind, both the 'white stockings' being on the
near side. General Liprandi, when questioning English prisoners
with a view to identify the English officer whom he had seen galloping
back, seems to have spoken of the horse as a chestnut *with white heels,*
only one of the witnesses saying that the Russian General asked as to
the rider of a chestnut with white *legs.*

‡ The death of Captain Lockwood (an excellent officer, who was aide-
de-camp to Lord Cardigan) has thrown difficulty in the way of knowing
where he was during a considerable period of the combat, except its very

Although the part of the enemy's line which Lord Cardigan meant to attack lay as yet very distant before him, it was evident, from the position of the flanking batteries betwixt which he must pass, that his brigade would not long be in motion without incurring a heavy fire; and, upon the whole, he seems to have considered that almost from the first his advance was in the nature of a charge.

Lord Cardigan's impression as to the nature of the task imposed upon him.

Followed immediately by his first line, and, at a greater distance, by the other regiments of his brigade, Lord Cardigan moved forward at a trot, taking strictly the direction in which his troops before moving had fronted, and making straight down the valley towards the battery which crossed it at the distance of about a mile and a quarter.

Advance of Lord Cardigan and the Light Brigade.

Before Lord Cardigan had ridden a hundred paces in advance, he encountered a sight which filled him with anger. Right before him he saw Captain Nolan audaciously riding across his front from left to right; but not content with a trespass which alone would have been shocking enough to Lord Cardigan's orderly mind, Captain Nolan, turning round in his saddle, was shouting, and waving his sword, as though he

The appearance of Captain Nolan in front of the brigade.

last phase; and there is an idea (not confirmed by Lord Cardigan or by Maxse) that he was carrying a message from his chief at the time when the advance began. In a letter addressed to the 'Times' newspaper, Maxse says that at the commencement of the advance, and again when the first line was 'three parts of the way down,' he observed Lockwood in his place some five or six horses' lengths to the right rear of Lord Cardigan, and that that was the last time he saw him. Major Mayow, the brigade-major, had been on the sick-list, and although, as we shall learn, he found strength enough upon seeing the prospect of an engagement, to join the brigade and take a signal part in the combat, he was busied, in general, with the troops, and did not ride much with the Staff.

CHAP.
X.
would address the brigade. We now know that
when Nolan thus strangely deported himself, he was
riding in a direction which might well give signifi-
cance to his shouts and his gestures; for, instead of
choosing a line of advance like that pursued by Lord
Cardigan, he rode crossing the front of the brigade,
and bearing away to the right front of our advancing
squadrons, as though he would go on to the spot on
the Causeway Heights where the Odessa regiment
His pro-bable ob-ject.
stood posted.* Regarded in connection with this significant fact, the anxious entreaties which he sought to
express by voice and by signs would apparently mean
something like this—'You are going quite wrong!
' You are madly going down this North Valley between
' flanking fires, where you won't have an enemy in
' your front for 'the next mile. This—the way you
' see me going—this is the direction to take for doing
' what Lord Raglan has ordered. Bring up the left
' shoulder, and incline to your right as you see me
' doing. This, this is the way to get at the enemy!'†

* This diagram, by an officer who was one of the nearest of all the
observers, points out the way in which Nolan's direction deviated from
that of Lord Cardigan :—

†Lord Cardigan, however, in writing addressed to myself, has distinctly confirmed the statements which show that Nolan was riding
diagonally *across* the front of the brigade. Supposing my interpre-

Failing, however, to surmise that Nolan's object C H A P. might be that of averting mistake and supplying a X. much-needed guidance, Lord Cardigan, at the time, only saw in the appeal of the aide-de-camp a ridiculous and unseemly attempt to excite the brigade—nay, even to hurry it forward. Considering, however, that Nolan must have been acting with a full knowledge of the enemy's position, as well as of Lord Raglan's true meaning, and that at the time of his appealing thus eagerly to our Light Cavalry by gesture and voice, he was not only on the right front of our line, but was actually bearing away diagonally in the very direction of the Causeway Heights, there is plainly

tation to be right, the desire of an officer not only to have his chief's order faithfully executed, but likewise to save our superb Light Brigade from self-destruction, might well excuse Nolan's interference ; but it may be also observed that there had obtained at our Headquarters a practice of sending an officer of the Quartermaster-General's Staff to guide Lord Lucan (topographically) in the execution of the orders entrusted to him ; and on that special ground, as well as for the more general reason, Nolan might have imagined that he was warranted in trying to save the brigade from the error of taking a route which he knew to be the wrong one. His attempt no doubt was made at a very late moment ; but I have no reason for supposing that Nolan had the least idea of the mistake which was about to be perpetrated, until he saw the brigade begin to advance *without having first changed front.* After that (if my interpretation be right) he did not lose a moment in his efforts to rescue the brigade from the error into which he then saw it falling. He had just been speaking to Morris, announcing to him, in what I understand to have been a sufficiently cool and collected way, that he meant to accompany the brigade ; but the moment the brigade began to advance without having first inclined its front towards what Nolan knew to be the true point of attack he began to move diagonally across the front, and this so fast and with such appearance of excitement—excitement very natural to one who was then in the very act of discovering the fatal error, and eagerly trying to stop it whilst yet it was possible to do so— that Morris shouted out to him, 'That won't do, Nolan ! we've a long ' way to go, and must be steady.'

CHAP.
X.
more room for surmising that the aide-de-camp's
anxiety had been roused by seeing our squadrons
advance without having first changed their front, and
that what he now sought was to undo the mistake of
Lord Lucan, to bend our troops from the path which
led down the fatal North Valley, and make them incline to their right—make them so incline to their
right as to strike the true point of attack which Lord
Raglan had twice over assigned.

Nolan's
fate.
But a Russian shell bursting on the right front of
Lord Cardigan now threw out a fragment which met
Nolan full on the chest, and tore a way into his heart.
The sword dropt from his hand; but the arm with
which he was waving it the moment before still remained high uplifted in the air, and the grip of the
practised horseman remaining as yet unrelaxed still
held him firm in his saddle. Missing the perfect hand
of his master, and finding the accustomed governance
now succeeded by dangling reins, the horse all at once
wheeled about, and began to gallop back upon the
front of the advancing brigade. Then from what had
been Nolan—and his form was still erect in the saddle,
his sword-arm still high in the air—there burst forth
a cry so strange and appalling that the hearer who
rode the nearest to him has always called it 'un-
'earthly.' And in truth, I imagine, the sound resulted
from no human will, but rather from those spasmodic
forces which may act upon the bodily frame when
life, as a power, has ceased. The firm-seated rider,
with arm uplifted and stiff, could hardly be ranked
with the living. The shriek men heard rending the

air was scarce other than the shriek of a corpse. This dead horseman rode on till he had passed through the interval of the 13th Light Dragoons. Then at last he dropt out of the saddle.

An officer of the Guards, who set down at the time in his journal what he had learnt of this part of the battle, went on to say lightly in passing, that the blame of the error would be laid upon Captain Nolan, because the Captain was dead. Whether based on sound reason or not, the prophecy was amply fulfilled. None, so far as I know, have yet questioned that, when wrought into anger by the reception given to Lord Raglan's order, the aide-de-camp was guilty of a high military offence — the offence of openly taunting a general officer in front of his troops; and the limit of the evil thus done will never be measured, for no man can reckon and say how much an insulting apostrophe may have tended to disturb the judgment of the Lieutenant-General upon whom at that moment the fate of our cavalry was depending; but when this has been freely acknowledged, it is hard to see any other or heavier share of the blame that can justly be charged against Nolan's memory. The notion of his not understanding the order he brought, the notion of his mistaking a mile and a quarter of unoccupied valley for those occupied heights which our cavalry was to try to recover, the notion of his seeking to annul Lord Raglan's order in regard to the captured guns, the notion of his intending (by a taunt and an outpointed hand) to send our troops down the North Valley—all these, it would seem, for reasons already

C H A P.
X.

disclosed, are too grossly improbable to be worthy of acceptance; and unless error lurks in fair inference, he was in the very act of striving to bend the advance of our squadrons, and bring them to the true point of attack, when death came and ended his yearnings for the glory of the cavalry arm.

II.

The shell which slew Nolan was the first, I believe, of the missiles which our squadrons, now advancing, encountered; and the gunners on the Fedioukine Hills were still only awakening—awakening almost incredulously—to the singular occasion which their foe seemed coming to offer them, when—unknown at the time to our people—a móvement was made by the Russians, which shows with how sound a judgment Lord Raglan had acted when he ordered, and ordered twice over, the advance of our cavalry.

Movement on the part of the enemy which shows the exact adaptation of Lord Raglan's written orders to the exigency of the hour.

In both of the two last orders, as we saw, the position of the enemy on the Causeway Heights was assigned as the ground which our horsemen should endeavour to win; and although our Light Cavalry, now advancing at a trot, had been launched from the first in a wrong direction, yet the ulterior purpose of pushing the attack down the valley had not yet so developed itself as to be discernible by the enemy. To him for the moment, and until our troops had moved down a distance of some hundreds of yards, this superb advance of our cavalry was so far similar to the advance which Lord Raglan had directed, and which Liprandi was plainly expecting, that at the CHAP. mere sight of our squadrons there began to take place, X. on the part of the Russians, that very surrender of ground—nay, that very surrender of captured guns— which Lord Raglan had expected to obtain when he sent down his third and fourth orders. The weak and protruding column of infantry by which Liprandi had hitherto clung to the line of the Causeway Heights, and of the captured redoubts, began all at once to curl up. As already we know, the head of that column was formed by the Odessa Regiment, a force numbering four battalions, which stood drawn up on the heights near the Arabtabia Redoubt.* Well, upon the approach of our Light Brigade' those battalions at once fell back, abandoned the defence of the Arabtabia, retreated to such a distance as to be a good way in the rear of even the Redoubt 'Number Two,' and threw them- selves at length into hollow squares, thereby ap- parently indicating that they expected the triumphant advance of our squadrons along the very route which Lord Raglan had assigned, and that, so far at least as concerned the westernmost portion of Liprandi's morning conquest, they had no mind to obstruct our cavalry in its task of effecting a recapture.† It would

---

* Otherwise called the 'Number Three' Redoubt.

† In General Todleben's plan—not in the text of his book—this re- treat of the Odessa Regiment upon the approach of our Light Brigade is faithfully recorded ; but the 'Legende' of the official 'Atlas de la Guerre d'Orient,' which discloses a great amount of careful labour and inquiry on the part of the officers who undertook to record and illustrate the Russian movements at Balaclava, has put the same fact into words ; and as I consider that the retrograde movement of the Odessa Regiment is the most satisfactory proof that could well be furnished of the sound

CHAP. be hardly an overstrained use of language to say that
  X.
       without hearing Nolan, or seeing the paper he carried,
       the Russians understood Lord Raglan's order, and
       (until they saw it annulled by the advance of our
       troops down the valley) were full ready to conform to
       its pressure.

Even at this late moment, and after all the misconception that had occurred, if Lord Lucan had turned
at last in the direction assigned to him by his written
orders, he would have found himself master at once of
two out of the seven captured guns, with (apparently)
a rich opportunity of not only securing the ulterior
recovery of the two other lost redoubts and the five
other English guns, but also inflicting upon Liprandi
a calamitous defeat;* for although the enemy's right
wing was untouched, and although, towards his left,
he still held his ground from Kamara to the second
redoubt, yet the means on which he had relied for
connecting the head of his column with the troops of
General Jabrokritsky had been ruined by the defeat
of his cavalry at the hands of Scarlett's dragoons.
His grasp of the field was relaxing; and indeed it
could hardly be otherwise, for now that the Allies in

judgment with which Lord Raglan acted when he, twice over, ordered
his cavalry to advance to the line of the redoubts, I venture to give the
passage : 'A l'approche de la cavalerie légére Anglaise, le regiment
' d'Odessa a quitté sa position près de la Redoute No. 4 [*i.e.*, in front of
' the Redoubt No. 3, see the plan]. Ses battaillons se sont formés en carré
' plus en arrière.' See the plan. Of course I am not entitled to quote the
French Atlas as an authoritative record of Russian movements, but, as I
have said, the statement is in strict accordance with Todleben's plan.

    * That men may judge how far such a surmise may be warranted, I
invite an examination of the accompanying plan.

force were completing their descent into the plain of CHAP, Balaclava, Liprandi's continued obtrusion of troops in the direction of the Causeway Heights was no longer warranted by his relative strength.

X

* It is distressing to be forced to learn that at this critical moment, when Fortune proffered a victory, Sir George Cathcart was still disobeying the order to 'advance immediately ' and recapture the redoubts.' He was still halted by the No. 4 Redoubt with the main body of his infantry. The Riflemen he had sent out skirmishing were, some of them, very near to the work when the fire which the enemy had thence been directing came all at once to an end. This change resulted, as we now know, from the retreat of the Odessa battalions; but Cathcart still remained halted. Indeed, before long he drew in his Riflemen, and informed the Staff Officer that he should advance no further.† Thus, from the enemy's temporary alarm on the one side, and on the other from the recusancy of Cathcart, it resulted that the

* The footnote ante, p. 65, applies to this interpolation as well as to the one there occurring.

† Having heard General Airey tell Cathcart that Lord Raglan wished him to recapture the redoubts, and being under orders to remain with Sir George, the Staff Officer, somewhat later, thought it right to ask Cathcart whether he would not proceed to the No. 3 Redoubt (the Arabtabia), but Cathcart said 'No,' he would not advance further; for, though he felt sure he could recapture all the redoubts, including even the 'Number One,' no advantage would accrue, because the operation would cause him to lose some men, and the position being much too extended, the works would have to be evacuated after dark. He said his mind was quite made up, and that he would write to Lord Raglan. I do not find the note amongst Lord Raglan's papers. Before men condemn Lord Raglan for not bringing Cathcart to an account for his conduct on the day of Balaclava, it will be well for them to know that on the morrow—the very time when investigation on this subject might have been otherwise going on—there came a despatch from the Home Government which was calculated to make him stay his hand. See the chapter respecting Cathcart and the Dormant Commission contained in Vol. V. of the 'Invasion of the Crimea.'

CHAP. Arabtabia and the next Redoubt beyond—that is, the one
  X.   called 'Number Two'—remained for a while unoccupied by
either Russians or English.

***

Gradual
awaken-
ing of the
Russians
to the op-
portunity
which
our Light
Brigade
was offer-
ing them.

At first, as was natural, the enemy's gunners and
riflemen were so far taken by surprise, as to be
hardly in readiness to seize the opportunity which
Lord Cardigan was presenting to them; and indeed
for some time, the very extravagance of the operation masked its character from the intelligence of the
enemy, preventing him from seeing at once that it
must result from some stupendous mistake; but the
Russians at length perceived that the distance between
our Heavy Brigade and Lord Cardigan's squadrons was
every moment increasing, and that, whatever might
be the true meaning of the enterprise in which our
Light Cavalry had engaged, the red squadrons were
not under orders to give it that kind of support which
the Englishman calls 'thoroughgoing.'. This once
understood, the enemy had fair means of inferring
that the phenomenon of ten beautiful squadrons moving down the North Valley in well-ordered lines, was
not the commencement of anything like a general
advance on the part of the Allies, and might prove,
after all, to be hardly the result of design. Accordingly, with more or less readiness, the forces on the
Causeway Heights, the forces on the Fedioukine Hills,
and the twelve-gun battery which crossed the lower
end of the valley, became all prepared to inflict upon
our Light Cavalry the consequences of the fault which

propelled it. It is true that the main body of the Russian cavalry, drawn up in rear of the confronting battery, had been cowed by the result of its encounter with Scarlett's dragoons; but, when that has been acknowledged as a qualification of what is coming, it may be said that the three sides of the quadrangle in which our cavalry moved, were not only lined with Russians, but with Russians standing firm to their duty.

Soon the fated advance of the Light Brigade had proceeded so far as to begin to disclose its strange purpose — the purpose of making straight for the far distant battery which crossed the foot of the valley, by passing for a mile between two Russian forces, and this at such ugly distance from each as to allow of our squadrons going down under a doubly flanking fire of round-shot, grape, and rifle-balls, without the opportunity of yet doing any manner of harm to their assailants. Then, from the slopes of the Causeway Heights on the one side, and the Fedioukine Hills on the other, the Russian artillery brought its power to bear right and left, with an efficiency every moment increasing; and large numbers of riflemen on the slopes of the Causeway Heights who had been placed where they were in order to cover the retreat of the Russian battalions, found means to take their part in the work of destroying our horsemen. Whilst Lord Cardigan and his squadrons rode thus under heavy cross-fire, the visible object they had straight before them was the white bank of smoke, from time to time pierced by issues of flame, which

CHAP.
X.

Powerful fire opened upon the advancing brigade from both flanks.

CHAP. marks the site of a battery in action; for in truth
the very goal that had been chosen for our devoted
squadrons—a goal rarely before assigned to cavalry—
was the front of a battery—the front of that twelve-
gun battery, with the main body of the Russian
cavalry in rear of it, which crossed the lower end of
the valley; and so faithful, so resolute, was Lord
Cardigan in executing this part of what he understood to be his appointed task, that he chose out one
of the guns which he judged to be about the centre
of the battery, rode straight at its fire, and made this,
from first to last, his sole guiding star.

Officers
acting
with the
two regi-
ments of
the first
line.

With the two regiments constituting the first line,
there rode the following officers; Besides Captain
Oldham, the officer commanding the 13th Light
Dragoons, the officers with the regiment were—
Captain Goad, Captain Jenyns, Captain Tremayne,
Lieutenant Percy Smith (acting Adjutant), Lieutenant
Edward Lennox Jervis, Cornet Montgomery, and
Cornet Chamberlayne; * whilst with the 17th Lancers
there were Captain Morris (in command of the
regiment), Captain Robert White, Captain Winter,
Captain Webb, Captain Godfrey Morgan, Lieutenant
Thomson, Lieutenant Sir William Gordon, Lieutenant
Hartopp, Lieutenant Chadwick (Adjutant), Cornet
Wombwell,† and Cornet Cleveland.

---

* Cornet G. M. Goad was present with this regiment in the earlier
part of the battle, but at the time when our cavalry moved westward,
after the loss of the Turkish redoubts he was disabled from the effect of
a fragment of shell which struck his charger and caused the animal to
fall over him.—*Note to 2d Edition.*

† Wombwell, though near his own regiment—being on its right

Pressing always deeper and deeper into this pen of fire, the devoted brigade, with Lord Cardigan still at its head, continued to move down the valley. The fire the brigade was incurring had not yet come to be of that crushing sort which mows down half a troop in one instant, and for some time a steady pace was maintained. As often as a horse was killed or disabled, or deprived of the rider, his fall, or his plunge, or his ungoverned pressure, had commonly the effect of enforcing upon the neighbouring chargers more or less of lateral movement, and in this way there was occasioned a slight distension of the rank in which the casualty had occurred; but, in the next instant, when the troopers had ridden clear of the disturbing cause, they closed up, and rode on in a line as even as before, though reduced by the loss just sustained. The movement occasioned by each casualty was so constantly recurring, and so constantly followed by the same process,—the process of re-closing the ranks, that, to distant observers, the alternate distension and contraction of the line seemed to have the precision and sameness which belong to mechanic contrivance. Of these distant observers there was one—and that too a soldier—who so felt to the heart the true import of what he saw that, in a paroxysm of admiration and grief, he burst into tears. In well-maintained order, but growing less every instant, our squadrons still moved down the valley.

Their pace for some time was firmly governed.

CHAP.
X.

Continued advance of the brigade.

The pace.

flank—was not doing duty with it, because as we saw he was on Lord Cardigan's Staff.

CHAP.
X.

When horsemen, too valorous to be thinking of flight, are brought into straits of this kind, their tendency is to be galloping swiftly forward, each man at the greatest pace he can exact from his own charger, thus destroying, of course, the formation of the line ; but Lord Cardigan's love of strict, uniform order was a propensity having all the force of a passion ; and as long as it seemed possible to exert authority by voice or by gesture, the leader of this singular onset was firm in repressing the fault.

Thus when Captain White, of the 17th Lancers (who commanded the squadron of direction), became 'anxious,' as he frankly expressed it, 'to get out of ' such a murderous fire, and into the guns, as being ' the best of the two evils,' and endeavouring, with that view, to 'force the pace,' pressed forward so much as to be almost alongside of the chief's bridle-

Lord Cardigan's rigid way of leading the brigade.

arm, Lord Cardigan checked this impatience by laying his sword across the Captain's breast, telling him at the same time not to try to force the pace, and not to be riding before the leader of the brigade. Otherwise than for this, Lord Cardigan, from the first to the last of the onset, did not speak nor make sign. Riding straight and erect, he never once turned in his saddle with the object of getting a glance at the state of the squadrons which followed him ; and to this rigid abstinence—giving proof, as such abstinence did, of an unbending resolve—it was apparently owing that the brigade never fell into doubt concerning its true path of duty, never wavered (as the best squadrons will, if the leader, for even an instant, appears to be uncertain of purpose), and was guiltless of even inclining to any default except that of failing to keep down the pace.

So far as concerned the first line, this task was now becoming more and more difficult. When the 13th Light Dragoons and the 17th Lancers had passed so far down the valley as to be under ef- fective fire from the guns in their front, as well as from the flanks right and left, their lines were so torn, so cruelly reduced in numbers, as to be hardly any longer capable of retaining the corporate life or entity of the regiment, the squadron, the troop; and these aggregates began to resolve themselves into their component elements—that is, into brave, eager horsemen, growing fiercely impatient of a trial which had thus long denied them their vengeance, and longing to close with all speed upon the guns which had shattered their ranks. The troopers here and there could no longer be restrained from darting forward in front of the officers; and the moment this licence obtained, the ceremonious advance of the line was soon changed to an ungoverned onset. The racing spirit broke out, some striving to outride their comrades, some determining not to be passed.

In the course of the advance, Lieutenant Maxse, Lord Cardigan's second aide-de-camp, was wounded; and when the line had come down to within about a hundred yards of the guns, Sir George Wombwell, the extra aide-de-camp, had his horse killed under him. We shall afterwards see that this last casualty did not end the part which Wombwell was destined to take in the battle; but for the moment, of course,

CHAP. it disabled him, and there was no longer any Staff-
X.   officer in the immediate personal following of the
General who led the brigade.

Continued
advance of
Lord Car-
digan and
his first
line.

But although he rode singly, and although, as we
have seen, he rigidly abstained from any retrograde
glance, Lord Cardigan, of course, might infer from
the tramp of the regiments close following, and
from what (without turning in his saddle) he could
easily see of their flanks, that the momentum now
gathered and gathering was too strong to be mode-
rated by a commander; and, rightly perhaps avoiding the effort to govern it by voice or by gesture,
he either became impatient himself, and drew the
troops on more and more by first increasing his
own speed, or else yielded (under necessity) to the
impatience of the now shattered squadrons, and closely
adjusted his pace to the flow of the torrent behind
him. In one way or in the other, a right distance
was always maintained between the leader and his
first line. As before, when advancing at a trot, so
now, whilst flinging themselves impetuously deep into
the jaws of an army, these two regiments of the first
line still had in their front the same rigid hussar
for their guide, still kept their eyes fastened on the
crimson-red overalls and the white near hind-leg of
the chestnut which showed them the straight, honest
way—the way down to the mouths of the guns.*

Lord Cardigan insists that he was not the originator

---

* The chestnut had two 'white stockings,' both rather high up the
leg. Both these ' white stockings' were on the near side, and to people
following Lord Cardigan the white stocking behind was, of course, the
one which most caught the eye.

of the high speed which they reached in this part of their onset; whilst some, on the other hand, say that the squadrons never ceased from their duty of studiously watching the leader, and that the swiftness of Lord Cardigan was the cause which hurried forward the line. The truth, perhaps, is intermediate; for it seems not unlikely that the rapid pace of the leader, and the eagerness of the squadrons behind him, were causes which acted and reacted alternately the one on the other; but with whomsoever originating, and whether dictated by a sound warlike judgment, or by mere human instinct, the desire to move more and more swiftly was not unwarranted. Even at the cost of sacrificing military order, for the moment, it was seemingly wise, after all, in the straits to which our squadrons had been brought, to let every man close upon the battery with all the speed he could gather.*

Alone, in a sense, though close followed, and with no regimental labour on his hands, Lord Cardigan had more leisure for thought than the chief part of those he was leading; and for that reason simply, if not for any other, there is an interest in hearing him say how it fared with him mentally at the time of undergoing this trial. He has not been reluctant to disclose the tenor of the ideas which possessed themselves of his mind whilst he thus led his troops down the valley. From moment to moment he was an expectant of death; and it seems that death by some cannon-ball dividing his body was the manner

CHAP.
X.

* This I understand to be an opinion now recognised as sound by officers most competent to judge.

C H A P.
X.
of coming to an end which his fancy most constantly harboured; but there is a waywardness in the human mind which often prevents it from laying a full stress on any one thought, however momentous; and despite the black prospect of what the next moment might bring, Lord Cardigan—not knowing that his anger was with the dead—still dwelt, as he rode, on the incident which had marked the commencement of the advance—still raged, and raged against Nolan for having ridden in front of him, for having called out to his troops.* By thus affording distraction to one who supposed himself doomed, hot anger for once, it would seem, did the work of faith and philosophy.

Lord Cardigan and his first line had come down to within about eighty yards of the mouths of the guns, when the battery delivered a fire from so many of its pieces at once as to constitute almost a salvo. Numbers and numbers of saddles were emptied, and along its whole length the line of the 13th Light Dragoons and 17th Lancers was subjected to the rending perturbance that must needs be created in a body of cavalry by every man who falls slain or wounded, by the sinking and the plunging of every horse that is killed or disabled, and again by the wild, piteous intrusion of the riderless charger appalled by his sudden freedom

* The accuracy of Lord Cardigan's impression as to the thought chiefly occupying his mind at this time is confirmed by what we know from other sources of the first utterances to which he gave vent after coming out of the charge. No one was more struck than Lord Cardigan was by the strange and 'unearthly' shriek which Nolan had uttered; but oddly enough, he failed to infer that the cry was one immediately preceding death.

coming thus in the midst of a battle, and knowing not
whither to rush, unless he can rejoin his old troop,
and wedge himself into its ranks. It is believed by
Lord Cardigan that this was the time when, in the 13th
Light Dragoons, Captain Oldham, the commander of
the regiment, and Captain Goad, and Cornet Montgomery, and, in the 17th Lancers, Captain Winter*
and Lieutenant Thomson, were killed—when Captain
Robert White and Captain Webb and Lieutenant Sir
William Gordon were struck down.† The survivors
of the first line who remained undisabled were feeble
by this time, in numbers scarce more than some
fifty or sixty ;‡ and the object they rode at was a
line of twelve guns close supported by the main body
of the Russian cavalry, whilst on their right flank as
well as on their left, there stood a whole mile's length
of hostile array, comprising horse, foot, and artillery.
But by virtue of innate warlike passion—the gift, it
would seem, of high Heaven to chosen races of men—

* Captain Winter about this time was seen alive and in his saddle,
but it seems probable that he had then already received his mortal
wound.

† Sir William Gordon survived and recovered, but afterwards retired from active service. I have heard that he was an officer of great
ability, with an enthusiastic zeal for his profession ; and his retirement
has been quoted to me by cavalry men as an instance of the way in
which the perverse arrangements of our military system tend to drive
able men from the service. It seems that (upon principles analogous
to those adopted by the trades-unions) the sacred rights of mediocrity
are maintained with a firmness which too often defeats the patient
ambition of a highly gifted soldier.

‡ The grounds of this necessarily rough computation are, 1st, the
strength of the two regiments as ascertained at the muster after the
battle ; and 2d, the absence of proofs showing that any numerous casualties occurred in these two regiments at a later moment.

C H A P.
X.

the mere half of a hundred, carried straight by a resolute leader, were borne on against the strength of the
thousands. The few, in their pride, claimed dominion:
Rushing clear of the havoc just wrought, and with
Cardigan still untouched at their head, they drove
thundering into the smoke which enfolded both the
front of the battery and the masses of horsemen
behind it.

III.

The advance of the three regiments acting in support.

Whilst the first line thus moved in advance, it was
followed, at a somewhat less pace, by the three regiments which were to act in support. The officers
present with these regiments—I take them from left

Officers present with the 11th Hussars.

to right—were as follows: With the 11th Hussars,
besides Colonel Douglas who commanded the regiment, there rode Captain Edwin Cook, Lieutenant
Trevelyan, Lieutenant Alexander Dunn, Lieutenant
Roger Palmer, and George Powell Haughton. With

With the 4th Light Dragoons.

the 4th Light Dragoons, besides Lord George Paget
who commanded the regiment, there were present
Major Halkett, Captain Alexander Low, Captain
George John Brown, Captain Portal, Captain Hut-
ton, Lieutenant Sparke, Lieutenant Hedworth Jolliffe,
Cornet Wykeham Martin,* Cornet William Affleck
King, and Cornet Edward Warwick Hunt. With

---

* Thackeray, who once chanced to meet this young officer in society,
spoke of him as coming up to the very idea which he (Thackeray) had
formed of a ' brave, modest soldier.' Cornet Wykeham Martin survived
the Crimean War, but died young, and deeply loved. He was the son
of the member for Newport, and the brother of the member for Ro-
chester.—*Note to Second Edition.*

the 8th Hussars (which had only three of its troops
present), there rode, besides Colonel Shewell who
commanded the regiment, Major de Salis, Captain
Tomkinson, Lieutenant Seager (the Adjutant), Lieutenant Clutterbuck, Lieutenant Lord Viscount Fitzgibbon, Lieutenant Phillips, Cornet Heneage, Cornet
Clowes, and Cornet William Mussenden.

Of the regiments thus acting in support the foremost was the 11th Hussars. In obedience to the
order personally delivered to Colonel Douglas by Lord
Lucan, the regiment had altered its relative position;
and, instead of forming the left of the first line, it
now advanced in support of the 17th Lancers. Next
came Lord George Paget's regiment, the 4th Light
Dragoons. Whilst entrusting to Lord George Paget
the charge of what he had intended to be his second
line—that is, the 4th Light Dragoons and the 8th Hussars—Lord Cardigan had said, with what was taken
to be a somewhat marked emphasis, ' I expect your
' best support; mind, Lord George, your best support! '
Lord George said, ' Of course, my lord, you shall have
' my best support;' but the eager injunction he had
received so continued to ring in his ears during the
critical minutes which followed, that he was more
careful to keep near the first line than to preserve
his connection with the 8th Hussars. His order to
the 8th Hussars had been, ' 4th Light Dragoons will
' direct;' and this order of course, if obeyed, would
have sufficiently maintained the connection between
the two regiments; but the instruction, it would
seem, had not been effectually heard, or, at all events,

CHAP. was not kept in mind; for the officers of the 8th
X. Hussars apparently entertained a belief that theirs
was the directing regiment of the line in which it
had to act. Whatever the cause, it is certain that
Colonel Shewell was most resolute in keeping down
the pace of the regiment, and would not allow it to
assume the same speed as the 4th Light Dragoons.
Also, it happened, from some unknown cause, that the
regiment bore more towards its right than did the
4th Light Dragoons; and from the difference of pace
thus combined with the difference of direction, it resulted that both the interval and the distance which
separated the two regiments were suffered to bo con-
tinually increasing. For some time Lord George
Paget laboured with voice and gesture to call on,
and call in to his side the diverging regiment; and
it seems that he despatched a message to Colonel
Shewell with the same object; but his efforts were
vain; and presently the increasing pace of the first
line·made him give his whole care to the duty of
following it with a sufficient closeness; for the sound
of that ' Mind, Lord George, your best support ! ' still
haunted his memory, and it seemed to him that there
was no evil so great as the evil of lagging behind.

Nor was the task of bringing and keeping the regiment to the pace of the first line so easy as it might
seem at first sight; for the squadron-leaders, being
both of them men of singular firmness, would not suffer themselves nor their troops to be hurried by stress
of fire, nor even by the impatience of their chief; and
therefore, whilst Lord George was labouring to force

the pace, and from time to time crying 'Keep up!'
the two imperturbable squadron-leaders so ignored
any difference there might be for such purpose between wearisome practice at home and desperate service in battle, that without remission or indulgence
the teachings of Hounslow Heath and the Curragh
were repeated in this fatal valley. The crash of
dragoons overthrown by round-shot, by grape, and by
rifle-ball, was alternate with dry technical precepts :
'Back, right flank!' 'Keep back, Private This!'
'Keep back, Private That!' 'Close in to your cen-
'tre!'. 'Do look to your dressing!' 'Right squadron,.
'Right squadron, keep back!'

The increasing distance between the 4th Light
Dragoons and the 8th Hussars soon became so great
as to make Lord George Paget discard for the time
all idea of reuniting them into one line ; and, accordingly, with his now isolated regiment, he continued to
press forward at a rate which was in great measure
dictated to him by the speed of the first line. He
observed, however, that in his front there was another
regiment which had also become isolated ; for, in obedience to Lord Lucan's direction—a direction never
communicated to Lord George Paget—the 11th Hussars had by this time dropped back, so as to be acting
in support to the left of the first line. In these circumstances, Lord George Paget determined that, by
advancing in support to the 13th Light Dragoons,
and by somewhat accelerating his pace, he would try
to align himself with the 11th Hussars. In coming
to this determination Lord George was governed only

CHAP. by the exigency of the occasion; but it so happened
X.
that, without knowing it, he was bringing the disposition of the 'supports' to that exact form which
his Divisional General had intended to order; for as
soon as Lord George should succeed in overtaking the
11th Hussars, the second line would be formed, as Lord
Lucan had intended, by two regiments. Meantime,
however, and up to the moment when Lord George's
purpose attained to completion, the three regiments now
following the first line were in echelon of regiments.*

When the 8th Hussars began to encounter the riderless horses dashing back from the first line, there was
created some degree of unsteadiness, which showed
itself in a spontaneous increase of speed; but this
tendency was rigorously checked by the officers, and
they brought back the pace of the regiment to a good
trot. Of the three officers commanding the three
troops, one—namely, Captain Tomkinson—was at this
time disabled. Another, Lord Fitzgibbon, was killed;
and several men and horses fell; but Lieutenant
Seager and Cornet Clowes took the vacant commands,
and those of this small and now isolated regiment
who had not been yet slain or disabled moved steadily
down the valley.

In some respects this advance was even more try-

* Thus :—

11th Hussars.

4th Light Dragoons.

8th Hussars
(less one of its troops). .

ing to the supports than to the first line; for al- C H A P.
though the supports were destined to suffer much ___X.___
less than our first line from the twelve Cossack guns
in their front, yet, passing as they did between batteries and numbers of riflemen and musketeers, where
the gunners and the marksmen were now fully on
the alert, they incurred heavy loss all the time from
the double flank fire through which they were moving; and yet did not (as did ultimately the first line)
come under such stress of battle as to be warranted in
cutting short their probation by a vehement and un-
controlled rush. Throughout their whole course down
the valley the officers and the men of the 11th Hussars,
the 4th Light Dragoons, and the 8th Hussars never
judged themselves to be absolved from the hard task
of maintaining their formation, and patiently endur-
ing to see their ranks torn, without having means for
the time of even trying to harm their destroyers.
These three regiments, moreover, were subjected to
another kind of trial from which the first line was
exempt; for men not only had (as had had the first
line) to see numbers torn out of their ranks, and
then close up and pass on, but were also compelled to be witnesses of the havoc that battle had
been making with their comrades in front. The
ground they had to pass over was thickly strewn
with men and horses lying prostrate in death, or from
wounds altogether disabling; but these were less
painful to see than the maimed officers or soldiers,
still able to walk or to crawl, and the charger moving
horribly with three of his limbs, whilst dragging

CHAP. the wreck of the fourth, or convulsively labouring
X. to rise from the ground by the power of the fore-
legs when the quarters had been shattered by round-
shot.

And, although less distressing to see, the horses
which had just lost their riders without being themselves disabled, were formidable disturbers of any
regiment which had to encounter them. The extent
to which a charger can apprehend the perils of a
battle-field may be easily underrated by one who
confines his observation to horses still carrying their
riders; for, as long as a troop-horse in action feels
the weight and the hand of a master, his deep trust
in man keeps him seemingly free from great terror,
and he goes through the fight, unless wounded, as
though it were a field-day at home; but the moment
that death or a disabling wound deprives him of his
rider, he seems all at once to learn what a battle is
—to perceive its real dangers with the clearness of
a human being, and to be agonised with horror of
the fate he may incur for want of a hand to guide
him. Careless of the mere thunders of guns, he
shows plainly enough that he more or less knows the
dread accent that is used by missiles of war whilst
cutting their way through the air, for as often as
these sounds disclose to him the near passage of
bullet or round-shot, he shrinks and cringes. His
eyeballs protrude. Wild with fright, he still does not
most commonly gallop home into camp. His instinct
seems rather to tell him that what safety, if any, there
is for him must be found in the ranks; and he rushes.

at the first squadron he can find, urging piteously,
yet with violence, that he too by right is a troop-
horse—that he too is willing to charge, but not to be
left behind—that he must and he will 'fall in.' Sometimes a riderless charger thus bent on aligning with
his fellows, will not be content to range himself on
the flank of the line, but dart at some point in the
squadron which he seemingly judges to be his own
rightful place, and strive to force himself in. Riding,
as it is usual for the commander of a regiment to do,
some way in advance of his regiment, Lord George
Paget was especially tormented and pressed by the
riderless horses which chose to turn round and align
with him. At one time there were three or four of
these horses advancing close abreast of him on one
side, and as many as five on the 'other. Impelled
by terror, by gregarious instinct, and by their habit
of ranging in line, they so 'closed' in upon Lord
George as to besmear his overalls with blood from
the gory flanks of the nearest intruders, and oblige
him to use his sword.

Familiar pulpit reflections concerning man's frail
tenure of life come to have all the air of fresh truths
when they are pressed upon the attention of mortals
by the 'ping' of the bullet, by the sighing, the hum-
ming, and at last the 'whang' of the round-shot,
by the harsh 'whirr' of the jagged iron fragments
thrown abroad from a bursting shell, by the sound—
most abhorred of all those heard in battle—the sound
that issues from the moist plunge of the round-shot
when it buries itself with a 'slosh' in the trunk of a

CHAP. man or a horse.   Under tension of this kind pro-
X. longed for some minutes, the human mind, without
being flurried, may be wrought into so high a state of
activity as to be capable of well-sustained thought;
and a man, if he chose, whilst he rode down the
length of this fatal North Valley, could examine and
test and criticise—nay, even could change or restore
that armour of the soul, by which he had been accustomed to guard his serenity in the trials and dangers
of life.

One of the most gifted of the officers now acting
with the supports was able, whilst descending the
valley, to construct and adopt such a theory·of the
divine governance as he judged to be the best-fitted
for the battle-field.   Without having been hitherto
accustomed to let his thoughts dwell very gravely
on any such subjects of speculation—he now all
at once, whilst he rode, encased himself body and
soul in the iron creed of the fatalist; and, connecting destiny in his mind with the inferred will of God,
defied any missile to touch him, unless it should come
with the warrant of a providential and foregone
decree.   As soon as he had put on this armour of
faith, a shot struck one of his holsters without harm-
ing him or his horse ; and he was so constituted as to
be able to see in this incident a confirmation of his
new fatalist doctrine.   Then, with something of the
confidence often shown by other sectarians not engaged in a cavalry onset, he went on to determine
that his, and his only, was the creed which could
keep a man firm in battle.   There, plainly, he erred;

and, indeed, there is reason for saying that it would
be ill for our cavalry regiments, if their prowess were
really dependent upon the adoption of any highly spiritual or philosophic theory. I imagine that the great
body of our cavalry people, whether officers or men,
were borne forward and sustained in their path of
duty by moral forces of another kind—by sense of
military obligation, by innate love of fighting and of
danger—by the shame of disclosing weakness—by
pride of nation and of race—by pride of regiment,
of squadron, of troop—by personal pride; not least,
by the power of that wheel-going mechanism which
assigns to each man his task, and inclines him to give
but short audience to distracting, irrelevant thoughts.

But, whatever might be the variety of the governing motives which kept every man to his duty
through all the long minutes of this trying advance,
there was no variety in the results; for what it was
his duty to do, that every man did; and as often as a
squadron was torn, so often the undisabled survivors
made haste to repair it. The same words were ever
recurring—'Close in! Close in!' 'Close in to the
'centre!' 'Close in!'

It was under this kind of stress—stress of powerful
fire on each flank, and signs of dire havoc in front—
that the three regiments (in echelon order, but with
an always diminishing distance between the 11th
Hussars and the 4th Light Dragoons) moved down to
support the first line. Except that the pace of the
8th Hussars was more tightly restrained than that of
the 11th Hussars or the 4th Light Dragoons, the con-

CHAP. ditions under which the three regiments respectively
X. acted were, down to this time, much alike. Sustaining all the way cruel losses without means of reprisal,
but always preserving due order, and faithfully running the gauntlet between the fire from the Causeway
Heights and the fire from the Fedioukine Hills, they
successively descended the valley.

IV.

The near
approach
of our first
line to the
battery.

Lord Cardigan and his first line, still descending at
speed on their goal, had rived their way dimly through
the outer folds of the cloud which lay piled up in
front of the battery; but then there came the swift
moment when, through what remained of the dim-
ness, men at last saw the brass cannons gleaming
with their muzzles towards the chests of our horses;
and visibly the Russian artillerymen—unappalled by
the tramp and the aspect of squadrons driving down
through the smoke—were as yet standing fast to
their guns.

By the material obstacle which they offer to the
onset of horsemen, field-pieces in action, with their
attendant limber-carriages and tumbrils behind them,
add so sure a cause of frustration to the peril that
there is in riding at the mouths of the guns, that,
upon the whole, the expedient of attacking a battery
in front has been forbidden to cavalry leaders by a
recognised maxim of war. But the huge misconception of orders which had sent the brigade down this
valley was yet to be fulfilled to its utmost conclusion;

and the condition of things had now come to be such that, whatever might be the madness (in general) of charging a battery in front, there, by this time, was no choice of measures. By far the greater part of the harm which the guns could inflict had already been suffered; and I believe that the idea of stopping short on the verge of the battery did not even present itself for a moment to the mind of the leader.

Lord Cardigan moved down at a pace which he has estimated at seventeen miles an hour, and already he had come to within some two or three horses' lengths of the mouth of one of the guns—a gun believed to have been a twelve-pounder; but then the piece was discharged; and its torrent of flame seemed to gush in the direction of his chestnut's off fore-arm. The horse was so governed by the impetus he had gathered, and by the hand and the heel of his rider, as to be able to shy only a little at the blaze and the roar of the gun; but Lord Cardigan being presently enwrapped in the new column of smoke now all at once piled up around him, some imagined him slain. He had not been struck. In the next moment, and being still some two horses' lengths in advance of his squadrons, he attained to the long-sought battery, and shot in between two of its guns.

There was a portion of the 17th Lancers on our extreme left which outflanked the line of the guns, but with this exception the whole of Lord Cardigan's first line descended on the front of the battery; and as their leader had just done before them, so now our horsemen drove in between the guns; and some then

CHAP.
X.

Lord Cardigan's charge into the battery at the head of his first line.

CHAP.
X.

at the instant tore on to assail the grey squadrons drawn up in rear of the tumbrils. Others stopped to fight in the battery, and sought to make prize of the guns. After a long and disastrous advance against clouds and invisible foes, they grasped, as it were, at reality. What before had been engines of havoc dimly seen or only inferred from the jets of their fire and their smoke, were now burnished pieces of cannon with the brightness and the hue of red gold—cannon still in battery, still hot with the slaughter of their comrades.* In defiance of our cavalry raging fiercely amongst them, the Russian artillerymen with exceeding tenacity still clung to their guns. Here and there indeed gunners were seen creeping under the wheels for safety, but in general they fought with rare devotion, striving all that men could, in such conditions of fight, against the sabres and lances of horsemen. They desired at all hazards to save their Czar's cannon from capture by removing them in haste from the front; and apparently it was to cover this operation—an operation they had already begun to attempt—that the gunners, with small means of resistance, stood braving the assaults of dragoons.

V.

It so happened that Captain Morris, the officer in command of the 17th Lancers, was advancing in front

---

* There is reason for believing that the pieces were twelve-pounders. Their metal had that reddish tinge which is observable in the sovereigns coined of late years by the English Mint.

of his left squadron, and thence it resulted that the portion of the regiment which outflanked the battery fell specially under his personal leadership.*

As soon as Morris had ridden so far through the smoke as to be able to see beyond it, he found that he had before him—with no line of guns intervening—a body of regular cavalry, and he seems to have understood that the force thus immediately opposed to him consisted of not less than two squadrons;† though he could not apparently see whether these two squadrons stood isolated or were acting in conjunction with other bodies of horse. We now know, however, that the body of horse Morris had on his front was one overlapping the battery, and connected with the right wing of that great body of Russian cavalry which stood posted across the valley in rear of the guns. On the other hand, the portion of the 17th Lancers which was thus confronted by the right wing of the Russian cavalry could hardly have numbered more than some twenty horsemen;‡ and

* Before the change by which Lord Lucan reduced the three regiments of the first line to two, the centre of the 17th Lancers was the centre of the line; and, Lord Cardigan's proper position being then in front of that centre, Captain Morris thought it right to avoid being unduly near the general of the brigade by placing himself in front of his left squadron. Having once taken that place, he kept it, notwithstanding the change.

† In words, so far as I know, Morris spoke only in general terms of the force as a 'body of cavalry;' but whilst lying in bed ill from his many wounds he contrived (though his arm was fractured) to sketch a little plan of the combat; and in this the Russian force immediately opposed to him is represented in a way which indicates the presence of not less than two squadrons.

‡ It is known that, besides the whole of the right squadron of the 17th Lancers, a large portion of the left squadron (probably not much less than a troop) was confronted by the battery, and entered it; and if

C H A P.   this scanty force, being now at the close of a rapid ad-
   X.
———   vance carried on for more than a mile under destructive fire, was not moving down with such weight and
compactness—nor even, in truth, at such a high rate
of speed—as to be able to deliver that shock which is
the object of a cavalry charge.   It was plain, however,
that, with all such might as was now possible, the
blow must be dealt; for the Russian horsemen, by remaining halted, were offering once more to the English that priceless advantage which they had given to
Scarlett in the earlier part of the day.   The density
of the smoke had prevented the commander of the
17th Lancers from seeing that three-fourths of his
horsemen were confronted by the battery; * and he
apparently believed that, in executing a charge against
the enemy's cavalry, he would be carrying with him
the whole remains of his regiment. †

Morris's   Be this as it may, Morris, turning half round in his
charge.   saddle, called out to his people, and said, 'Now re-
'member what I have told you, men, and keep to-
'gether.'   Then he put his spurs into 'Old Treasurer,'
and, followed by that fraction of the regiment which
ranged clear of the battery, drove full at the squadron
confronting him.

also it be true, as I imagine it must be, that by far the greater part of
the casualties which ultimately reduced the regiment to a strength of
only 37 had already occurred, it would seem to follow that there can
hardly be any wide error in the surmise which puts the force engaged
in Morris's charge at a number not exceeding twenty.
    * This is proved, as I think, by a little sketch-map in which he con-
veyed his impression as to the position of the guns.
    † This is inferred from the fact mentioned in the foregoing note and
from the general tenor of Colonel Morris's narrative.

In resistance to the onset of a handful of Lancers thus descending upon their close serried ranks, the Russians still remained halted ; and in the moments which passed whilst galloping down to attack them, Morris used to the utmost his well-practised eyes without being able to discern any one sign of wavering. The only movement he could detect in the enemy's ranks was of a kind showing readiness to join in close combat. The Russian troopers in front of him were perceptibly drawing their horses' heads in the direction of the bridle-arm, as though seeking to gain larger space for the use and free play of their swords.

In the direct front of the ranks thus awaiting the charge of our horsemen, there was sitting in his saddle a Russian who seemed to be the 'squadron-leader. Morris drove his horse full at this officer, and in the instant which followed the contact, the sword of the assailant had transfixed the trunk of the Russian, passing through with such force that its hilt pressed against the man's body. The handful of men whom Morris was thus leading against the Russian cavalry followed close on their chief, drove full down at the charge on the enemy's array of Hussars, and so broke their way into his strength as to be presently intermingled, the few with the many—the twenty gay, glittering Lancers, with the ranks of the dusky grey cavalry.

Seeing perhaps, with more or less distinctness, that they were undergoing an attack from only a handful of Lancers, some portions of the Russian Hussars whose

CHAP. ranks had thus been invaded did not choose to con-
   X.   fess themselves vanquished, although their array had
been broken, and these remained on the ground, but the
rest galloped off; and their English assailants, or such
of them as were yet undisabled, swept on in pursuit.

Scarcely, however, had this happened, when those
Russian Hussars who had not given way were joined
by numbers of Cossacks pouring in from the flank;
and they now once more had dominion of the very
ground where their ranks, half a minute before, had
been broken by Morris's charge. For the moment
there was nothing to hinder the enemy from capturing any of the English who here remained wounded
and disabled.

Morris   Of these Morris himself was one; and his misfor-
wounded
and taken   tune was a consequence of the determination which
prisoner.   induced him to 'give point' to his adversary. 'I
'don't know,' he would afterwards say—'I don't
'know how I came to use the point of my sword, but
'it is the last time I ever do.' When his sword,
driving home to the hilt, ran through the Russian
squadron - leader whom he had singled out for his
first adversary, the Russian tumbled over on the off
side of his horse, drawing down with him in his fall
the sword which had slain him; and since Morris,
with all his strength, was unable to withdraw the
blade, and yet did not choose to let go his grasp of
the handle, or to disengage himself from the wrist-
knot, it resulted that, though still in his saddle, he
was tethered to the ground by his own sword-arm.*

* Thrust home with the momentum belonging to a horse charging

Whilst thus disabled, Morris received a sabre-cut on
the left side of the head which carried away a large
piece of bone above the ear, and a deep, clean cut
passing down through the acorn of his forage-cap,
which penetrated both plates of the skull. By one or
other of these blows he was felled to the ground, and
for a time he lay without consciousness. As soon as he
had regained his senses, he found himself lying on
the ground; but his sword was once more in his
power, for by some means (to him unknown) it had
been withdrawn from the body which before held it
fast, and being joined to him still by the wrist-knot,
was now lying close to his hand. He had hardly
recovered his senses and the grasp of his sword when
he found himself surrounded by Cossacks thrusting
at him with their lances. Against the numbers thus
encompassing him Morris sought to defend himself by
the almost ceaseless 'moulinet,' or circling whirl of
his sword, and from time to time he found means to
deliver some sabre-cuts upon the thighs of his Cossack
assailants. Soon, however, he was pierced in the
temple by a lance-point, which splintered up a piece
of the bone, and forced it in under the scalp. This
wound gave him great pain ; and, upon the whole, he
believed that his life must be nearly at its end; but
presently there appeared a Russian officer, who interposed with his sword, striking up two or three of Cossack lances, and calling out loudly to Morris, with

down at high speed, the blade, it would seem, must have been forced
through so much bone and muscle, as to be held fast against any mere
pull which Morris could apply.

CHAP. assurances that if he would surrender he should be
X.
saved. Accordingly Morris yielded up his sword, and
became a prisoner of war.

Other in-   At nearly the same time, and not far from the same
cidents in
this part   spot, another officer of the 17th Lancers fell alive into
of the
field.   the hands of the enemy. This was Lieutenant Chadwick. Before he reached the line of the battery, his
charger had received so many wounds, and lost so much
blood, as to be all but incapable of stirring, though yet
remaining on his legs. In spite of the singular and
tormenting disadvantage of thus having under him an
almost immovable horse, Chadwick found means to
defend himself for some time against the stray Cossacks and other dragoons who, óne after another, beset
him; but at length he was caught in the neck by a
Cossack lance, which lifted him out of his saddle, and
threw him to the ground with such force as to stun
him. When his senses returned, and whilst he still
lay on the ground, he succeeded in defending himself
with his revolver against a Cossack who sought to
despatch him; but presently, from the direction of
our right rear, other Cossacks, to the number of eight
or ten, rode down yelling, with lances poised, and to
these (when they circled around him, and made signs
that he might have quarter if he would throw down
his pistol) Lieutenant Chadwick at length surrendered.

At this time, and in this part of the field, several of
the wounded English who lay on the ground without
means of defending themselves were despatched by
the Cossacks; but I have not been compelled to learn

that men were guilty of acts such as these where any C H A P. Russian officer was present.

It was before our supports had come down, and whilst the English were still combating in the battery or pushing their onset beyond it, that the enemy, for a moment, was thus able to exercise dominion in rear of Lord Cardigan's first line.

VI.

Of those who swept on at the instant without staying to subdue the resistance of the artillerymen, Lord Cardigan from the first had been one. After charging into the battery, he continued his onset with but little remission of speed; and although the smoke was so thick as to put him in danger of crushing his legs against wheels, he pierced his way through at a gallop between the limber-carriages and the tumbrils, by a gangway so narrow as hardly to allow a passage for two horsemen going abreast. Of necessity, therefore, his people who had hitherto followed him strictly now had to seek out other paths for their still continuing onslaught. Some, by bending a little, when necessary, to their right or to their left, found gangways more or less broad for their passage through the ranks of the artillery-carriages, and others made good their advance by sweeping round the flanks of the battery, but a few only were able to follow close on the track of their leader, and all these, sooner or later, were cut off from him by the incidents of battle.

In this way it happened that Lord Cardigan had

Continued advance by Lord Cardigan in person.

His isolation.

C H A P.
X.

His advance towards a large body of Russian cavalry.

already become almost entirely isolated, when, still pursuing his onward course, he found himself riding down singly towards a large body of Russian cavalry, then distant, as he has since reckoned, about eighty yards from the battery. This cavalry was retreating, but presently it came to a halt, went about, and fronted. Lord Cardigan stopped, and at this time he was so near to the enemy's squadrons that he has reckoned the intervening distance at so little as twenty yards. The same phenomenon which had enforced the attention of some of Scarlett's dragoons in the morning now presented itself under other conditions to Lord Cardigan. All along the confronting ranks of the grey-coated horsemen, he found himself hungrily eyed by a breed of the human race whose numberless cages of teeth stared out with a wonderful clearness from between the writhed lips, and seemed all to be gnashing or clenched. It is believed that this peculiar contortion of feature, so often observed in the Russian soldiery, was not, in general, an expression of anything like brutal ferocity, but rather of vexation, and keen, eager care, with a sense of baffled energy. Lord Cardigan himself imagines that, with the feelings of the Russian troopers whilst eyeing him, the thought of gain possibly mingled; for his pelisse being rich, and worn close at the time like a coat, showed a blaze of gold lace to the enemy.

It can rarely occur to any man to be able to recognise a friend or acquaintance across the dim barrier of distance or smoke which commonly divides hostile armies in a modern battle-field; but in the part of the

valley to which Lord Cardigan's onset had brought CHAP.
X.
him the air was clear, and I am assured that an
officer of the house of Radzivill, then serving with
the Russian cavalry, was able to recognise in the
gorgeous hussar now before him, that same Earl of
Cardigan whom he had formerly known or remarked
during the period of a visit to England.* This offi- Endeav-
cer says that he ordered some Cossacks to endeavour our to
take him
to capture his London acquaintance, enjoining them prisoner.
specially to bring in their prisoner unhurt, and that,
the better to whet their zeal, he promised them a
tempting reward.

Certainly, the bearing of the Cossacks who now
came forward against Lord Cardigan was very much
what might have been expected from men who had
received such instructions as these. Two of them
only, in the first instance, came up close to him,
and these not, as I gather, in a truculent way, for
they seemed as though they would have liked to make
him prisoner. Lord Cardigan, however, showing no
signs of an intention to surrender, they began to assail
him with their lances, and for a moment his demeanour was like that of a man who regarded the
movements of the Cossacks as disorderly rather than
hostile; for—full of high scorn at the wretchedness
of their nags—he sat up stiff in the saddle, and kept
his sword at the slope. Presently, however, he found
himself slightly wounded by a thrust received near the
hip, and in peril of being unhorsed by a lance which

* My informant assures me that he had this from Prince Radzivill
himself.

CHAP. caught hold of him by the pelisse, and nearly forced
   X.   him out of his saddle. Yet that last effort seems
to have been made by a Cossack who was himself
almost in retreat; for the man at the time had his
back half turned to Lord Cardigan, and the thrust he
delivered was the one known to science by the name
of the 'right rear point.' The assailant had possibly
learnt by this time that his comrades a little way off
were flying from the English cavalry, and that he
must not be too slow in conforming.

The move-
ment in
retreat by
which he
disengag-
ed himself
from his
Cossack
assailants.
It was right, of course, that instead of submitting
to be taken prisoner, or to be butchered by overwhelming numbers, Lord Cardigan, being nearly alone,
and altogether unaided, should disengage himself, if
he could, from the reach of his assailants by a sufficing
movement of retreat, and this he accordingly did; but
before he had galloped far back, and whilst still on
the Russian side of the battery, he found that he
already had extricated himself from personal moles-
tation, and had leisure to determine what next he
would do.

The devo-
tion with
which,
down to
this time,
Lord Car-
digan had
led his
brigade.
Being now on the verge of that period in the battle when Lord Cardigan's course of action became
such as to leave room for question and controversy, if
not for unsparing blame, I would here interpose, and
say that, home down to the moment when he found
himself almost alone in the presence of the enemy's
cavalry, he had pursued his desperate task with a rare,
and most valorous persistency. And English officers,
I know, will take pleasure in learning that, from the
moment when he quietly said, 'The brigade will ad-

'vance,' to the one when, nearly alone in the presence of the enemy's cavalry, he stiffly awaited his assailants with his sword at the slope, Lord Cardigan performed this historic act of devotion without word or gesture indicative of bravado or excitement, but rather with the air of a man who was performing an everyday duty with his everyday courage and firmness.*

VII.

When Lord Cardigan had withdrawn himself from the reach of his Cossack assailants, he still continued to retire, and passed once more through the battery into which he had led°his brigade. He then saw men of the 13th Light Dragoons and the 17th Lancers retreating in knots up the valley, and he apparently imagined that the horsemen whom he thus saw retiring constituted the entire remnants of his first line. There, however, he erred. So far as I have learnt, there was no group of English horsemen still remaining 'effective' which, at this time, had moved to the rear; and indeed I have never yet heard of any one ascertained exception of either officer or man which

Lord Cardigan's return through the battery.

His predicament.

* During the advance down the valley, Captain Morris, who could not have been under a bias favourable to the commander of the brigade (see *ante*, p. 171), was on the left rear of Lord Cardigan, and at no great distance from him. When asked as to the manner in which Lord Cardigan had led the brigade, Morris used to say, 'Nothing 'could be better. He (Lord Cardigan) put himself just where he 'ought, about in front of my right squadron, and went down in capital 'style.' When specially asked whether Lord Cardigan had led 'quietly,' Morris answered, 'Quite so; just as it ought to be—in short, like 'a gentleman'—'an expression from his lips conveying much,' so says the narrator of the conversation, 'to any one who knew him.'

CHAP.
X.

ought to forbid me from saying in general terms that the Light Dragoons and the Lancers whom Lord Cardigan saw retreating were, all of them, men disabled —men either disabled by their own wounds, or else by the wounds of their chargers. It must be remembered, however, that the number of men thus in one way or other disabled was so huge in proportion to the whole strength of the regiments, as to give a seeming, though fallacious ground for the wrong impression which their appearance produced upon Lord Cardigan's mind. It is certain enough, as we shall afterwards learn more fully, that effective remnants of the 13th Light Dragoons and of the 17th Lancers pushed on their attack down the valley in the direction of the aqueduct; but Lord Cardigan solemnly declares—and declares, I believe, with truth—that, at the time, he could see none of his first line except those who, being most of them already some way towards the rear, were retreating up the slope of the valley. In these circumstances, he satisfied himself that, so far as concerned the business of rallying or otherwise interfering with the shattered fragments of his first line, there was nothing he could usefully do, without first following their retreat.

But then Lord Cardigan, though acting as the more immediate leader of the first line was also in command of the whole brigade, and had charge, amongst others, of the three regiments which formed his supports. Was he warranted in leaving those regiments to fight their way in, or to fight their way out without giving them the advantage, if any, which the presence of their Brigadier might confer?

Lord Cardigan answers this question by propound- C H A P.
ing the theory that his primary duty was with the X.
first line, and by also asserting that he could nowhere
see his supports. He determined to follow the horsemen whom he saw falling back. Without seeing
occasion to deliver any order, or to hold up his sword
for a rally, he continued the movement by which he
had withdrawn himself from the Cossacks, and re-
mounted the slope of the valley.

It might be thought that, since he left a main part
of his brigade in the fangs of the Russian army, Lord
Cardigan, when resolved to fall back, would have
sought, to turn his retrograde journey to a saving
purpose by flying to Lord Lucan or General Scarlett,
and entreating that some squadrons might be pushed
forward to extricate the remains • of his brigade.
Perhaps, though he has not so said, he exerted the
utmost resources of his mind in the endeavour to
see what, if anything, could be done for the salvation
of his troops, then engulfed, as it were, in a hostile
army, and was painfully driven to the conclusion that
no reinforcements could help them; but, so far as I
know, he has not been accustomed to speak of any
such mental efforts. Resolved as he was from a sense
of personal honour to execute to the letter, and without stint of life whatever he might make out to be
his clear duty, he yet never seemed to attain to such
a height above the level of self as to feel what is
called public care. And certainly his own account,
if taken as being complete, would tend to make
people think that, although, as might be expected,

CHAP. he was magnanimously regardless of his mere personal
  X. safety, yet in other respects, he much remembered
himself, and all but forgot his brigade. It occurred
to him, he says, at the time, that it was an anomalous thing for a General to be retreating in the
isolated state to which he found himself reduced,
and he therefore determined to move at a pace
decorously slow.

His   Whatever were his governing motives, and what-
retreat.
ever was his actual pace, he rode back alone towards
the spot where Scarlett at this time was halted.*
The first words he uttered were characteristic, and
gave curious proof that the anger provoked by an
apparent breach of military propriety had not been
at all obliterated by even the ' Light Cavalry Charge.'
He began to run out against the officer who had
galloped across his front at the commencement of
the onset, and was continuing his invective when
Scarlett stopped him by saying that he had nearly
ridden over Captain Nolan's dead body†. Lord

* It is stated by General Scarlett that Lord Lucan was present at
this time; but Lord Lucan, on the other hand, has stated that Lord
Cardigan did not ride up to or approach him until afterwards when all
was over. Whoever is acquainted with the tenor of the affidavits filed
in Cardigan v. Calthorpe will see, from my use of the word ' towards,'
instead of ' to,' that I avoid adopting, and also avoid contradicting, the
passage of Lord Lucan's affidavit in which he says : he saw Lord
Cardigan pass up the valley at a distance from him of about 200 yards.
If Lord Lucan's impression in that respect be accurate, Lord Cardigan
must have made a loop movement, passing first up the valley and then
riding back to Scarlett.

† General Scarlett states that ' immediately previous ' to this conversation he had pointed out to Lord Lucan a body of troops (which he
took to be the 4th Light Dragoons and the 11th Hussars) retreating
under the Fedioukine Hills.

Cardigan afterwards resumed his westerly movement, C H A P. and rode back to the neighbourhood of the ground X from which his brigade had advanced.

Supposing Lord Cardigan to be accurate when he says that he could neither see any still-combating remnants of his first line, nor any portion of his supports, there are two monosyllables—more apt than the language of scholars—by which hunting-men will be able to describe his predicament, and to sum up a good deal of truth in a spirit of fairness. For eight or ten minutes, Lord Cardigan had led the whole field, going always straight as an arrow: he then was 'thrown out.' Perhaps if he had followed the instincts of the sport from which the phrase has been taken, he would have been all eye, all ear, for a minute, and in the next would have found his brigade. But with him, the sounder lessons of Northamptonshire had been overlaid by a too lengthened experience of the soldiering that is practised in peace-time. In riding back after the troops which he saw in retreat up the valley, he did as he would have done at home after any mock charge in Hyde Park.

It will always be remembered that he who retired from the now silenced battery was the man who, the foremost of all a few moments before, had charged in through its then blazing front, and that that very isolation which became the immediate cause of his misfortune, was the isolation, after all, of a leader who had first become parted from his troops by shooting on too far ahead of them.

Lord Cardigan was not amongst the last of the

C H A P. horsemen who came out of the fight; and his move-
___X.___ ment in retreat was so ordered as to prevent him from
sharing with his people in the combats which will
next be recorded. It must therefore be acknowledged that his exit from the scene in which he had
been playing so great a part was at least infelicitous,
and devoid of that warlike grace which would have
belonged to it if he had come out of action only a
little while later with the remnant of his shattered
brigade; but despite the mischance, or the want of
swift competence in emergency, which marred his
last act, he yet gave, on the whole, an example of
that kind of devotion which is hardly less than absolute. He construed his orders so proudly, and obeyed
them with a persistency at once so brave and so fatal,
that—even under the light evolved from a keen,
searching controversy—his leadership of this singular
charge still keeps its heroic proportions.

VIII.

The
Lancers
who had
charged
under
Morris.

The handful of men which had charged under Morris
pursued the defeated Hussars in the direction of our
left front, and drove them in on their supports; but
when the Russians found out that their heavy squadrons were suffering pressure from what, after all, was
no more than a small knot or group of horsemen, they
turned upon their assailants; and the little band of
Lancers then beginning at last to retreat, came back
intermixed more or less with the enemy's grey-coated
horsemen.

Presently they were met by some men of their own CHAP.
regiment who turned with them, and joined their X.
retreating movement.* The united groups of these
17th Lancer men were pursued by the Russian cavalry, and soon found also that they were threatened
on their flank by a large number of Cossacks. † To
avoid being cut off by those Cossacks, they inclined
sharply towards their then left, but in vain, for the
Cossacks closed upon them. They, however, fought
their way through their assailants, and made good
their retreat, passing up the valley obliquely towards
the ground where Scarlett was posted.

The zest of the first line, having broken straight into
the battery, had either engaged themselves in the task
of spearing and cutting down the obstinate artillerymen, or else had pushed forward betwixt the limbers
and the tumbrils to assail the cavalry in rear of the
guns. These men of the first line, however, were all The
broken up into small groups and knots, or else acting, combat-
each singly, as skirmishers. stituting
the main
One of these groups had in it some of those very remnants
few men of the 13th Light Dragoons who yet remained line.
undisabled, and Captain Jenyns, then in command of The
the regiment, endeavoured to keep it together; but under
the largest fraction of the first line consisted of that Jenyns.
part of the 17th Lancers, which, not having been en- Group
gaged in Morris's charge, and not having yet pressed mén of the

* The men they thus met were those who (as will be presently mentioned) were acting under Sergeant O'Hara.

† These apparently were the Cossacks who had poured in from the
flank and were able to take prisoners as already described whilst the
Lancers who charged under Morris were passing on in pursuit.

C H A P.
___X.___

17th Lancers.

on against the enemy's cavalry, was engaged with the Russian artillerymen in the battery. Morris, himself, as we saw, having first been cut down, had fallen into the hands of the enemy; and, there being but few other officers at this time who remained alive and undisabled, the men knew of nothing better to do than to try to complete their capture of the battery.

At the part of the battery which had been entered by these men of the 17th Lancers, the Russian artillerymen were limbering up and making great exertions to carry off their guns, whilst our Lancers, seeing this, began to busy themselves with the task of hindering the withdrawal of the prey, and in particular the leftermost portion of them, under the direction of Sergeant O'Hara, were stopping the withdrawal of one of the guns which already had been moved off some paces,

Mayow's assumption of command over these.

when a voice was heard calling, 'Seventeeth! Seventeenth! this way! this way!'

The voice came from Mayow, the officer who held the post of brigade-major; but also it chanced that, with the first line, Mayow was the officer next in seniority to the commander of the brigade (whom he could not, he says, then see), and it was in that condition of things that he took upon himself to direct the operations of this still fighting remnant.

Mayow's order to the men.

Mayow judged that if these men remained combating in the battery they would be presently overwhelmed by the cavalry which he saw in his front, and that, desperate as the expedient might seem, the course really safest and best was at once, with any force that could be gathered, to attack the Russian horsemen

whilst still they were only impending, and before they
became the assailants. Therefore warning the Lancers
that if they remained in the battery they would presently be closed in upon and cut to pieces, he called
upon them to push forward.   He was obeyed; but
from the way in which, at the time, he chanced to be
carrying the pistol then held in his hand, his order
was in part mistaken ; for O'Hara supposed that the
brigade-major, by pointing, as he seemed to be doing,
towards his left front, must be intending to order an
advance in that direction. Accordingly O'Hara, with
the Lancers acting under his immediate guidance,
moved off towards his left front, and there then only
remained about fifteen men who continued to act
under Mayow.

Putting himself at the head of these last, Mayow led
them against a body of Russian cavalry which stood
halted in rear of the guns.* With his handful of
Lancers he charged the Russian horsemen and drove
them in on their second reserve, pushing forward so
far as to be at last some five hundred yards in the
rear (Russian rear) of the battery, and in sight of the
bridge over the aqueduct on the main road which
led to Tchorgoun.

It may well be imagined that, intruding, as he was,
with less than a score of horsemen, into the very
rear of the Russian position, and dealing with a
hostile cavalry which numbered itself by thousands,
Mayow was not so enticed by the yielding, nay,

CHAP.
X.

Men under
O'Hara.

Mayow's
charge.

His ad-
vance in
pursuit.

* This was probably the body which went about and fronted when
Lord Cardigan in person approached it.

CHAP.
X.
fugitive, tendency of the squadrons retreating before him, as to forget that the usefulness of the singular venture which had brought him thus far must depend, after all, upon the chance of its being supported. He

His halt. halted his little band; and whether he caught his earliest glimpse of the truth with his own eyes, or whether he gathered it from the mirthful voices of his Lancers saying something of 'the Busby-bags com- 'ing,' or 'the Busby-bags taking it coolly,' he at all events learnt to his joy that exactly at the time when he best could welcome its aid, a fresh English force was at hand.* The force seen was only one squadron, but a squadron in beautiful order ; and, though halted when first discerned, it presently resumed its advance, and was seen to be now fast approaching.

Opera-
tions of
the forces
actively
supporting
the first
line.
It will now be convenient to observe the operations of the troops which were actively supporting Lord Cardigan's first line, and to take them in the order of from left to right.

IX.

The feel-
ings with
which the
French
saw our
Light Cav-
alry ad-
vance
down the
North
Valley.
It was with a generous admiration, yet also with a thrilling anxiety, and with a sentiment scarce short of horror, that the French saw our squadrons advance down the valley, and glide on, as it were, to destruc- tion; but especially was strong feeling aroused in that warlike body of horse which stood ranged, as

* The 'Busby-bag' is the familiar name for the head-gear of the English Hussar, and—upon the *pars pro totâ* principle—for the Hussar himself.

we know, on the left rear of the ground whence our
Light Brigade had advanced.

Though originating in arrangements somewhat similar to those by which our Irregular Cavalry in India is constructed, and though mounted on Algerine horses, the horsemen called 'the Chasseurs d'Afrique' were French at the time now spoken of, and they constituted an admirably efficient body of horse; but if all the four regiments which composed it were equal the one to the other in intrinsic worth, the one which had had the fortune to be in the greatest number of brilliant actions was the 'Fourth.' From the frequency, with which the corps had chanced to be moved in Algeria, it went by the name of the 'Traveller' regiment. From the period of its merely rudimentary state in 1840, home down to this war against Russia, the career of the regiment had been marked by brilliant enterprises. When the Duc d'Aumale performed that famous exploit of his at Taguin, overruling all the cautions addressed to him by general officers and resisting the entreaties of his Arab allies (who implored him to wait for his infantry), it was with this 'Fourth' regiment of the African Chasseurs, supported only by some Spahis or native horsemen, that the youthful Prince broke his way into the great esmala of Abdel Kader, swept through it like a hurricane, overtook and defeated the enemy's column, cut off its retreat, rode down the Emir's new battalions of regular infantry, and made himself master of all.* After the Duc d'Aumale himself, no one perhaps knew better

* In May 1843.

The Chasseurs d'Afrique.

The celebrated 4th regiment of the Chasseurs d'Afrique.

C H A P.
X.
General
Morris.

what this famous regiment could do than that very General Morris, the officer commanding the whole of the French Cavalry Division, and now present in person with his first brigade ; for he it was who with this superb 'Fourth,' and one other of the regiments of the Chasseurs d'Afrique, had issued at the battle of Isly from that famous amassment of troops which Bugeaud used to call his 'boar's head,' and carried by his onslaught sheer ruin into the army of Morocco.

This was the General who had ridden down to be present in person with the troops of his first brigade, and this 'Fourth' was one of the two regiments of the Chasseurs d'Afrique of which the brigade consisted. General d'Allonville commanded the brigade.

During the earlier moments of the fatal advance down the valley, it could not but be difficult to infer that the operation was to be one of an irrational kind, there being at first no clear reason for imagining that the Light Brigade would really descend betwixt the open jaws of the enemy, instead of proceeding, as Lord Raglan had ordered, to recapture the lost Turkish

His deter-
mination.

heights ;* but when, after some time, Morris saw that our Light Brigade was still moving straight down the valley, and avoiding the heads of both the enemy's columns in order to run the gauntlet between them, he could not, of course, help perceiving that a terrible error was in course of perpetration. He was

* I have already said that at the point whence our Light Brigade advanced, the angle of difference between the right road and the wrong one was only about twenty degrees ; and it well might be some time before a spectator could convince himself that the brigade was really going down the valley.

not, however, a man to see this and stand aghast, CHAP.
doing nothing to succour the English. He resolved X
to venture an enterprise in support of Lord Cardigan's attack, and on one side at least of the valley—Lord Lucan was on the other with his Heavy
Dragoons—to endeavour to silence the enemy's fire.
The force which he determined to assail was the one
which lay the nearest to him—the one under General
Jabrokritsky on the slopes of the Fedioukine Hills;
and the immediate object of his intended attack was
a battery (divided into two half-batteries of four guns
each) which was guarded on its right by two battalions of foot and on its left by two squadrons of
Cossacks.*

General Morris chose for this service his famous
'Fourth' or 'Traveller' regiment of the Chasseurs
d'Afrique; and General d'Allonville, the officer in
command of the brigade, was himself to conduct the
attack.

Accordingly, the chosen regiment moved forward D'Allon-
under D'Allonville. The front of the assailing force attack.
was formed by two squadrons of the regiment under
the immediate command of Major Abdelal, and these
were supported by the two remaining squadrons of
the regiment under Colonel Champeron. Champeron's
two squadrons were in echelon; and it seems that,
though acting in support to the first line during the
earlier part of the advance, these two squadrons, upon
approaching more closely to the enemy, were to incline
away to their left, and then, again bringing round the

* The two battalions of foot were 'Black Sea Cossacks.'

C H A P.
   X.

left shoulder, to fall upon the two battalions of foot
which constituted the infantry support to the guns.

The ground about to be invaded was much broken
and scrubby, being encumbered with a tall under-
growth reaching up to the girths of the saddles; but
the want of smooth even turf was not likely to be
discomposing to men who had learnt war in the ranges
of the Atlas. . Abdelal's two squadrons, advancing
briskly in foraging order, and bringing round the left
shoulder whilst moving, broke through the enemy's
line of skirmishers, and having by this time a front
which was nearly at right angles with the front of the
Russian guns, drove forward with excellent vigour
upon the flank of the nearest half-battery, and already
were near to their goal, when, with singular alacrity,
the guns of the half-battery thus attacked, and those
also of the other half-battery which had not been
directly assailed, were limbered up by the Russians
and briskly moved off at a trot, whilst the two battalions of foot which constituted the infantry supports
to the guns fell back all at once, without waiting for
the impact of Champeron's two squadrons then rapidly
advancing against them; and, moreover, the Cossack
squadrons on the left of the battery which constituted its cavalry supports went about and began to
retreat.

Then, to arrest the overthrow with which he seemed
menaced, or to cover the retreat of his guns, General
Jabrokritsky in person put himself at the head of two
battalions of that famous 'Vladimir' regiment which
had proved itself well just five weeks before in its

PLATE 4

BATTLE OF BALACLAVA.

The Light Cavalry attack at its culminating moment.
Charge of d'Allonville with the 4th Chasseurs d'Afrique.

EXPLANATION.

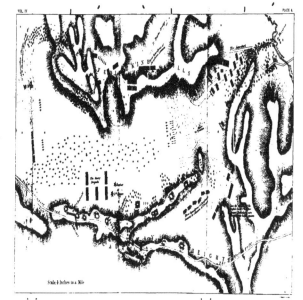

Scale ½ Inches to a Mile

fight with our troops on the Alma, and proceeded to C H A P. X. hazard the somewhat rare enterprise of advancing with foot-soldiers against cavalry; but already the object of General Morris had been attained, and— exactly, as it would seem, at the right moment— he caused the 'recall' to be sounded. In an instant the victorious squadrons glided back to' their place in the brigade; and it soon appeared that the losses, though involving certainly a considerable deduction of strength from a body of only a few hundred horsemen, were small in proportion to the brilliancy of the service these squadrons had rendered., They had ten men killed (of whom two were officers) and twenty-eight wounded; but in the course of the swift moments during which these losses befell them, they had neutralised (for the requisite time) the whole of the enemy's infantry on the Fedioukine Hills, had driven his artillery there posted into instant retreat, and in this way had not only done much towards the attainment of a general victory, but, failing that result, had prepared for our Light Brigade, whenever the moment for its retiring up the valley should come, a complete immunity from one at least of the two flanking fires under which it had been condemned to advance.

Moderate extent of the losses sustained by D'Allonville in proportion to the service rendered.

Well imagined, well timed, undertaken with exactly apt means, performed with boldness as well as with skill, and then, suddenly, at the right moment, arrested and brought to a close, this achievement was not only brilliant in itself, but had the merit of being admirably relevant, if so one may speak, to the then

The brilliancy of this achievement of the Chasseurs d'Afrique.

CHAP.
X.

passing phase of the battle, and became, upon the whole, a teaching example (on a small scale) of the way in which a competent man strikes a blow with the cavalry arm. The troops engaged in this enterprise were not the fellow-countrymen of those whose attack they undertook to support; but that is a cir-cumstance which, far from diminishing the lustre of the exploit, gave it only a more chivalrous grace. The names of General Morris and General d'Allonville are remembered in the English army with admiration and gratitude.

X.

The 11th Hussars.

When the 11th Hussars had so far descended the valley as to be close to the battery, it appeared that the right troop of their right squadron was confronted by some of the Russian guns, whilst all the rest of the regiment outflanked the line of the battery, and had clear ground before it. Meeting little or no obstruction to their progress from the mounted and dismounted artillerymen who were busy with their teams in the hope of carrying off their Czar's precious ordnance, this right troop passed in through the battery, and pushed on beyond the limbers and tumbrils which were in rear of the guns. Then the regiment was halted.

The Russians who stood gathered in the most immediate proximity to the 11th Hussars were a confused number, including, it seems, artillerymen and cavalry. They were in a state of apparent helplessness; and one of their officers, not disguised, as was

usual, in the grey outer-coat of the soldiers, but CHAP.
wearing the epaulettes of a full colonel, came up,   X.
bare - headed, to the stirrup of Lieutenant Roger
Palmer, and voluntarily delivered his sword to him.
Palmer handed over the sword to a corporal or
· serjeant at his side, and did not of course molest the
disarmed officer, though the condition of things was
not such as to allow of taking and securing prisoners.

It soon appeared, however, that this tendency to
utter surrender was not as yet general; for when the
crowd cleared and made off, it disclosed to the 11th
Hussars some squadrons of Russian Lancers formed
up and in perfected order.*

The 11th Hussars re-formed their ranks and made
ready to charge; whilst on their part the Russian
horsemen brought their lances smartly down as though
for an immediate attack. They did not, however,
advance. Repeating the mistake already committed
that day in the face of Scarlett's dragoons, and again
under Morris's charge, and again under Shewell's,
they remained at a halt, awaiting the attack of our
horsemen. Douglas seized the occasion thus given

---

* These were not Cossacks, but regular Lancers. A reader who might
be comparing this narrative with the official accounts of the Russians,
would have some right to ask what Lancers these could be, because
Jeropkine's Lancers (called by the Russians the 'Combined Lancers')
were not in this part of the field, and the official accounts mention no
other Lancers. It is, however, a fact proved decisively by the evidence
of our officers, that both in the heavy cavalry charge and upon this
occasion, squadrons of Lancers (not Cossacks) were present. Supposing
that the Russian official accounts did not actually omit any forces really
present, the solution, I believe, is this : portions of the Russian Hussars
had been converted into Lancers, without undergoing a corresponding
change in the official designation of the force.

CHAP.
X.

him, and led down his Hussars at the charging pace. For a while, the Russians awaited him with a great steadfastness, and it seemed that, in a few moments, there must needs be a clash of arms; but when our Hussars had charged down to within a short distance of them, the Russians, all at once, went about and retreated. Far on, and into the opening of the gorge which divides the aqueduct from the eastern base of the Fedioukine Hills, the 11th moved down in pursuit.

On the immediate right of the 11th Hussars, and so little in rear of them (by the time they had reached the battery) as to be separated by a distance of no more than some twenty or thifty yards, Lord George Paget was advancing with the 4th Light Dragoons. For some time this regiment had been driving through a cloud of smoke and dust, which so dimmed the air as to hide from them all visible indications of the now silent battery; but upon their nearer approach, the Czar's burnished brass pieces of ordnance were almost suddenly disclosed to view; and our Light Dragoons saw that, at the part of the battery they confronted, the mounted men there appearing were artillery drivers trying to carry off the guns. Then an officer of the regiment—and one, too, strange to say, who had hitherto been most inexorably rigid in enforcing exactness—brought his hand to the ear, and delivered a shrill ' Tallyho! ' which hurled forward the hitherto well-ordered line, and broke it up into racing horsemen. In the next instant, with an ungoverned rush, our dragoons broke into the battery.

The 4th Light Dragoons.

Their entrance into the battery.

There, with the artillery teams, brought up for the purpose, and by means of the lasso harness, the Russians were making extreme exertions to carry off their guns; and, since these people were not only bold, strong, and resolute, but contending for an object very dear to them, a fierce struggle began. In their eagerness to be putting forth their bodily strength by cutting and slashing, very many of our men neglected the use of the point ; and, for the most part, the edge of the sabre fell harmless upon the thick grey outercoats of the Russians. In the midst of the strife, one young cornet—Cornet Edward Warwick Hunt —became so eager to prevent the enemy from hauling off one of the pieces that, after first 'returning' his sword, he coolly dismounted, and at a moment when the six wretched artillery horses and their drivers were the subject of a raging combat, applied his mind with persistency to the other end of the traces or ' prolong,' and sought to disengage the gun from the harness; a curious act of audacity in the thick of a fight, for which, unless I mistake, his colonel both damned and admired him. There were some amongst our men, and even amongst our officers, who performed hideous wonders in the way of slaughter; for the Russians were under such cogent obligation to save their Czar's cherished ordnance from capture, and were, many of them, so brave and obstinate, that even the sense of being altogether unequal to strive against an onslaught of English cavalry did not suffice to make them yield. There was one of our officers who became afflicted, if so one may speak, with what

CHAP. has been called the blood-frenzy. Much gore be-
X. smeared him, and the result of the contest was such
as might seem confirmatory of the vulgar belief as to
the maddening power of human blood. This officer,
whilst under the frenzy, raged wildly against human
life, cutting down, it was said, very many of the obstinate Russians with his own reeking hand.* Other
officers of a different temperament made use of their
revolvers with a terrible diligence.

From his bearing at this time, it seemed that Lord
George Paget scarce approved this kind of industry on
the part of his officers. At all events, he so acted as
to convey the impression that he reserved his energy
and attention for the purposes of command, and did
not conceive it his duty (except in actual self-defence)
to become, with his own hand, a slayer of men.

As might be expected, the obstinacy of the Russians,
interrupted in their task of carrying off the guns, was
very unequal; and if some fought so hard as to involve
our people in the combat we have just been speaking
of, there were others who attempted no active resistance. Several drivers, for instance, threw themselves
off their horses, and so crept under them, as in that
way to seek and find shelter. In the end our Dragoons
got the mastery, and not only succeeded in preventing
the withdrawal of all the pieces of cannon which they
had seen in the line of the battery at the time of their
entering it, but also arrested and disabled some other

---

* I have heard that, after the battle, when this officer had calmed
down, there was so great a reaction in his nervous system, that he burst
into tears, and cried like a little child.

guns—already a little way from the front—which the enemy was in the act of removing. The business of repressing the enemy's obstinate endeavours to carry off his guns was of such duration that again there interposed a long distance between the 4th Light Dragoons and the regiment (the 11th Hussars) with which Lord George Paget had sought to align himself; for whilst the 4th Light Dragoons remained combating on the site of the battery, Colonel Douglas, as we know, was advancing; but his task in the battery being almost complete, Lord George with a part if not with the whole of his troops, now pressed forward once more in the hope of being able to combine the next operations of his regiment with those of the 11th Hussars. CHAP. X Farther advance of Lord George Paget.

The 8th Hussars, we remember, was on the extreme right of the forces advancing in support. Reduced to one-half of its former strength by that triple fire through which it had been passing, but still in excellent order, and maintaining that well-steadied trot which Colonel Shewell had chosen as the pace best adapted for a lengthened advance of this kind, this regiment had continued its advance down the valley, had moved past the now silent battery at a distance of a few horses' lengths from its (proper) left flank, had pressed on beyond it some three or four hundred yards, and by that time had so passed through the jaws of the enemy's position, as to be actually for the moment in a region almost out of harm's way—in the region, if so one may speak, which lies behind the north wind.* Colonel Shewell then halted the regiment. The 8th Hussars.

* I need hardly say that the idea of referring to the 'country of the

CHAP.
X.

Making only now one squadron—and that a very weak one—its remains stood formed up to their front.

Colonel Shewell, it seems, had the hope that an order of some kind would presently reach him; and he well might desire to have guidance, for the position into which he had pushed forward his regiment was somewhat a strange one. On three sides—that is, on his front, and on the rising grounds which hemmed in the valley on either flank—Colonel Shewell saw bodies of the enemy's cavalry and infantry; but the Russian forces in front of him, both horse and foot, were in retreat, and numbers of them crowding over the bridges of the aqueduct. Yet nowhere, with the exception of his regiment, now reduced to a very small squadron, could he descry any body of our cavalry in a state of formation, though before him, in small knots or groups, or acting as single assailants, he saw a few English horsemen who were pressing the retreat of the enemy, by pursuing and cutting down stragglers.

After continuing this halt during a period which has been reckoned at three, and also at five, minutes, Colonel Shewell resumed his advance.

These remains of the 8th Hussars formed the small but still well-ordered squadron, which we saw coming down towards the spot where Mayow had checked the pursuit, and halted his small group of Lancers.

'Hyperboreans' as a modern illustration, belongs to Mr Lowe. See his celebrated speech in the House of Commons, 1866.

XI.

It seems right to survey the circumstances in which the Allied forces stood at this critical and interesting period of the combat. At the bare apprehension of the advance against the Causeway Heights which Lord Raglan had twice over ordered, Liprandi, as we saw, had retracted the head of the column there established in the morning, and had probably at this time no higher hope than that of being able to retreat without seeing his infantry and artillery involved in the overthrow which was sweeping his cavalry out of the field. On the Fedioukine Hills, the head of Jabrokritsky's column was rolling up under D'Allonville's brilliant attack. In the low ground between the Causeway Heights and the Fedioukine Hills, the condition of things was this: Having intruded itself, as we know, a mile deep into a narrow valley, hemmed in on three sides by Russian forces of all arms, our Light Cavalry Brigade had overthrown all the forces which before confronted it, and was disposed for the moment as follows: The still combating remains of the first line were broken into groups and small knots, numbering perhaps, altogether, after the retreat of the men acting under O'Hara, as many as thirty. Of these, some were combating in a desultory way, with little other purpose than that of defending themselves, and endeavouring to make out what best they could do in the confusion; but others, as we saw, were hanging upon the skirts of the Russian squadrons, and, in effect, pressing on the retreat by

CHAP.
X.
assailing the people who lagged. The group of some fifteen men under Mayow had coherence enough, as we saw, to be able to put to flight the body of horse which encountered them.

On our extreme left, Colonel Douglas, with his 11th Hussars, now counting a little more than 50 sabres, was pursuing the retreat of the Russian Lancers which had given way under his charge; and on his right rear, Lord George Paget (having quelled the attempts of the Russians to carry off their guns) was advancing with a part at least of the 4th Light Dragoons, a regiment now reckoning, perhaps, about the same numbers as the 11th Hussars. These two regiments formed our left; and although at this moment they were not so placed as to be visible the one to the other, the direction of Douglas's advance was so far known to Lord George Paget as to make it likely that the two regiments might find means of acting together in concert, with a force, when united, of about 100 sabres. In the event of their doing so, Lord George Paget, as the senior officer, was the one who would be entitled to take the command.

Towards our centre, we had no troops at all in a state of formation; but on our extreme right, as we know, the 8th Hussars, now reduced to a strength of about 55, and commanded by Colonel Shewell, was advancing towards the group under Mayow. The event proved that this group of fifteen under Mayow was still in a state of coherence which rendered it capable of acting with military efficiency in concert with other troops, and it may therefore be said that Colonel Shewell (who was senior to Mayow) CHAP. had under his orders a force of about 70 sabres. X.

Altogether, these undisabled combatants numbered perhaps about 220 or 230, of which only about 170 were in a state of formation. The two wings (if so we may call disconnected forces) were not visible the one to the other, and no communications passed between them.

In the absence of any general who might come to take in person the direction of these combatants, Lord George Paget, as we saw, was the senior officer on our left; on our right, Colonel Shewell.

From before the 230 English horsemen thus thrust *The re-* into the very rear of the enemy's position, the bulk of *treat of* that powerful body of Russian horse which numbered *sian cav-* itself by thousands was strangely enough falling back. *alry.* We now know that the retreat was much more general than our people at the time could perceive, and that, excepting Jeropkine's six squadrons of Lancers, almost the whole of the enemy's cavalry had been not merely beaten but routed.* Apparently

---

* Liprandi, in his despatch, admits the retreat of his cavalry, but says that the movement was a ruse of General Ryjoff's to draw the English on. 'The English cavalry,' he says, 'appeared more than 2000 ' strong. Its impetuous attack induced Lieutenant-General Ryjoff [the ' commander of the Russian cavalry] to turn back upon the route to ' Tchorgoun to draw the enemy.' General de Todleben, however, discards that way of explaining the retreat, and says frankly that our Light Cavalry utterly overthrew the bulk of the Russian cavalry. Using the word ' Cardigan,' in a sense importing the Light Brigade, he says : ' Car- ' digan flung himself against the Don Cossack battery which was in ' advance, sabred the gunners, then charged our cavalry, utterly over- ' threw it [*la culbuta*], and advanced far beyond the line of the redoubts ' in pursuit of our cavalry, which retreated towards Tchorgoun.'

CHAP.
X.

also, as indeed might well be, these fugitive squadrons carried panic along with them as they rode ; * for away, on the eastern slopes of Mount Hasfort, where no English could dream of pursuing, battalions of infantry were thrown into hollow squares, as though awaiting from moment to moment a charge of victorious cavalry.

Thus much some brave men were able to do towards wringing an actual victory from even the wildest of blunders.

The need there was of fresh troops in order to clench the victory.

Thus much ; but considering that this singular overthrow of the many by the few was occurring, after all, a mile deep in the enemy's realms, and that, even although partly rolled up, the forces of Jabrokritsky on the north, and of Liprandi on the south, yet lined on both sides, the lower slopes of the valley, it was evident, of course, that the ascendant of little more than two hundred horsemen now driving whole thousands before them would only prove momentary and vain, unless it should be upheld by fresh troops coming down in support, or else by an attack on the Causeway Heights of the kind which Lord Raglan had ordered. Were the red squadrons coming to clench the victory, and by victory to rescue their comrades ?

We must turn to the commander of our cavalry, and to the regiments of the Heavy Brigade, with which he was present in person.

* See the plan taken from General de Todleben. To eyes accustomed to such things, it expresses an almost headlong retreat more forcibly than words.

Plate 7.

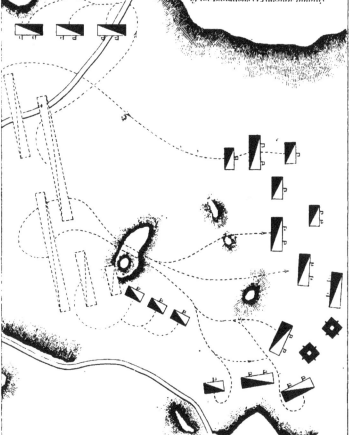

NOTE

The Insertion of this Plan must not be taken as a representation that it is accurate, the object is to impart to others that general impression in regard to the nature of the Rout which seems to have prevailed amongst those to whom Gen! Todleben appealed for Information.

THE PART OF

GENERAL DE TODLEBEN'S

PLAN

Which shews the state of Rout into which the main body of the Russian Cavalry was thrown by the English Light Cavalry Charge and the hollow squares formed in resistance to our Horsemen, by two Battalions of Russian Infantry

XII.

Amongst all those struggles between the judgment
and the feelings by which man is liable to be tortured,
hardly any can be more distressing than that which
rends the heart of a chivalrously-minded commander
who is bringing himself to determine that, in obedience to the hard mandates of Duty, and for the
preservation of the troops which still remain in his
hands, he will suffer an adventured portion of his
force to go on to its fate unsupported ; and especially
must he be troubled in spirit if the words which
drove.his people into a desperate path were words
from his own lips.

Wild as was the notion of sending a force to run
the gauntlet between the Fedioukine Hills and the
Causeway Heights, yet, supposing the sacrifice to be
irrevocably vowed, Lord Lucan seems to have formed
a good conception of the way in which it could-best
be performed. He saw that in such an undertaking
extension of front was an object of vastly less importance than the maintenance of an unfailing connection
between the troops employed along the whole line of
the advance. In short, he considered that the first
line should be followed at intervals by successive lines
of support, all forming the links of a chain so connected that, happen what might, the whole British
cavalry would be a body of troops acting together
under one commander, and constituting a powerful
unit. It was in part execution of this plan that he
had divided the Light Brigade into three lines ; and,

Lord La-
can.

CHAP.
X.
intending to effect a corresponding disposition of Scarlett's Dragoons, he trusted that the several links thus
provided would form an unbroken chain of sufficing
length.

The advance of our cavalry, however, had gone on
but a short time when it became apparent that Lord
Cardigan's severe and increasing pace was much
greater than that which Lord Lucan had adopted for
the Heavy Dragoons; and the Russians who lined
the two ranges of heights were not only quick in
their perception of this difference, but sagacious
enough to infer from it a want of connecting purpose
in the movements of the two brigades. The moment
was approaching when it would be necessary for Lord
Lucan to make a painful choice, and either to con-
form with his Heavy Dragoons to Lord Cardigan's
pace, or else—a cruel alternative—to let the chain
break asunder.

In his own person—and the keenness of his far-
reaching sight made him apt for this service—Lord
Lucan strove hard to prolong the connection between
his two brigades by riding on in advance of his Heavy
Dragoons, and following his Light Cavalry with
straining eyes; but he had not long passed the Number Four Redoubt when he was rudely compelled to
perceive that he had entered on the path of destruction already traversed by his Light Cavalry, and was
drawing forward his Heavy Dragoons to the verge of
a like disaster. His aide-de-camp, Captain Charteris
—fulfilling an incurable presentiment—fell dead at
his side; Lord William Paulet, his Assistant-Adjutant-

General, was struck, or unbonneted by a shot or a C H A P.
shell; Major M'Mahon, his Assistant-Quartermaster- $\underbrace{\quad X \quad}$
General (not, however, at quite the same time), had
his horse struck by grape; and Lord Lucan himself
was wounded in the leg by a musket-ball, his horse
being also struck by shot in two places.*

Lord Lucan was not, however, disabled by the
wound; and, continuing his advance, he passed
quickly so far down the valley as to be on ground
nearly parallel with the Arabtabia Redoubt :† but the
distance between his two brigades, which he thus, as
it were, sought to span or bridge over by his personal
presence, was increasing with each stride of our Light
Cavalry squadrons. Growing more and more faint
to the sight, those splendid, doomed squadrons were
sinking and sinking into the thick bank of smoke
which now closed in the foot of the valley; and
even if no new motive had interposed, Lord Lucan
could scarcely have withheld his decision many moments more. What happened, however, was that,
upon looking back, he perceived the Royals and
the Greys to be undergoing a destructive cross-fire;
and then, at all events, if it had not done so before,
the terrible question forced itself upon him, and
peremptorily exacted a decision. Should he risk The ques-
                                                   tion now
the loss of his second brigade by flinging it after forced
his first, or submit to one disaster (if disaster it was upon his
                                                         attention.

* The apparently absolute indifference of Lord Lucan under this fire
was specially remarked by an officer — not at all an admirer of his
divisional chief—whose testimony enabled me to make the statement
contained in a former page—p. 10.
† The same as Number Three Redoubt.

CHAP. to be) for the sake of avoiding fresh hazards? He
X.   was the link which connected one brigade with the
other; and so long as he might choose to hold fast
to each, he would be realising his own conception of
the several successive supports, and sustaining his
Light Cavalry :force with the power of his Heavy
Brigade : but also he would be grievously imperilling
this, his second and last brigade, by drawing it down
with him into the gulf where his first brigade seemed
disappearing.   Should he, then, hold fast or let go?

His deci-   He let go.   Elsewhere, the reasons which governed
sion.   him shall be given in his own ampler words; but the
sentence which he uttered at the moment contains the
pith of his argument.   Determining. that the Greys
and the Royals should at once be halted, he said to
Lord William Paûlet, 'They have sacrificed the Light
'Brigade : they shall not the Heavy, if I can help it.'

The Greys   It was only after two successive movements in re-
and the
Royals   treat that the Royals and the Greys were relieved
ordered to
fall back. from the·fire to which they had been exposed.

Severity of   This fire had indeed been heavy; and—under
the fire
which had conditions very trying to horsemen—both regiments
been sus-
tained by sustained it with a firmness so admirable, that even
these regi-
ments.   the out-dazzling splendour of their morning's achievement did not blind a skilled judge of such things to
the merit of this warlike endurance.

In the Royals alone—and this was a more than
decimating loss—as many as twenty-one were disabled
by death, or by wounds inflicted upon themselves or
their horses.   Colonel Yorke, the commanding officer,
received a wound which cruelly shattered his leg, and

he was disabled for life.* So also was Captain George CHAP. Campbell. Captain Elmsall and Lieutenant Hartopp were, both of them, wounded severely; and Lieutenant Robertson had a horse shot under him.

Lord Lucan had come to the conclusion that 'the 'only use to which the Heavy Brigade could be 'turned was to protect the Light Cavalry against 'pursuit in their return;' and he judged that for that service the position to which he had now brought back the Heavy Dragoons was sufficiently advanced. There, accordingly, the brigade remained halted.

Lord Lucan's conclusion as to the only use that could now be made of the Heavy Dragoons.

The brigade kept halted accordingly.

Lord Lucan being present in person, General Scarlett had no authority to determine upon the extent to which his brigade should be ventured in supporting the advance of the Light Cavalry; and at the time when the Heavy Dragoons received their first order to retreat, he was still unaware of the decision which had produced this result. Yielding to a natural eagerness, he had ridden forward some sixty yards in advance of his brigade; and I imagine that he and Colonel Beatson (the aide-de-camp then at his side) must have been the last of those acting with the Heavy Dragoons to whom the advancing brigade remained visible.† They saw our Light Cavalry fade

* In support of Lord Lucan's impression respecting the part taken by the Royals in the Heavy Cavalry charge the alleged acquiescence of Colonel Yorke in words addressed to him by Lord Lucan will be probably insisted upon. If that should happen, it will be well to remember that the shattering and terrible wound above mentioned long made it impossible for Colonel Yorke to undertake any such task as that of remonstrating against Lord Lucan's words.

† This was the time when General Scarlett (finding suddenly that

CHAP.
X.

away into the smoke which hung thick at the foot of the valley.

This parting was disruption—disruption in the very crisis of the exigency—disruption of that chain which hitherto had been binding into one the strength of the whole English cavalry.

To repress the idea of going down with fresh troops to the rescue, to abstain from all part in the combat below the battery where the Light Brigade was engulfed, to allow the communication between the two brigades to remain broken without risking even one squadron in an attempt to restore it—this, all this, was the import of the painful decision to which, by a sense of hard duty, Lord Lucan had found himself driven.

Our present knowledge of what was going on at the foot of the valley tends to show that a decision in the opposite direction would have been likely to produce good and brilliant results ; * but that same present knowledge which we now have is exactly what at the time was most wanting : and of course

his brigade was retiring, and not knowing that the movement had been ordered by Lord Lucan) sent back his trumpeter with orders to sound the halt. At the sound the brigade instantly halted, and fronted beautifully, as at parade. As I have named Colonel Beatson, let me here say that I have abundant proofs before me of the warmth with which General Scarlett expressed his grateful recognition of the Colonel's services in the Crimea ; and it is only from the want of that detailed information which none but the Colonel himself—who is now (1868) in India— would be able to give me that I have been prevented from narrating the part that he personally took in the battle. See in the Appendix papers illustrative of his distinguished services.

* See the state of the field as shown *ante*, p. 275, and the plan illustrating the statement.

it is no more than right that the soundness of an
officer's judgment should be viewed in its relation to those circumstances only which were fairly within the range of his knowledge or surmise when he had to make his resolve.*

The Heavy Dragoons at this time were but little if at all vexed by fire; and there was nothing to distract their thoughts from the Light Brigade, or from the pain of dwelling on their own condition as bystanders withheld from the combat. At first, the grey boundary of their sight was from time to time pierced by the flashes from the battery at the foot of the valley; the thunder of the guns was still heard, and the round-shot, óne after another, came bowling along up the slope; but next there followed a time when the cloud at the foot of the valley remained blank without issues of flame, when a terrible quiet had succeeded to the roar of artillery, when no token of the fight could be seen, except a disabled or straggling horseman or a riderless charger emerging here and there from the smoke. Thenceforth the cause of anguish to those who gazed down the valley was no longer in what they could now see or hear, but in what they otherwise knew, and in what they were forced to imagine. They knew that beyond the dim barrier, our Light Brigade was ingulfed. On the thought of what might be its fate they had to be dwelling, whilst they themselves remained halted.

Our Heavy Dragoons at the time when the Light Brigade was out of sight at the foot of the valley.

* With respect to Lord Raglan's opinion as to the way in which Lord Lucan supported the Light Brigade, see his letter of the 16th of December 1854 in the Appendix.

XIII.

The Light
Brigade.

We descend once again to the borders of the aqueduct, where little more than two hundred of our
horsemen, divided into several bodies, were hanging
upon the retreat of almost the whole Russian cavalry;
but we go there, this time, with the knowledge that
the ascendant of the few over the many will not be
supported by the regiments which Lord Lucan was
keeping in hand.

Colonel
Mayow
and his
fifteen
lancers.

On our right, and on the line of the principal road
which led, over the bridge, to Tchorgoun, we left
Colonel Mayow with some fifteen men of the 17th
Lancers. Upon descrying the English squadron,
which had come down, as we saw, in the direc-

Their
junction
with the
8th Hus-
sars.

tion of his right rear, Mayow hastened to join it,
and was presently in contact with the squadron
which represented the 8th Hussars. It appeared that
Colonel Shewell, the commander of the 8th Hussars,
had not been killed or disabled; and, Mayow being
now once more in the presence of an officer senior to
himself, the temporary command which the chances
of battle had cast upon him came at once to an end.
He had been commanding less than a score of men
during only a few minutes; and yet, with these
means and within this limit of time, he had attained
to a height of fortune which is not always reached
by those who are described in the army lists as field-
marshals and generals. He had had sway in battle.

The fifteen men whom Mayow had brought with
him were ranged on the left of the 8th Hussars; and

this little addition brought up Colonel Shewell's C H A P.
strength to about seventy. The panic which was X.
driving from the field the whole bulk of the enemy's
horse plainly did not extend to the Russian infantry
on the eastern part of the Causeway Heights; for Liprandi's
looking back towards their then right rear, our Hus- on the
sars at this time were able to see the grey battalions Heights.
still holding their ground, in good order. Nor was
this all; for presently the glances cast back in nearly
the same direction disclosed some new-comers.

Three squadrons of Russian lancers were seen issu- Three
ing from behind one of the spurs of the Causeway of Jerop-
Heights and descending into the valley. Another Lancers
instant, and this body of Lancers was wheeling into ing in rear
line, and forming a front towards the Russian rear, Hussars.
thus interposing itself as a bar between the English
and their line of retreat. These three squadrons of
Lancers—the half of Colonel Jeropkine's regiment—
were the force which had been placed, as we saw,
in one of the folds of the Causeway Heights at the
time when Liprandi was making arrangements for
covering his retreat.

At the moment when Colonel Mayow joined the
8th Hussars, Colonel Shewell had asked him, 'where
'Lord Cardigan was;'* and Mayow having replied

* This question of 'Where is Lord Cardigan?' will be found recurring; but commanders of course cannot be everywhere at the same time,
and it must not be understood that when an officer asks this question, he
inferentially suggests ground of blame against the general for not being
visible at a particular moment and on a particular spot. It is right,
however, to mention these dialogues; because they show, or tend to
show, a devolution of authority creating fresh responsibilities. Thus,
for instance, it resulted from the dialogue given in the text that Colonel

Colonel
Shewell
the senior
officer in
this emer-
gency.

His
charge.

that he did not know, it resulted that Colonel Shewell, as the senior officer present, became charged with the duty of determining how the emergency should be met by the troops within reach of his orders. It does not, however, appear that there was much scope for doubt. After an almost momentary consultation with the senior officers present, including Colonel Mayow and Major de Salis, Colonel Shewell gave the word ' Right about wheel!' and the squadron, with its ad- · junct of fifteen Lancers, came round at once with the neatness of well-practised troops on parade. Colonel Shewell and Major de Salis put themselves in the front, and Lieutenant Seager commanded the one squadron into which, as we saw, the remains of the 8th Hussars had been fused. Mayow led the small band of Lancers' which had attached itself to the Hussars.

The seventy horsemen rode straight at the flutter-ing line of gay lances which the enemy was then in the very act of forming. The three Russian squadrons thus wheeling into line were at a distance from She-well of something less than 300 yards, and the two leading squadrons had already established their line, but the third squadron was still in process of wheel-ing. Once more in this singular battle of horsemen, our people had before them a body of cavalry which passively awaited the charge. With his seventy against three hundred, Shewell needed some such counterbalancing advantage as that; but he might

Shewell, as senior officer, became the commander of that part of the first line which was within reach of his directions.

THE BATTLE OF BALACLAVA.

have lost his occasion if he had been wanting in that C H A P.
swiftness of decision which is one of the main condi-   X.
tions of excellence in a cavalry officer, for it was to be
inferred that upon the completion of the manœuvre
by their third squadron, the Russians would charge
down on our people.

Colonel Shewell proved equal to the occasion. He
lost not one 'moment. He was a man whose mind
had received a deep impress from some of the contents of the Bible ; but those who might differ from
his opinions still recognised in him a man of high
honour who extended the authority of conscience to
the performance of military duties ; and it has not
been found in practice that a piety strictly founded
on the Holy Testaments (taken fairly, the one with
the other) has any such softening tendency as to unfit
a man for the task of fierce bodily conflict.*

As in the battles of old times, so now, and not for
the first time, this day, he who was the chief on one
side singled out for his special foe the man who
seemed chief on the other. Shewell had not the advantage of being highly skilled as a swordsman, and being
conscious of his deficiency in this respect, he asked
himself how best he could act. The result was that
he determined to rely upon the power which can be
exerted by sheer impact. He resolved that, whilst

* One of Shewell's companions in arms—a man well entitled to
deliver a judgment on the merits of his lost comrade—has said of him,
' I knew the man with whom I had to deal—I knew that I was dealing
' with one of the most honourable, the most gallant, the most consci-
' entious, the most single-minded man it has ever been my good fortune
' to meet with.'

VOL. IV.   T

CHAP.
X.

charging at the head of his little band of horsemen, he would single out the Russian officer whom he perceived to be the leader of the opposing force, and endeavour to overthrow him by the shock of a heavy concussion. To do this the more effectively he discarded the lessons of the riding-school, clenched a rein in each hand, got his head somewhat down; and, as though he were going at a leap which his horse, unless forced, might refuse, drove full at the Russian chief. The assailant came on so swift, so resolute, and, if so one may speak, with such a conscientious exactness of aim that, for the Russian officer who sat in his saddle under the disadvantage of having to await the onset, there remained no alternative at the last moment but either to move a little aside or else be run down without mercy by this straightforward pious hussar. As was only natural, the charger of the Russian officer shrank aside to avoid the shock; and Shewell, still driving straight on, with all his momentum unchecked, broke through the two ranks of the Lancers. He was well followed by his seventy horsemen. Upon their close approach some of the Russian Lancers turned and made off; but the rest stood their ground and received the shock prepared for them. By that shock, however, they were broken and overthrown. It is true that in the moment of the impact, or in the moments immediately following, men had, some of them, a fleeting opportunity for the use of the sword or the lance, and one at least of our Hussars received a great number of slight wounds from the enemy's spearheads; but the clash was brief. The whole of these three Russian

Defeat and flight of the Russian Lancers.

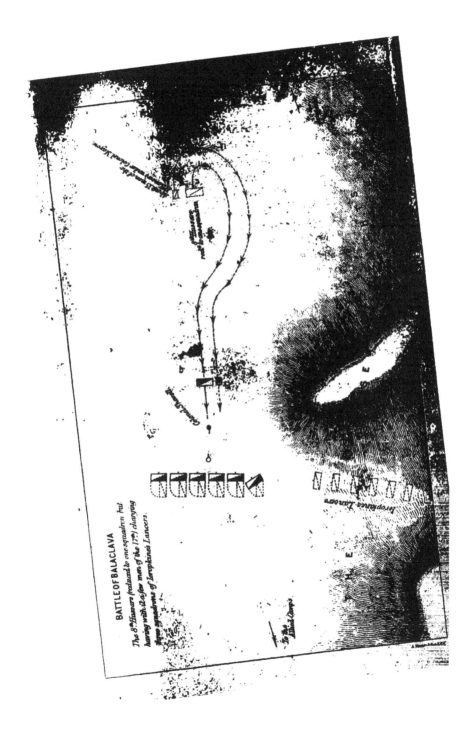

BATTLE OF BALACLAVA

The 8⁰ Hussars (reduced to one squadron but having with it a few men of the 17th) charging two squadrons of Jeropkine's Lancers.

squadrons were quickly in retreat, a part of them CHAP. going back into the fold betwixt the Causeway X. Heights, from which just before they had issued, whilst the rest fled across to the Fedioukine Hills; and there is reason for inferring that these last attached themselves to the other three squadrons of their regiment which had been posted, as we saw, on the northern side of the valley.

After having thus conquered their way through the Shewell's body of Lancers opposed to them, Colonel Shewell retreat. and those who had followed him in his victorious charge could see a good way up the valley; but their, eyes searched in vain for an English force advancing to their support; and, in truth, the very attempt which Jeropkine's Lancers had just been making, went far to show that no English succours were , near; for it is evident that the endeavour to cut off our Hussars by showing a front towards the Russian rear would never have been made by troops which were able to see a red squadron coming down to the support of their comrades. Therefore, having now cut open a retreat not only for themselves, but also for such of the other remnants of the Light Brigade as might be near enough to seize the occasion, Shewell's regiment and the men who had joined it continued to pursue the direction in which they had charged, in other words, to retire. Colonel Shewell, it seems, did not judge that the condition of things was such as to warrant any attempt at the usual operation of governing a retreat by fronting from time to time with a portion of the force; and those who remained

CHAP.
   X.
of the seventy had only to withdraw up the valley with such speed as they could.   In this movement they were followed by Captain Jenyns and the few men of the first line — men chiefly, it is supposed, of the 13th Light Dragoons—who had been acting under his guidance, or riding, at all events, near him.

When our retreating horsemen had ridden clear of Jeropkine's discomfited Lancers, they began once more to incur severe fire from those batteries on the Causeway Heights, and those rifles in the same part of the field which had thinned their ranks during the advance ; but they were not molested by cavalry, and they observed, without knowing the cause of the change, that there was silence on the Fedioukine Hills.*

It happened, as might be expected, that, in the trail of our small body of retreating Hussars, there were both mounted and dismounted men who had been so . disabled by their own wounds or by the wounds or the overwearied state of their horses as to be more or less lagging behind. The sight of these disabled horsemen did not so far tempt Jeropkine's defeated squadrons as to bring them all back into the valley ; but his Lancers, here and there coming singly, or else in small knots, pressed on for a time, in pursuit, and killed or took some of the stragglers. Amongst others moving on foot was Major de Salis. With a rare generosity he had given up his own charger to a disabled trooper of the 8th Hussars, and the Major was seen leading the horse whilst the wounded man sat in the saddle.

* This result, as we know, was owing to D'Allonville's attack with the Chasseurs d'Afrique.

Soon the efforts of the enemy's horsemen to kill or CHAP.
take any straggler they might find in their power X.
were checked by their own fellow-countrymen; for
the gunners who manned the batteries on the
Causeway Heights would not suffer their energies to
be paralysed by the presence of a few Russian Lancers,
intermixed here and there with our stragglers; and
when it became plain that Jeropkine's horsemen were
incurring fire from their own brethren, the trumpet
sounded the recall, and they desisted from their
efforts. Then some of our disabled horsemen, who
had been surrounded by Lancers, were enabled, after
all, to, escape. Thus, for instance, Lieutenant Phillips, who had just had his horse shot under him, and
Private Brown, who had been disabled in both hands,
were attacked by Lancers; and although Phillips was
able to keep off the assailants with his revolver, both
he and the soldier whom he was protecting must have
been on the point of being either despatched or taken,
when, the recall being sounded, the Lancers rode off,
and both Phillips and the soldier he had guarded
made good their way back to our lines.* In like manner also Lieutenant Clowes, whose horse had been
shot under him, and who was himself wounded by
grape, found himself freed from the Lancers who had
had him in their power; but he was so much exhausted
by loss of blood as to be unable to drag himself far.

---

* Major Phillips, it seems, believed the wounded man to be dead;
and is anxious to have it understood that ' beyond the mere accident of
' coming near at the time' he ' had no share in defending Brown.'—
Note to Second Edition.

CHAP.
X.

After the close of the battle he was picked up by the
Russians, and became, of course, their prisoner.

XIV.

The 11th
Hussars
and the
4th Light
Dragoons.

When last we were glancing at the state of the
combat on our extreme left, Colonel Douglas with his
11th Hussars was pursuing a body of the enemy's
cavalry far down towards the strip of low ground
which divides the eastern slope of the Fedioukine
Hills from the banks of the aqueduct; whilst Lord
George Paget, with the 4th Light Dragoons (excepting, it seems, a part of the regiment still busied in
resisting the enemy's attempt to carry off some of
the guns), was once more endeavouring to co-operate
with Colonel Douglas, and for that purpose pushing
on his advance in the right rear of the 11th Hussars. .
The 4th Light Dragoons was in a somewhat disorganised state, brought about by its recent combat
in the battery, where each man, speaking generally,
had been fighting in his own way.

Their
retreat.

Colonel Douglas had carried his pursuit far down
towards the bank of the aqueduct, when at length he
found himself confronted by bodies of cavalry too
large to be fair opponents for his little band of
Hussars. He therefore fell back; and the Russian
cavalry, in their turn, made a show of pursuing, but
in a harmless, irresolute way. Presently the 4th
Light Dragoons, whilst advancing, was met on its
left front by the 11th Hussars in retreat; and at the
sight of their comrades retiring, the men of the 4th

Light Dragoons being still in the disorganised state which had resulted from its desultory combat in the battery, were surprised into an act of imitation. They hesitated, stopped, and, without word of command, went about, aligning themselves in their retreat with the 11th Hussars.

Masses of the enemy's cavalry were at this time pursuing the 11th Hussars, and the foremost bodies of them were already within about forty yards, but in a disorderly state, and disclosing once more that appearance of hesitation and bewilderment which had been observed in the morning at the time of the Heavy Cavalry charge; but the enemy was overwhelmingly strong in numbers, and now that two English regiments had successively retreated before him, it was to be expected, of course, that he would begin to act with increasing boldness.

When Lord George Paget saw the enemy's horse at a distance of only some forty yards from our two retreating regiments, he judged the moment to be critical. With the whole power of his voice, he shouted out to his Dragoons, ' If you don't front, my boys, we ' are done !'

Lord Anglesea used to say that ' cavalry are the ' bravest fellows in the world in advance; but that ' when once they get into a scrape, and have their ' backs turned to the enemy, it is a difficult matter to ' stop and rally them.' If Lord George was perchance one of those who had heard this saying from the lips of his father, he could hardly have been without some misgiving. For once, however, the saying did not

CHAP.
X.

Its effect.

Discovery
of a body
of Russian
cavalry
formed up
across the
line of re-
treat.

hold good. The men of the two regiments who at this moment remained together were only, as was computed, about 70 in number, and not, as a body, in a good state of order; but nevertheless, at the word of command, they came to a halt, and began to front towards the enemy. It was at this time that the young Lieutenant Jolliffe did opportune service. Facing boldly towards the newly fronting troopers in despite of the numbers advancing against him from behind, he held up his sword for a rally, and so well used his voice as to be able to cause numbers of the 4th Light Dragoon men who were straggling and bewildered to understand what had to be done, and at once form up with their comrades. At the sight of the front thus presented to them, the Russians were instantly checked; and it is believed that our troops saved themselves from a crushing disaster by their ready obedience to Lord George Paget's appeal.

But during the very moments that were occupied by this operation of fronting towards the pursuers, it was becoming known to our officers and men that the enemy had interposed a fresh body of horse in a new, and indeed opposite, quarter. Roger Palmer—that young Lieutenant of the 11th Hussars to whom the Russian colonel had delivered his sword—was singularly gifted with long sight, and casting his glance towards our left rear, he saw in that direction, but at a distance of several hundred yards, a considerable body of cavalry, which he assured himself must be Russian. He reported this to his chief. Colonel

Douglas at first scarce believed that the squadrons C H A P.
thus observed could be Russian; and, it being per- X.
ceptible that the force consisted of Lancers, men were
able, for a while, to indulge a pleasant surmise, and
to imagine that the Lancers descried in our rear, at a
distance of several hundred yards, must be our own
'Seventeenth.' Presently, however, Roger Palmer
convinced Colonel Douglas that the head-gear of the
cavalry descried was Russian; and in another moment all doubt was at an end; for our officers and
men could then see that the newly-interposed troops
were formed up across the slope of the valley, with a
front towards the Russian rear, as though barring
the retreat of our people. So, there being then
certain knowledge that the English were between two
powerful bodies of Russian cavalry, it became necessary to use the very next moments in determining **Means for**
how to meet the emergency. Seeing Major Low **meeting**
the emer-
close to him on the left, Lord George Paget, it seems, **gency.**
exclaimed : 'We are in a desperate scrape. What
'the devil shall we do?' And in the next moment
Lord George seems to have perceived that the answer
to the question he had put should be elicited from
some one entitled to command.

It was evidently with that purpose in his mind,
and not from any notion of indulging in irony, that
Lord George then asked the same question which
had been put once before, but on the other side of the
valley—the question of 'Where is Lord Cardigan?'
Whatever were the terms of the answer elicited from
Major Low, it became plain that for the moment,

CHAP. at all events, no guidance was to be had from the
   X.   General commanding the Brigade, and that the
emergency must be met without the aid of Lord
Cardigan. * Lord George Paget was the senior
officer present; and the few rapid words which he
and Colonel Douglas found time to exchange were
enough to prove them agreed upon the course that
ought to be taken. †

It was determined that, with the whole of the little
band which had been formed from the remnants of
the two united regiments, our men should endeavour
as best they could to break through the newly-interposed force of Russian Lancers, and should do this
without persisting in the attempt to oppose a front to
the cavalry advancing from the opposite direction.
Our men well understood the predicament in which
they stood; and Lord George Paget holloaed out to
them, 'Well, you must go about, and do the best you
' can. Threes about!'

The order was obeyed, and both regiments now
fronted towards the body of Lancer which stood
barring their line of retreat. In both regiments
strenuous exertions were made to get the men together; and wherever, in this little band, an officer
sat in his saddle, there also there was a sword in the
air, and a voice commanding the rally. The force

* Of the purport of the answer given to this question I have not yet
obtained sufficing proof; but its alleged tenor will be found in the
affidavits of Edden and David Thomas.
† In the circumstances stated should it be judged that the whole of
the body thus acting in concert came out under the command of Lord
George Paget?

was joined by some troopers belonging to the first C H A P.
line.   X.

In the hastily-attempted array which was now in
some slight measure formed, the (proper) rear-rank
formed the front, and the officers had to follow, instead
of leading, their line. In such a position they were
evidently more likely than the rest of the force to be
cut off by the Russian Lancers : but this was not all ;
for behind them, as we know, and at a distance of
but a few yards, they had the bodies of the Russian
cavalry which had come up in pursuit from the neighbourhood of the aqueduct. Thus placed, our officers
were not only exposed beyond measure to the dangers
of the hour, but also shut back in positions unfavourable to the exercise of command.

With but little attempt at the preservation of
order, the English horsemen moved off at such speed
as they could command, driving straight towards the
thicket of lances which threatened to bar their
retreat. They presently began to incur the fire
of some Russian artillery ; but, upon the whole,
this effort of the enemy's gunners proved to be an
advantage to our people, for, without inflicting heavy
loss upon our retreating horsemen, it delivered them
from the pursuit of the cavalry in their then rear.
The body of Russian Lancers which stood barring the
retreat of our horsemen was that moiety of Jeropkine's
six squadrons which had been placed, as we saw, on
the north side of the valley, and in the fold of the
hills enclosing the road from Tractir ; but there is
reason for believing that these three squadrons had

CHAP.
X.

been ... by some portions at least, if not by the whole of those other three squadrons through which Colonel Shewell had broken.

Position of the interposed force.

Hitherto, the position taken up by the Lancers now undertaking to cut off Lord George Paget and Douglas had been exactly of the same kind as that of the three squadrons on the other side of the valley which attempted, and attempted in vain, to bar Colonel Shewell's retreat; for, just as their comrades had done before, these Lancers stood ranged with a front towards the Russian rear; but, upon the nearer approach of our people, the force they were going to assail disclosed a new plan of action; and it is not improbable that the overthrow which the first three squadrons had undergone, may have so far influenced Colonel Jeropkine as to cause this change in his tactics.

Its formation and apparent strength.

The force, it seems, was a double column of squadrons, having two strong squadrons abreast, and being two, if not three squadrons deep.* It was in a per-

* We saw that the portion of Jeropkine's Lancers which was originally placed on this side of the valley consisted of only three squadrons; but we also saw, that of the other three squadrons overthrown by Colonel Shewell some part at once crossed the valley, and it is evidently probable that they did this with the intention of joining their comrades in the gorge of the Tractir road. Also, those of the Lancers who at first fled southward, must have found in a few moments that they were flying from nothing; and it seems likely that they too would very soon turn or cross over the valley, to the point where their comrades were stationed. I am able to say, on good grounds, that the time which intervened between Shewell's combat and the affair I am now speaking of, was sufficient to allow of this movement taking place. Upon the whole, it seems probable that all the six squadrons of the regiment were at this time together, and if so, the column with its front of two, had a depth of three squadrons.

fect state of formation, and directly confronting our CHAP.
retreating horsemen; but when the remnants of the X.
two English regiments drew near them, the com-
mander of these Russian Lancers retracted all at once Its sudden
the right shoulder, and wheeled his squadrons half front.
back; so that, instead of continuing to oppose a
direct barrier in the face of our returning Dragoons,
his force now stood ranged in such way as to flank
the line of retreat, and became, in that way, much
more formidable than before. The movement was
executed with a precision which made the strength
of the close serried squadrons seem more than ever
overwhelming to the few score of English horsemen
now moving, each man as he could, with hardly a
trace of formation. The evident purpose of the manœuvre was to enable the Russian column to descend
upon the flank of the English, and overwhelm them
at the moment of passing. The direction in which
the English moved was such that, supposing it to
continue unchanged, the Russian column would have
a distance of about thirty yards to go through in
order to come down upon the flank of our horsemen
at the intended moment.

When he saw this manœuvre and detected its
purpose, Lord George Paget determined that he
would endeavour to oppose some semblance of a front
to the new front the enemy had formed; and accordingly he shouted to the men, 'Throw up your left
'flank!' But in the din which prevailed, his words,
it would seem, were but little heard; and, instead of
attempting, as they moved, to form up a front to-

CHAP.
X.

Advance and sudden halt of the column.

ward their right, our people, in the course they now took, inclined somewhat to their left.

At a moment which seems to have been rightly enough chosen, the Russian column commenced its advance, and descended at a trot to the very verge of the point where the two hostile forces thus moving at right angles with one another seemed going to meet; but then all at once the column was halted, and again the Russian horsemen displayed that same air of hesitation and bewilderment which our people had observed several times before on that day—hesitation and bewilderment not apparently resulting from any want of firmness on the part of the men, but rather from their not knowing what to do next.

When a body of cavalry has been moved forward some way at a gallop, or even at a trot, and then is brought to a halt, it very commonly happens that the flanks overshoot the centre, and render the line concave. It was so with the Russian column; and its right flank especially, at the moment of the halt, had swung forward in advance of the centre. Therefore now when our horsemen undertook to ride across the front of the column, they had before them some lancers on the extreme right of the enemy's line, who had so far edged forward as to be directly obstructing the path of retreat; but with this exception, the foe our men had to overcome or evade was entirely on their right flank.

The nature of the collision which

Then there occurred a contact of hostile forces for which, I imagine, it would be hard to find a parallel. In a very irregular body, and with a hardly per-

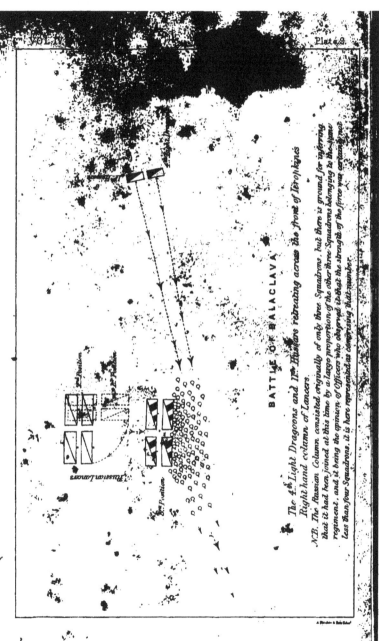

BATTLE OF BALACLAVA.

The 4.th Light Dragoons and 11.th Hussars retreating across the front of Ieropkyns
Right hand column of Lancers

N.B. The Russian Column. consisted originally of only three Squadrons, but there is ground for inferring that it had been joined at this time by a large proportion of the other three Squadrons belonging to the same regiment, and it being the opinion of Officers who observed it, that the strength of the force was estimated not less than four Squadrons, it is here represented as comprising that number.

Russian Lancers

3.rd Position

1.st Position

ceptible trace of their old line formation, the English
went on ; and the Russian mass then advancing a little,
or rather, it might be said, heaving forward, collision occurred. The body retreating grazed its right
flank against the enemy's front ; but, incredible as it
may seem, was allowed to scrape by, moving right
across the faces of the men in the foremost rank,
and receiving or parrying the thrusts of their lances
without undergoing any other than that momentary
attack which a lancer who remains strictly halted
can attempt against a dragoon in the act of galloping
past him. What happened was that those of the
English horsemen who chanced to be on the extreme
right of their retreating body, found themselves so
close to the enemy's lances as to have to fend them
off with the sabre ; but the number of attacks which
any one man had to encounter whilst passing along
the front of two squadrons, was not, it seems, so
great as might be imagined ; and Lord George Paget,
whose position exposed him more than most others,
had said that the number of lances which he had to
ward off with his sword did not exceed three or four.
It was well for our horsemen that the foe was on
their right flank, where the sword-arm could work
with advantage.*

Along the main part of the Russian front, each
collision, if so it can be called, which occurred, be-

CHAP.
X.

then oc-
curred.

* Since the period spoken of in the text, the broadsword exercise of
our cavalry has been so altered, under the suggestion, I believe, of Major
Miller (late of the Scots Greys) as to provide better guards than before
on the side of the bridle-arm.

component of a mass which had come to a halt; whilst every rider assailed was a rider in movement —a rider driving past the fixed column as swiftly as his tired beast could go, and rasped only, if so one may speak, by a thicket of lances in passing: but in that part of the enemy's right flank where his squadrons curled round in front of our people, the struggle which proved to be necessary for forcing a passage was somewhat less momentary; and Lieutenant Roger Palmer, for one, became engaged at that point in what may be called a personal combat. This brief combat ended, however, as did the other collisions, in the failure of every attempt to cut off the retreat of the English; and, without receiving much harm in the course of this singular traverse our people got past.* 'We got by them,' writes one of our officers,—'we got by them—how, I know ' not. It is a mystery to me. . . . There is one ' explanation, and one only—the hand of God was ' upon us!'

That is an explanation of the deliverance from a cavalry scrape which lies out of the reach of dispute; but if any gross mortals, intent on mere War-Office business were attempting to examine causation at the

---

* It is possible that men might have been unhorsed and killed by the Russian lancers without its becoming known that the deaths were so occasioned; but my impression is that few casualties resulted from this encounter.

terrestrial end of the chain, it might be useful for them to know in what stage of each combat it was that this hesitating embarrassment of the Russian cavalry so often evinced itself; and there is the more reason for the inquiry since the firmness of the Muscovite soldier is so well established as to exclude the explanation which might be applicable to the troops of a less valorous nation, if they were to be frequently disclosing incompetence in the critical moment of a combat. The bewilderment of the Russian cavalry has almost always disclosed itself at that very point where the lessons acquired in the exercise-ground, or even in mock battles at home, would carry the pupil no further; and hardly any instance of this could well be more striking than the one we have just seen displayed by Jeropkine's Lancers. Long and painfully trained, those docile Muscovites had come all at once to the border which divides the things that are military from the things that are warlike. Whenever they charged at St Petersburg under the eyes of father Nicholas, the son of Paul, they always, of course, stopped short without doing harm to those other troops of their Czar who might make-believe to oppose them. They had now done no less, but also no more. It might sound paradoxical to say that the remnants of these two English regiments owed their escape to the high state of discipline to which their adversaries had been wrought; but certainly if this Russian mass had consisted of an equal number of bold, angry ploughmen on horseback, with pitchforks in hand, the

CHAP.
X.

eight █████████ disordered dragoons who might try to br██ █████ the faces of their rough foes, would be in danger of incurring grave losses. As it was, our people found themselves saved yet again, as they had been saved before, by the bewilderment of troops who were too ' military ' to be warlike.

Continued course of the two retreating regiments.

It was something for our people to be no longer encountered in their homeward course by a barrier of hostile cavalry; but at the first aspect of it, their plight was still desperate; for being but few, and in disorder, and having a long extent of uphill ground which must be traversed before they would stand in safety, they were on horses now cruelly jaded; whilst the hostile squadrons behind them had not only the strength and the weight of numbers and of solid formation, but also were fresh.

However, those Russian artillerymen who had twice before guarded our cavalry by toiling for its destruction, now once more helped its retreat. It is true that, from a cause then unknown to our retreating horsemen (who, of course, had not witnessed the achievement of D'Allonville and his Chasseurs d'Afrique), the guns on the Fedioukine Hills which had shattered their ranks whilst advancing were now silent; but from the Causeway Heights on the opposite side of the valley there opened a diligent fire against the remnants of the two retreating regiments; and as before had occurred with other bodies of the enemy's cavalry, so now this new effort of the Russian artillerymen served to keep back Jeropkine's Lancers, and prevent them from undertaking the

destructive pursuit of our horsemen, which would
otherwise have been in their power.

Besides being scanty in numbers, these retreating remnants of the 4th Light Dragoons and the 11th Hussars were by this time so much broken up into small groups, or knots, or single horsemen, that they no longer presented to the enemy's gunners the broad easy mark that is offered by a regiment of cavalry in a state of formation ; but if there was now no formed squadron that could be opened and cleaved by shell or by round-shot, each dragoon individually still had to be reckoning on the death that might come the next moment; and this the last trial which the soldier passed through was that of riding for life, with the torment of being forced to ride slowly ; for he had to toil on uphill under a heavy fire, at the laggard and always decreasing pace which represented the utmost remaining power of his wearied horse.

The ground traversed by these remnants of the 4th Light Dragoons and the 11th Hussars was strewn with such ruins of brilliant squadrons as might well be more distressing to them than to any other regiment, except, perhaps, the 17th Lancers. Lord George Paget's and Colonel Douglas's regiments in the course of their advance had encountered ugly traces of battle, but they now, as they rode, saw the marks of a yet more terrible havoc ; and, this time a great proportion of those they saw dead, or dying, or cruelly disabled, were men of their own regiment. Amongst the wounded comrades and friends thus passed, some

CHAP. X.

were ... though feebly, some limping, some ... it was grievous to have to see the sti... ains of horses with the trappings upon t... th Light Dragoons or the 11th Hussars ... tly struggling to get up, though perhaps ... than one limb shattered, or floundering back with cruel weight upon their disabled riders. Of those who lay wounded and dying upon the ground thus retraced by our people, there was one who extended his arm, saying—but no, I pass on, and yet leave here the half-written sentence. There are some to whom it will speak.

As the pace of each rider had long since had no other limit than the last strength of his sinking horse, it resulted, of course, that, after a while, the single horseman and the groups or knots of those who kept together were divided by lengthened intervals. The greater number of them were still toiling on up the valley under heavy fire without knowing how much further they would have to go before they might call their lives their own, when at length—and this came by surprise—they all at once caught a glad sound. In their front they heard an English cheer. It ceased, but was presently followed by another, and then again by another. These greetings were the welcome bestowed by spectators upon each officer or group of horsemen coming up the incline, and returning, as it were, from out of the abyss.

Lord George Paget (whose wearied horse had long been failing him in pace) was one of the last of the shattered brigade who rode labouring in up the valley.

Some officers moved forward to greet him, and one of these was Lord Cardigan.

Lord George Paget then uttered an exclamation which has now no importance either historical or personal; but it had a bearing, some thought, upon a question formerly in controversy, and was therefore, at one time, so much spoken of that the suppression of the words (though they are now altogether immaterial) might confuse, and be misunderstood. Seeing Lord Cardigan approach composedly from an opposite direction, Lord George Paget exclaimed to him, ' Holloa! ' Lord Cardigan, weren't you there ?' Naturally, the bystanders smiled; but Lord Cardigan saw that no jest was intended, and answered at once with perfect simplicity and truthfulness as one soldier might to another.*

Lord George Paget now ventured—he seemed to be speaking in grief, and in apprehension of the dismal answer he might receive—he ventured to ask after the fate of the first line. ' I am afraid,' he said, ' there are no such regiments in existence as the 13th ' and 17th, for—I can give no account of them.'

Lord
George
Paget's
inquiry as
to the fate
of the first
line.

---

* According to the version which I prefer—and it does not much differ from others—Lord Cardigan answered, ' Wasn't I, though ?' and then turning to Captain Jenyns said, ' Here, Jenyns, did not you see me ' at the guns ?' Jenyns answered that he did; and he could well bear witness, because he was very near to Lord Cardigan at the moment of his entering the battery. The colloquy never had any importance, except in so far as it tended to show that there was an interval of time between the retreat of Lord Cardigan and that of Lord George Paget; and its value in that respect has been superseded by the ampler knowledge we now possess—knowledge placing the fact beyond the reach of doubt.

C H A P. Hardly, however, had he spoken, when he saw on the
X. brow of the hill some clusters of men standing by
their horses, and among them some Lancers. Then he
knew—for the English had only one Lancer regiment
—that, so far at least as concerned the 17th, the disaster fell short of extinction.

XV.

The escape
of Sir
George
Womb-
well.
One of those who returned to our lines with the
remnant of the 4th Light Dragoons had been a prisoner in the hands of the enemy. I speak of Sir
George Wombwell, then an extra aide-de-camp to
Lord Cardigan. When last we saw Wombwell he
was not far from the front of the battery, but his
charger had just been shot under him. He so quickly
succeeded in catching and mounting a stray horse as
to be able to join the 4th Light Dragoons when they
came on, and advance with them down to the guns.
There, however, his newly-caught horse was killed
under him (as his own charger had been some minutes
before), and, this time, he found himself surrounded by
twenty or thirty Russian Lancers, who took from him
his sword and his pistol, and made him prisoner. It
happened that Captain Morris (then also, as we know,
a prisoner, and with his head deeply cut and pierced
by sabre and lance) was brought to the spot where
Wombwell stood; and it is interesting to observe that,
in spite of his own dreadful condition, Morris had still
a word of timely counsel that he could give to a
brother officer. 'Look out,' he said to Wombwell—

'look out and catch a horse.' At that moment, two CHAP.
or three loose horses came up, and Wombwell, darting ___X___
suddenly forward from between the Russian Lancers
who had captured him, seized and mounted one of
these riderless chargers, and galloped forward to meet
the 4th Light Dragoons, which he then saw retiring.
He succeeded in joining the regiment, and, with it,
returned to our lines.

When Captain Morris (unhorsed and grievously The escape
wounded) found himself surrounded by Russian dra- of Captain
goons, it was to an officer, as we saw, that he surren- Morris.
dered his sword.* That officer, however, quickly dis-
appeared, and then the Russian horsemen—Morris
took them to be Cossacks—rushed in upon their prisoner, and not only robbed him of all he had about
him, but convinced him by their manner and bearing
.that they were inclined to despatch him. Morris,
therefore, broke away from them, and ran into the
midst of the thickest smoke he could see. Then,
a riderless horse passing close to him, Morris caught
at the rein, and was dragged by it a short distance,
but afterwards fell and became unconscious.

Upon regaining his senses Morris became aware ·of
the presence of a Cossack, who seemed as though he
had just passed him, but was looking back in a way
which seemed to indicate that he had seen the English officer move, and would therefore despatch him.
Morris gathered strength from the emergency, found
means to get on his feet, and once more sought shelter
in the thickest smoke near him. Whilst standing

* See *ante*, p. 248.

CHAP.
X.

there, he found himself almost run down by another loose charger, but was able to catch hold of the horse's rein, and to mount him. He turned the horse's head up the valley, and rode as fast as he could; but just as he fancied he was getting out of the cross-fire his new horse was shot under him, and fell with him to the ground, giving him a heavy fall, and rolling over his thigh. Then again for some time Morris was unconscious; and when he regained his senses, he found that the dead horse was lying across his leg, and keeping him fastened to the ground. He then 'set to 'work' to extricate his leg, and at length succeeded in doing so. Then, getting on his feet, he ran on as well as he could, stumbling and getting up over and over again, but always taking care to be moving up hill, till at last, when quite worn out, he found himself close to the dead body of an English Staff-officer, —the body, he presently saw, of his friend Nolan.

Remembering that Nolan had fallen at a very early period in advance of the brigade, Morris inferred that he must be nearly within the reach of his fellow-countrymen; so, being now quite exhausted, he laid himself down beside the body of his friend, and again became unconscious.

Besides the three deep ugly wounds received in his head, Morris, in the course of these his struggles for life had suffered a longitudinal fracture or split of the right arm, and several of his ribs were broken.*

There was a circumstance in the lives of Nolan and

* The longitudinal splitting of the arm was of the kind, which, it seems, is scientifically described as a 'Saliswitch fracture.'

Morris which made it the more remarkable that the dead body of the one and the shattered frame of the other should be thus lying side by side. On the flank march, Morris and Nolan, who were great allies, had communicated to each other a common intention of volunteering for any special service that might be required in the course of the campaign; and they found that each of them, in anticipation of the early death that might result from such an enterprise, had written a letter which, in that event, was to be delivered. Morris had addressed a letter to his young wife, Nolan had addressed one to his mother. Under the belief that the opportunity for hazardous service of the kind they were seeking might be close at hand, the two friends had exchanged their respective letters: and now, when they lay side by side, the one dead and the other unconscious, each of them still had in his pocket the letter entrusted to him by the other.*

When Morris recovered his consciousness he found himself in an English hospital tent.† Terribly as he had been wounded and shattered, he did not succumb.‡

---

* The letter found in the pocket of Nolan—*i.e.*, the one addressed to Mrs Morris by her husband—was sent through the usual channels; but it is presumed that counteracting intelligence was sent by the same post.

† I believe that the satisfaction of having taken the requisite steps for bringing in the shattered frame of his commanding officer is justly enjoyed by Sergeant O'Hara, the same officer whom we saw exerting himself at the battery captured by the first line. He had been informed by Private George Smith of the spot where Morris lay.

‡ Up to the commencement of the campaign Morris had been keeping himself in an almost constant state of high 'training;' and, by some, the possession of the bodily force that was needed for enabling him to go ·through what he did has been attributed in part to that cause,

XVI.

The remnants of the brigade at this time.

Amongst the remnant of our Light Cavalry, now once more gathering together, there was, of course, a sense of the havoc that had been made in what, half an hour before, was Lord Cardigan's splendid brigade; but, for a while, this feeling was much interrupted by the joy of seeing comrade after comrade trail in from out of the fight, and in spite of the ruin their force had incurred, the men were from time to time cheering.

Lord Cardigan's address to the men.

When the remnants of the brigade had formed up, Lord Cardigan came forward and said, 'Men !. it is a 'mad-brained trick,* but it is no fault of mine.' Some of the men answered, 'Never mind, my 'lord ! we are ready to go again.' Lord Cardigan replied, 'No, no, men ! you have done enough.'

The first muster of the Light Brigade after the charge.

It was upon one of the slopes which look south-ward towards Balaclava that the muster took place; and, for some time, stragglers and riderless chargers were coming in at intervals; but at length there was a numbering of horses, and afterwards the mel-

though the indomitable courage and determination of the man were probably his chief resource. Morris was able the following year to take part again in war service, and did not die till the July of 1858. The suppression of the Bengal mutinies had been the task which, in 1857, drew him and his regiment to the East; and it was to the climate of India that at length he surrendered his life. He was much thought of in our army as a valorous and skilled cavalry officer, and with so high a reputation for straightforwardness and accuracy, that once, when a general officer imprudently ventured to put himself in conflict with Morris upon a matter of fact, there was a smile at the 'impar congres- 'sus,' no one who knew Morris consenting to imagine it possible that he could be the one who mistook.

* According to another version, 'a great blunder.'

ancholy roll-call began. As often as it 'appeared
that to the name called out there was no one present to answer, men contributed what knowledge
they had as to the fate of their missing comrade,
saying when and where they last had seen him.
More or less truly, if they knew it not before, men
learned the fate of their friends from this dismal
inquest. And then also came the time for the final
and deliberate severance of many a friendship between
the dragoon and his charger; for the farriers, with
their pistols in hand, were busied in the task of
shooting the ruined horses.

CHAP.
X.

The kill-
ing of the
disabled
horses.

Upon counting the brigade, it appeared that the
force, which numbered 673 horsemen when it went
into action, had been reduced to a mounted strength
of 195; * and there was one regiment, it seems—
namely, the 13th Light Dragoons, which, after the
charge, mustered only ten mounted troopers. From
a later examination it resulted that, in officers and
men killed and wounded, the brigade had suffered
losses to the number of 247, of whom 113 had been
killed and 134 wounded; and that (including 43
horses shot as unserviceable on account of their
wounds) the brigade had 475 horses killed, besides
having 42 others wounded.†

The losses
suffered
by the
brigade.

* It will be vain to seek for any correspondence between the result
of the first muster and the casualties. Many wounded men and
wounded horses might be present at the muster; and on the other
hand, neither the unwounded men whose chargers had been killed, nor
the unwounded horses which came back into our lines without their
riders would contribute to the 'mounted strength' as ascertained at the
first muster.

† These figures may not agree exactly with other returns, but I have
good reason for believing them to be accurate.

CHAP.   It has been stated by one who had good means of
  X.   knowing the truth, that of all the officers acting with
the first line, those who came out of action without a
wound received by either the horse or the rider, were
only two in number.*

Lord Cardigan, as we saw, was wounded though
not disabled; and of the three officers who acted as
his aides-de-camp, one, Captain Lockwood, was killed;
another, Lieutenant Maxse, wounded; and the third,
Sir George Wombwell, as we before learned, had two
horses shot under him.

In the 4th Light Dragoons, Major Halkett and
Lieutenant Sparke were killed, and Captain Brown
and Captain Hutton were both wounded severely.†

In the 8th Hussars, Lieutenant Lord Fitzgibbon
was killed, and Lieutenant Clutterbuck, Lieutenant
Seager, and Cornet Clowes were wounded. Of the
ten officers who went into action with the regiment,
Colonel Shewell and Cornet Heneage were the only
two of whom it could be said that both they and
their chargers were unstricken.

In the 11th Hussars, Captain Cook, Lieutenant

---

* It should be observed that I do not adopt the statement as one
necessarily accurate; for the authority on which it rests though coming
from an official source is not itself strictly official, and there may have
been some omission.

† It is said that Captain Hutton was seen vigorously using his
sword in the battery at a time when he had his thigh broken.—*End of
Note to First Edition.* 'On returning from the guns, he was shot
' through the other thigh, and on reaching the English lines, from the
' desperate nature of his wounds, was lifted out of his saddle in a scarcely
' conscious state. His charger had eleven wounds.' Letter to me from
a near relative of Captain Hutton's.—*Note to Second Edition.*

Trevelyan, and Lieutenant Haughton were wounded. The wound of Haughton proved mortal.

In the 13th Light Dragoons, Captain Oldham, its commander, and Captain Goad, and Cornet Montgomery were killed.

In the 17th Lancers, Captain Morris, who commanded the regiment, was, as we saw, grievously wounded; Captain Winter and Lieutenant Thompson were killed; Captain Webb was mortally wounded; Captain Robert White was wounded severely; Lieutenant Sir William Gordon also was wounded; and Lieutenant Chadwick, as we saw, was both wounded and taken prisoner.

It is believed that the last man killed was Captain Lockwood, an officer who has been already mentioned as one of the three aides-de-camp of Lord Cardigan. For some time, there was a hope that he might be alive; and there is still some uncertainty in regard to his movements during the charge, and the way in which he met his death. At the moment when the Light Cavalry began its advance, he was probably in the performance of some duty which separated him from the other aides-de-camp.* Indeed, there is an idea that he rode to the ground where some of our battalions were halted, addressed a general whom he there found, and announcing that the Light Cavalry was about to engage in an ugly task, urged that it

CHAP.
X.

The supposed fate of Captain Lockwood.

* See, however, the statement by Maxse, the assistant aide-de-camp referred to *ante* at foot of p. 210, from which it appears that at the beginning, and afterwards when 'three parts of the way down,' Lockwood was in his place.—*Note to Second Edition.*

CHAP. should be supported by infantry.* Supposing that •
  X.   he did this, and that the brigade moved forward
before he returned to it, he would have been likely
to gallop off in all haste down the valley to regain
his place near Lord Cardigan; but all I have learnt
is, that some time after the retreat of Lord Cardigan, and indeed at a moment when all the remains
of the brigade had already come out of action, Captain Lockwood rode up to Lord Lucan, and, speaking in a way which disclosed anxiety and distress as
though for the fate of his chief, said, ' My Lord, can
' you tell me where is Lord Cardigan?' and that,
upon Lord Lucan's replying that Lord Cardigan
had passed him some time,' Lockwood rode away.
It is imagined that he must have mistaken the
meaning of the answer, and that, regarding it as
an intimation that Lord Cardigan had again advanced, he must have galloped down the fatal valley,
and there met his death; for he was never afterwards seen in the English camp, either dead or alive,
and the Russians did not number him among their
prisoners. He was an excellent officer, much valued in
the 8th Hussars, the regiment to which he belonged.

   Seeing that our squadrons drove into the heart,
nay into the very rear of the enemy's position, and
then had no means of retreat unless they could cut
their way back through his interposed forces, the

---

* It seems to have been understood that Lockwood made the supposed
request at the instance of Lord Cardigan; but this Lord Cardigan
entirely denies. The answer of the general thus appealed to was, it is
said, to the effect that he had no authority.

strangest feature in the statistics of the battle is the list of prisoners. With our cavalry so completely in their fangs as to have it a mile and a quarter deep in their position, the Russians took hardly one prisoner who had not been disabled by his own wounds or those inflicted upon his horse. They took but fifteen unwounded prisoners altogether; and I believe that almost all these—if not indeed all, without even a single exception—were men whose horses had been killed or disabled.

The small number of prisoners taken by the Russians.

Another strange circumstance of this combat is the comparative impunity which the remnants of our Light Cavalry were suffered to enjoy after once they had closed with the enemy. A detailed statement of the casualties which occurred after the seizure of the battery could hardly be furnished; but I am persuaded that they were few. It was in descending the valley that our people incurred the main loss.

The small amount of loss sustained by our troops after once closing with the enemy.

XVII.

Who brought the first line out of action? If an unwary civilian were to put this question to a soldier, he might find that, without knowing it, he was using a phrase so technical as to bring upon himself a technical and somewhat illusory answer.* But if it be

Who brought the first line out of action?

---

* In the military art there is a very inconvenient want of words and phrases with an exclusively technical import; and the result is that soldiers find themselves obliged to affix technical meanings to ordinary expressions—a practice insuring ambiguity, and tending, of course, to misconceptions. When a military man speaks of a regiment, or any other force, and says that he 'brought it out of action,' he does not

CHAP.
X.

asked who gave to the main fighting remnants of the
first line that guidance and help by which they were
ultimately extricated from the enemy's gripe, the
answer must be based upon a knowledge of those
occurrences which I have sought to record. From
this I imagine it will be gathered that, although
there were individuals of the first line who came
out on the northern side of the valley with the 4th
Light Dragoons and the 11th Hussars, the number
—a very small number—which could best be regarded as representing the first line, was that which
came out on the south of the valley with the 8th
Hussars. It was only during the period of the
advance from the battery to the neighbourhood of
the aqueduct, and of the movement back thence to
where stood the 8th Hussars, that Colonel Mayow
had, in any sense, the charge of the first line. As
soon as he had joined Colonel Shewell, he was in the
presence of his military superior; and he acknowledges, apparently, that any command which he had
been assuming in his character of senior officer then
came at once to an end. It seems plain that the
main undisabled remnant of the first line was extricated from the power of the enemy by Colonel
Shewell of the 8th Hussars.

And who
brought
out the
supports?

With regard to the supports, there was no co-
operation at the close of the combat between the force

mean that he did anything particular; all he means is, that he came
out senior officer. In that, the merely technical sense of the phrase,
Lord Cardigan, of course, was the officer who 'brought the first line
'out of action.'

on our right and the force on our left, and 'they came C H A P.
out in two distinct bodies. The 8th Hussars on our ___X.___
right was brought out by Colonel Shewell its commanding officer. On our left there were two regiments which co-operated in their retreat, and with
these, Lord George Paget was the senior officer.*

XVIII.

Immediately after the muster, Lord Cardigan rode *Interview between*
up to Lord Raglan in order to make his report. Lord *Lord Rag-*
Raglan said to him, in a severe and very angry way, *Lord Car-*
' What did you mean, sir, by attacking a battery in *digan.*
' front, contrary to all 'the usages of warfare, and the
' customs of the service ? '

Lord Cardigan answered : ' My Lord, I hope you
,' will not blame me, for I received the order to attack
' from my superior officer in front of the troops ; ' and
he then proceeded to give an account of the part he
had taken.

Subsequently, and after full inquiry, Lord Raglan
not only determined that the justification thus offered,
was sound, but also, it seems, formed an opinion that *Lord Rag-*
Lord Cardigan's whole conduct in the affair of the *lan's opin-*
charge had been admirable. ' Lord Cardigan,' he *Lord Car-*
wrote in private, some five days after the action, *in the*
charge.

* The question whether Lord George as senior officer acquired the
command of the whole body formed by the two co-operating regiments
(the 4th Light Dragoons Lord George's own regiment, and the 11th
Hussars commanded by Colonel Douglas) is one of a technical kind
which soldiers can best determine ; but the facts on which the solution
depends are given *ante*, p. 298.

CHAP. 'acted throughout with the greatest steadiness and
   X.   'gallantry, as well as perseverance.'

Interview   Upon meeting Lord Lucan at a later moment,
between
Lord Rag- Lord Raglan said to him, 'You have lost the Light
lan and
Lord   Brigade!'
Lucan.
             Lord Lucan at once denied that he had lost the
Light Brigade; and, as the ground for his denial, stated
that he had only carried out the orders, written and
verbal, conveyed to him by Captain Nolan.

Then it was that Lord Raglan is said to have uttered a sentence which, supposing it to be accurately
reported, did certainly supply Lord Lucan with fair
means of raising a controversy, and even gave him,
as many may think, a kind of 'argumentative victory.
The Commander of the Forces had no copy of either
the 'third' or the 'fourth' order; and, for that reason alone, even if there were no other, he might not
improbably desire to avoid or defer all discussion
founded upon the wording of the documents. Accordingly, he did not say, as he might have done:
'I ordered—I ordered in writing—that the cavalry
'should advance and take advantage of any oppor-
'tunity to recover the heights, and you kept it halted
'for more than half an hour. I ordered—I ordered
'in writing—that the cavalry should advance rapidly
'to the front, that it should follow the enemy, and
'try to prevent him from carrying away the guns,
'meaning of course, as you well know,* our lost Eng-
'lish guns, and yet with this order in your hand you

* For proof that Lord Lucan did know this, see the footnote *ante*,
p. 192.

'caused Lord Cardigan to go down the valley instead C H A P.
'of advancing upon the "heights," and to attack the ⎯⎯ X ⎯⎯
'front of a distant Russian battery, after running the
'gauntlet for a mile and a quarter between crossing
'fires.' What Lord Raglan did say according to
Lord Lucan, was to this effect: 'Lord Lucan, you
'were a Lieutenant-General, and should therefore
'have exercised your discretion, and, not approving
'of the charge, should not have caused it to be
'made.'

Whatever, abstractedly speaking, may be the value
of the reason thus said to have been adduced by Lord
Raglan, it was evidently one so far open to question
as to give Lord Lucan an excellent opportunity of
raising a controversy against his chief. Up to that
moment, the predicament of Lord Lucan was simply
the predicament of a man who had misconceived his
instructions, and imagined that he must advance
down the valley instead of trying to recover the
heights; but now, all at once, if his impression of
what Lord Raglan said be accurate, he found himself
raised into the position of one who, being mortal,
and having like other mortals committed an error,
has had the good fortune to be rebuked for it in
terms fairly open to question; and he was as competent as any man living to make vigorous use of the
advantage thus gained. Accordingly, when opportunity offered, he argued with great cogency against the
theory that he should have disobeyed an order which
he could not approve, urging soundly that Lord
Raglan's survey of the field from the high ground of

CHAP.
X.
the Chersônese was necessarily much more complete than that which could be commanded by any one in the plain below; and that to venture to disobey the order under such circumstances, would have been to disobey a General who was not only armed with the superior authority of a Commander-in-Chief, but also with superior knowledge.

Thus then it resulted that, independently of the substantial merits of the question as they stood at the time of the combat, Lord Lucan was so much advantaged afterwards by the alleged tenor of the blaming words as to be able to place himself—not, of course, in the right, but—still in the attitude of one who can take fair exception to the terms in which his chief has reproved him.

XIX.

General Liprandi's questions respecting the exploit of the Light Brigade.

It might be thought at first sight that, correlatively with the anger and the pain evinced by Lord Raglan, there would be exultation on the part of Liprandi; but this was not so. On the contrary, he seems to have been thrown into a state of angry vexation; and perhaps, after all—for in war reputation is strength—he was right in believing that the deduction of three or four hundreds from the numerical strength of our Light Brigade could be no sufficing compensation to him for the moral disaster sustained by the main body of his powerful cavalry—the disaster of having been overthrown and put to flight by the desultory and uncombined onsets of scanty numbers of horsemen.

Perceiving, as he could not fail to do, the unspeakable rashness, or rather self-destructiveness, of the charge, he was disposed to attribute it to the maddening power of alcohol ; and it would seem that he was rendered all the more indignant by imagining that the disgrace of his cavalry—his cavalry numbered by thousands—was the result of a drunken freak. He found himself obliged to abandon that somewhat easy mode of accounting for heroism when he had examined our prisoners. Upon his asking them whether they had not been made drunk before the charge, they were able to assure him with truth that the men of our Light Cavalry (as also, indeed, those of Scarlett's brigade who had defeated General Ryjoff in the morning) were not only guiltless of having touched any strong drink, but had been actually fasting all day.* For proof of this they appealed to the state of their haversacks when taken from them, which contained their untouched rations, including their untouched ration of rum.

Liprandi showed a strong wish to learn the name and rank of an English officer who had been seen retreating on a chestnut horse with white heels; and upon questioning the English prisoners on the subject, he was told by some of them that the officer so seen was Lord Cardigan. Upon receiving this answer General Liprandi remarked that nothing but the ad-

---

* It was just when they were about to be dismissed to their breakfasts that our cavalry were called upon to advance ; and from that time until the Light Cavalry charge they were either kept moving or on the alert.

C H A P. vantage of having a good horse could have saved the
X.   rider from the Cossacks who pursued him. *

XX.

Duration
of the
combat
called the
'Light
'Cavalry
'charge.'

Lord Rag-
lan's 'pri-
vately ex-
pressed
opinion
of the
charge.

It has been computed that the onset, the combat,
and the retreat, which are popularly comprised under
the name of the 'Light Cavalry charge,' lasted twenty
minutes.† What was suffered and done in that time I
have sought to record. I will add the opinion respecting this singular passage of arms which was spontan-
eously and in private expressed by the English Commander. With but two small brigades of cavalry
under his orders, Lord Raglan° had cogent reason for
thinking bitterly of an operation by which one of them
had been shattered ; and, when writing confidentially
to the Secretary of State, he declared that the result,
of the Light Cavalry charge was a 'heavy misfortune'
—a misfortune he felt 'most deeply.'‡ In conversation at Headquarters he not unfrequently expressed his
painful sense of the disaster ; and foreseeing the enthu-

* Supposing that the prisoners were right in identifying the rider
of the chestnut horse as Lord Cardigan, Liprandi's words add another
corroboration (if any such were needed) to Lord Cardigan's account
of the circumstances under which he began his retreat. There is
only one witness — Thomas King — who connects the retreat of the
rider of the chestnut horse with the time ' when the second line were
' going down.'

† This was General Scarlett's computation, and it has been generally adopted as likely to be right. Lord Cardigan at first used to
speak of twenty-five minutes as the probable period, but he afterwards
—and with great urgency—insisted that General Scarlett's computation
was the right one.

‡ Private letter to Duke of Newcastle, Oct. 28, 1854.

siastic admiration which the feat would excite in Eng- C H A P.
land, he used sometimes to lament the perverseness
with which he believed that his fellow-countrymen
would turn from the brilliant and successful achievement of Scarlett's brigade to dwell, and still dwell,
upon the heroic, yet self-destructive exploit of Lord
Cardigan's squadrons; but the truth is that, apart
from thoughts military, there was a deep human interest attaching to the devotion of the man and the
men who, for the sheer sake of duty, could go down
that fatal north valley as the English Light Cavalry
did.   This feeling on the part of others Lord Raglan
might þe willing to repress, but he could not help
sharing it himself; and despite all his anger and
grief, despite the kind of protestation he judged it
wholesome to utter for the discouragement of rash
actions on the part of his officers, I still find him
writing in private of the Light Cavalry charge that
it 'was perhaps the finest thing ever attempted.'*

The well-known criticism delivered by General General
Bosquet was sound and generous.   He said of the criticism
charge, 'It is splendid; but it is not war.'† He charge.
spoke with a most exact justice; but already the
progress of time has been changing the relative sig-
nificance of that glory and that fault which his terse
comment threw into contrast.   What were once the
impassioned desires of the great nations of the West
for the humbling of the Czar are now as cold as the

* Oct. 30, 1854.

† ' C'est magnifique ; mais ce n'est pas la guerre.' This was said by
General Bosquet to Mr Layard in the field, and at the time of the charge.

329

C H A P.
X.

ashes which remind men of flames extinguished; and
our people can cease from deploring the errors which
marred a battle, yet refuse to forget an achievement
which those very errors provoked. Therefore the perversity which sent our squadrons to their doom is
only after all the mortal part of the story. Half-
forgotten already, the origin of the 'Light Cavalry
'Charge' is fading away out of sight. Its splendour
remains. And splendour like.this is something more
than the mere outward adornment which graces the
life of a nation. It is strength—strength other than
that of mere riches, and other than that of gross numbers—strength carried by proud descent from one
generation to another—strength awaiting the trials
that are to come.

CHAPTER XI.

Divining apparently that the disaster incurred by our Light Cavalry would chill the ardour of the Allies, Liprandi not only determined to reverse that movement of retreat from the Causeway Heights which Lord Raglan had so swiftly detected, but even wished, it would seem, to make a show of seriously offering resistance to the Allies if assailed in that part of the field. He therefore countermarched the Odessa regiment to the ground near the Arabtabia Redoubt,* from which it had been withdrawn at the approach of our cavalry, and he moved such additional troops to the same ground as brought up his force on that part of the Causeway Heights to a strength of eight battalions, supported by artillery.

CHAP. XI.

Liprandi's counter-march of the Odessa battalions.

It is probable that Sir Colin Campbell detected this change of disposition on the part of the enemy; for he came to the Duke of Cambridge, and, with a good deal of earnestness, entreated his Royal Highness to dissuade Cathcart from attacking the redoubts. His Royal Highness declined to interfere; but it is probable that Sir Colin Campbell may have found some

* The Number Three Redoubt.

CHAP.
XI.
other channel by which to convey his advice.* At all events, no attack took place. I do not imagine that Sir Colin meant to express any opinion against duly concerted measures for the recovery of the heights, but only to deprecate an isolated attack upon ground where the enemy had just concentrated a large part of his force.

Delibera-
tions of
General
Canrobert
and Lord
Raglan.
However, General Canrobert and Lord Raglan had a force in the plain which, by this time, was so disposed that they might undertake the recapture of the heights, and they were called upon to determine whether or not it would be well for them to use their power. Lord Raglan, I believe, still desired to do so ; but the loss of the Light Cavalry Brigade, though it did not impair the power of the Allies to recapture the heights, was a reason which made it more difficult than before to maintain an extended dominion in front of Bala- clava. Indeed it was evident that the dominion which had there been exercised could now be no longer maintained without either relaxing the siege, or else determining that a portion of the French covering army should come down to take charge in the plain ; and it is evident that this was a condition of things which would fairly entitle General Canrobert to even more than his usual weight in the Anglo-French counsels.

Now, General Canrobert, as we know, had con- ceived from the first that the advance of the Russians into the plain of Balaclava was a mere snare by which

* I believe he came himself and spoke to Cathcart.—*Note to 3d Edition.*

they were trying to lure him down from the Cher- CHAP.
sonese ; and it must be acknowledged that, if looked XI.
at in a too narrow spirit, the reasons which could be
adduced against any attempt to recapture the forts
had a great appearance of cogency. It was said that,
with their limited strength, and the great business
of the siege in hand, the Allies could not afford the
troops needed for occupying ground so distant as that
on which stood the redoubts ; that if they were that
moment in possession of the heights, policy would
require that they should give them up the next day ;
and that, plainly, it must be unwise for belligerents,
whose, whole prospects depended upon the speedy capture of Sebastopol to undertake a combat for the recovery of ground which they could not afford to occupy.

In its direct bearing upon what may be called the
, merely material view of the question, the argument
was possibly sound ; but it had the defect which the
great Napoleon in the successful part of his career so
well knew how to avoid—the defect of leaving out
from the reckoning all allowance for those moral
forces which govern the actions of men. The events of
the day had been such, that if they should be followed
by the extrusion of the enemy from the sites of the
Turkish redoubts and the recapture of the English
guns, the Russians, it was plain, would have to go out
of action not only with the distinct consciousness of a
defeat, but of a defeat rendered bitter and humiliating
by the overthrow of their powerful cavalry ; whereas,
if Liprandi should be left in possession of the hillocks, and the small iron guns which he had been

able to capture, he might plausibly claim a victory, and would have some real trophies to show in the Theatre Square at Sebastopol. It is true enough that no such nominal victory as this was calculated to give mighty confidence to Liprandi's own little army—the men who composed it knew the truth too well—but it was for the defenders of Sebastopol rather than for the field army that moral force was vitally needed; and in Sebastopol, as we now know, the 'victory of Balaclava,' and the guns which, though taken from the Turks, could still be truly called 'English,' were well fitted to be received as blessings of unspeakable value. They could not fail to give heart to the men—whether soldiers, or sailors, or people—who were engaged in defending the place; and on the other·hand it may be taken for granted that if the tidings of so slender a 'victory' as that of Balaclava could bring all this accession of moral strength to the beleaguered town, the opposite effect that must have been produced by Liprandi's defeat would have been fully proportionate.

The determination of the Allies. It was determined that the Russians should be left in undisturbed possession of the ground which they held.

Sir George Cathcart, who had brought his division to the ground near the Redoubt 'Number Four,' now caused the work to be manned once more by the Turks; and his riflemen took part in a fusilade which appeared to have the effect of silencing two Russian guns.

At about four o'clock the firing came to an end;

but all grave contention had ceased from the moment C H A P.
when the Allied Commanders determined to acquiesce __XI.__
in Liprandi's conquest. He held without further challenge all three of the captured redoubts; and retained
to a point so far westward his dominion on the Causeway Heights as to be able to forbid free communication between Balaclava and the main Allied camps
by the line of the Woronzoff road.

With the condition of things now shown, both the Close of
the battle.
Allies and the Russians were so far content that they
allowed the battle to end.

CHAPTER XII.

I.

CHAP.
XII.

The kind
of import-
ance
which can
be attach-
ed to the
battle of
Balaclava.

IF the scope of this conflict were to be measured by numbering the forces engaged, and the men killed, wounded, or taken, a much slighter record than the one I have framed would be fully enough for the purpose; but from its effect in cramping the English at Balaclava, and exalting the spirit of Sebastopol, this first effort of Prince Mentschikoff's resurgent field-army exerted much power over the subsequent course of events; and, on the other hand, the battle comprised several fights which so happily elicited the quality of the soldier, whether English, French, Russian, or Turk, as to have a distinct present bearing on the warlike repute of each nation engaged, and therefore, of course, on its strength, and therefore, again, on its welfare. Under that kind of aspect the glory of fights which sprang out of sheer chance or mistake may come to be of higher moment to England than the objects and the vicissitudes of a somewhat fanciful war long since at an end. What are now the 'four points of Vienna' when compared with the achievement of Scarlett's dragoons and Cardigan's Light Cavalry charge?

Told more shortly, the story is this: Marching by C H A P.
two unconnected routes in the early morning, a por-XII.
tion of Liprandi's forces established batteries with Summary of the
which they cannonaded the Turkish redoubt on Can-battle.
robert's Hill. Upon being apprised of this movement
Lord Raglan at once sent down two divisions of foot ;
but time must necessarily elapse before the troops
thus despatched could come into action ; and, in the
meanwhile, there were no English forces with which
to support the Turks in their defence except our
division of cavalry and its attendant troop of horse-
artillery.

The, question was, Whether Lord Lucan, with the
cavalry arm alone, could and would aid the Turks in
warding off for a few hours the impending attack ?
With the approval of Sir Colin Campbell, he abstained
,from launching any of his squadrons in arrest of the
enemy's progress ; and our horsemen, though compelled to be spectators of what followed, were not
suffered to interpose as assailants.

Being thus let alone by our cavalry, and but
slightly molested, if molested at all, by its attendant
troop of horse-artillery, the Russian infantry proceeded to storm the work on Canrobert's Hill, and
by the strength of their overwhelming numbers they
succeeded in carrying it, though not until the brave
little Turkish garrison of not more than 500 or 600
men had lost, in killed only, as many as 170.

Upon seeing the fate of the redoubt on Canrobert's
Hill, the Turks posted in the three next adjoining
works abandoned them at once to the Russians. The

enemy having speedily entered them, dismantled and afterwards quitted the one called 'Number Four,' but kept the other three in his grasp, together with their seven English guns.

As the Russians advanced, our cavalry fell back; and Lord Lucan had just taken up a position in the South Valley, where his troops would cover Balaclava, when, by an order sent down from Headquarters, all his squadrons were drawn in under the steeps of the Chersonese; but that last order again was presently followed by another, which directed that eight squadrons of Heavy Dragoons should countermarch towards Kadiköi, and aid the defence of the gorge.

Notwithstanding the rapid and almost brillant success which had hitherto rewarded his enterprise, Liprandi did not hold to the purpose, if ever he had it, of really attacking Balaclava. Yet by arraying his powerful cavalry, with its attendant batteries, across the North Valley, he not only showed a good front to the troops coming down from the Chersonese, but connected himself by his right with the slopes of the Fedioukine Hills; and as Jabrokritsky was there establishing himself, it might be said that the Russians at this time were an army taking up a position.

Their array was apparently meant to be the commencing stage of a deliberate, well-conducted retreat.

Since the Russians were attempting nothing against Balaclava, and the Allies had as yet no division of infantry far advanced on the plain, there resulted a pause in the battle.

The Russian cavalry however, having before it a

great tract of unoccupied ground, was—without any
very large purpose—induced to advance up the valley; and (after detaching on its way the four squadrons which descended towards Sir Colin Campbell and quickly turned aside from his fire) this great body of horse continued to move forward till it came within range of the Chersonese batteries ; when, after incurring two shots, it turned aside to its left and gained the top of the Causeway ridge.

Then ended that part of the battle which was governed by design, and Chance began to have sway.

It happened that whilst countermarching towards Kadiköi, in obedience to the order last mentioned, General Scarlett with six of his squadrons had reached that part of the South Valley which lay directly under the Russians now crowning the ridge.

That which followed was the great fight between the Russian cavalry and our Heavy Dragoons. The Russian cavalry, upon being overthrown, did not merely retreat to the ground whence it came, but moved off far away to the rear with its attendant batteries, leaving the two protruding columns of Liprandi and Jabrokritsky in a state of severance the one from the other—two wings without a body— and each of them very open to attack.

Lord Raglan instantly saw his opportunity, and ordered—in writing—that the cavalry should advance and take advantage of any opportunity to recover the heights. This direction not having been executed by the commander of our cavalry, was followed, after

CHAP.
XII.
an interval, by the yet more peremptory order which Nolan brought down from Lord Raglan.

Upon the delivery of this order there occurred the strange scene which ended in Lord Lucan's conceiving that, instead of attacking the heights, it was his duty to send Lord Cardigan and his Light Brigade down the fatal North Valley, and to follow himself in support with the Heavy Dragoons. The first moments of Lord Cardigan's forward movement proved the wisdom with which Lord Raglan had ordered an attack on the Causeway Heights; for when the Russians perceived the advance of the Light Brigade, without yet being able to foresee its actual destination, the Odessa battalions—those battalions which stood on the spot to which Lord Raglan had directed the attack—retreated at once from the forward position they had occupied on the Causeway Heights, and formed square a good way to the rear.

The Light Brigade continued to move forward; and, for a time, Lord Lucan was anxiously following its advance with a portion of his Heavy Dragoons; but afterwards (though still holding his Heavy Dragoons in readiness to cover his Light Cavalry during a portion at least of its anticipated retreat) he judged that it was his duty to save the rest of his squadrons from the disasters which the Light Brigade was incurring, and determined that Lord Cardigan's attack must thenceforth remain unsupported.

Lord Cardigan persisted in his advance down the valley; and then followed the rest of the operations which constitute the 'Light Cavalry Charge.' It

was in advancing down the length of the valley that CHAP.
our Light Cavalry incurred their main losses, and were $\underbrace{\text{XII.}}$
reduced to a third of their strength; but the remnant
of the brigade seized the battery at the foot of the
valley, overthrew the main body of the Russian
cavalry, and forced their way back through the rest
of them, owing much of their immunity in retreat
to the brilliant achievement of D'Allonville and his
famous ' Fourth Chasseurs d'Afrique.'

Emboldened by the disaster which our Light Cavalry incurred, and possibly, also, by visible signs of
hesitation in the counsels of the Allies, Liprandi
began to reverse his movement of retreat. The
Odessa battalions countermarched to the ground
from which they had been withdrawn, and some
additional troops were established on the line of the
Causeway Heights.

For reasons based on the difficulty of holding a
wide extent of ground in the plain of Balaclava, the
Allies determined to acquiesce in Liprandi's conquest
of the redoubts; and with that decision — though
vain shots were afterwards fired—the battle came to
an end.

II.

In ground, the Allies lost the outer line of defence The loss
which the English by the aid of the Turks had pro- of ground
vided for Balaclava; and with it, they so lost their by the
sustained
Allies.
freedom of action in the country they had made bold
to invade, as to be thenceforth confined during several

CHAP. months within very narrow limits, and that, too, with
XII. great strictness. They remained, of course, in the
occupation of the whole of the Chersonese; but there
was a question, as we shall hereafter see, of actually
abandoning Balaclava; and although the proposal to
that effect was ultimately discarded by the Allies, the
scope of their dominion on the land side of the place
became so contracted as only to include the marine
heights on our right, and just so much ground in front
of the place as was necessary for maintaining its communications with the Chersonese by the way of 'the
'Col.'

In submitting to be thus extruded from the Causeway Heights, the Allies gave up the control of the
Woronzoff road, and the time was at hand when this
loss would become a cause of cruel sufferings to the
English army.

The casu-
alties re-
sulting
from the
battle.
The Allies lost in killed and wounded about 600
officers and men, besides some fifteen unwounded
English and a small number of Turks who were taken
prisoners.* The Russians, it seems, lost in men killed
and wounded about 627.†

Trophies
taken by
the Rus-
sians.
The Russians took out of the redoubts captured
from the Turks seven cast-iron English guns. Also,
Liprandi was enabled to send to his chief the welcome
trophy of a Turkish standard.

* I am not aware that any one unwounded Englishman having under
him an unwounded horse was taken prisoner.

† This includes some who were only 'contusionnés,' and also fifteen
missing. I include those last because I believe that all who were
'missing' had been either killed or wounded. The basis of the statement as to the Russian losses is the official return, to which (by adopting it) General de Todleben gives the weight of his authority.

It may here be recorded, and recorded with grati- C H A P. tude, that the English prisoners, upon the whole, were XII. treated with great kindness; and I will mention a touching example of good feeling displayed by the poor Muscovite soldiers. Simple, untutored men, they yet had heard so much of the ways of other nations as to be aware that the Englishmen did not live on that strange waxy substance which goes by the name of 'black bread;' and their kindly natures were so moved by the thought of this that they generously subscribed out of their humble pittances to buy white loaves for the prisoners.*

With the knowledge of the kindness thus extended to our own people, it is painful to have to add that the Turkish prisoners were ill treated.

Treatment of the prisoners taken by the enemy.

III.

With which of the two contending forces did the victory rest? If it be believed that—however irreso- lutely—the Russians entertained the design of trying to break into Balaclava, the failure of their attempt would be a circumstance strongly bearing upon the question; for when they ventured to descend into that South Valley by which Balaclava might be ap- proached, they were instantly stopped at one point by the 93d Highlanders, and superbly defeated at another by Scarlett's dragoons. If that were all, it might

With whom the victory?

* General de Todleben communicated this to me, and I have great confidence in the accuracy of the statement. The statement must not be understood as applying specially to the prisoners taken at Balaclava.

CHAP.
XII.
seem to follow that the palm was with those who repulsed the attacks; but, on the other hand, it must be remembered that our Light Cavalry after seizing the twelve-gun battery and routing the main body of the enemy's horse was itself obliged to retreat, and that the Russians, though worsted in combat after combat, still were suffered to remain in possession of the ground, the redoubts, and the trophies which they had won in the first hour of the morning. Upon the whole, therefore, it will probably be thought that there was no such decisive inclination of the balance as to give to one side or the other the advantage which men call a 'victory.'

The effect of the battle upon the self-confidence of the Russians.
But, apart from the mere name of victory, one of the weightiest effects of a battle is the change which it commonly works in the self-confidence of the opposing forces; and under this aspect of its consequences the result of the day's fighting in the plain of Balaclava was somewhat anomalous; for the action consisted of five several combats not effectually brought into one by any pervading design; and, excepting only the first, there were none of these combats which ended without shedding glory on the Allies, and inflicting something like humiliation on the enemy. Therefore the effect of the day's conflict was such as to be disheartening—oppressively disheartening—to those of the Russians who actually fought in it; and it is probable that for a long time afterwards it would have been impracticable to make the Russian cavalry act with anything like confidence in the presence of a few English squadrons; but, on the other hand, the

facts were such that, without any actual misstatement of them, they could be narrated in a way highly en- couraging to all Russians who were not on the field, and especially encouraging to the soldiery, the seamen, and the people upon whose spirit the fate of Sebasto- pol was depending. Liprandi could dwell upon the brilliant assault and capture of the work on Can- robert's Hill, and upon the fall of the other re- doubts; could pass lightly over the conflicts which his cavalry hazarded with the Highlanders and with Scarlett's dragoons; could speak frankly of the won- drous pertinacity evinced by our Light Cavalry in its road to destruction; could state that, in the teeth of all the forces brought down by the Allies, he had persisted in holding the line of the captured re- doubts; could show that he was thus pressing close , upon the English camp at Balaclava; and could end by producing the captured guns and the captured standard as fit tokens of what had been achieved. Despatched from the camp of a relieving army to a beleaguered town, such a narrative as this, with the many and brilliant adornments which rumour would abundantly add, might well carry heart to the gar- rison; and we now know that the tidings and the trophies of the battle brought such joy and encour- agement to the people defending Sebastopol as to aggravate, and aggravate heavily, the already hard task of the besiegers.

With each hour of the lapsing time from the night of the 20th of September, that store of moral power over the enemy which the Allies acquired by their

CHAP.
XII.

victory had been almost ceaselessly dwindling; and although it be granted that, so far as concerned all those Russians who were assailed by our cavalry, or by D'Allonville's Chasseurs d'Afrique, the old spell was superbly renewed, it is yet, I think, true that with the rest of the enemy's forces, and especially in the lines of Sebastopol, our patience under the capture which deprived us of the Turkish redoubts and the English guns which had armed them did much to destroy what was left of the ascendant obtained on the Alma.

SUPPLEMENTARY CHAPTER.

LORD CARDIGAN.

IN general, there is but little disposition on the part of the world to analyse any great feat of arms with the notion of seeing exactly how much was done by the troops, and how much by their leader. Under the ordinary and popular aspect of warlike conflicts, the actions of the chief and his soldiery are blended into one glowing picture; and since it is easier, and even more interesting to contemplate the prowess of one man than the compound deserts of a thousand, the result most commonly is that, without truly learning what guidance was given by the commander, mankind are content to assign him an enormously large share of the glory which he and his people have earned. In the instance of the Light Cavalry charge, this was the more especially likely to be the case, because the General in immediate command of the assailing troops was their actual, bodily leader. I imagine that if Lord Cardigan had remained silent, no painful scrutiny would have been ever applied to the actions of the man who rode the foremost of all between two flanking fires into the front of the twelve-gun battery, and

the glory allotted to the chief would have been nearly
as free from question as the glory of his martyred
brigade. But, as in the disposal of his daily life Lord
Cardigan had separated himself from his troops by
choosing to live in that home of comparative luxury
which a well-supplied yacht could afford, whilst not
only his officers and men but even his immediate
commander, lay always camped out in the plain, so
also in the graver business of upholding his fair fame
as a soldier by argument, assertion, and proof, he
acted in such manner as to sever himself from that
very brigade with which his renown had been blended.

Under stress of ill health, he returned to England.
There, as may well be supposed, he was greeted with
the wildest enthusiasm; and then began the long process by which he mismanaged his military reputation.
By consenting to be made the too conspicuous and
too solitary hero of public ovations; by giving to the
world his own version of the famous Light Cavalry
charge; by showing—he showed this quite truly—
how well he had led the attack, but omitting—and
there was the error of errors—to speak of that separation which I have called being 'thrown out;' by
continuing in this course of action until he provoked hard attacks; by submitting to grave speci-
fied charges, or meeting them with mere personal
abuse; by writing letters to newspapers; by sending
complaints to the Horse Guards; by making himself
the bitter antagonist of officers, nay, even of regiments, where claims for the least share of glory
seemed clashing at all with his own; and finally by

a process of tardy litigation exploding, after eight years of controversy, in one of the law courts at Westminster, he at length forced the world to distinguish between his brigade and himself. He forced men, if so one may speak, to decompose the whole story of the 'Light Cavalry Charge;' and one result is, that the narrator of that part of the combat which began when the chief went about, is driven against his will to an unaccustomed division of subjects, having first to go home with the leader, and then travel back to the fight. In such conditions, it is not possible to do real justice by merely saying what happened. It would, be cruel, and wrong to speak dryly of Lord Cardigan's retreat without giving his justification. Accordingly, at the very moment of narrating his retreat I began to show how he defended it; and I ,now think it right to impart the nature of his justification with more fulness than could well be allowed me whilst yet in the midst of the story.

So long as he moved down the valley under the guidance of what he understood to be an assigned duty, no danger seemed to appal him, and of a certainty none bent him aside from his course. That which afterwards baffled him was something more perturbing than mere danger to one whose experience had been military without being warlike. What he encountered was an emergency. Acting apparently with the full persuasion that the leadership of his first line was the one task before him, he all at once found that of that first line he could see nothing, except some horsemen in retreat, and already a good way up

the valley.* It did not, it seems, appear to him that
by holding up his sword for a rally he could draw
any stragglers to his side, and he had no aide-de-
camp, no orderly with him. What was he to do?†
Well indeed might it be said that the emergency
was an unforeseen one, for what manual had ever
explained how a cavalry leader should act if all the
troops he could see were out of his reach, and he had
no one at his side by whom he could send an order?

Lord Car-
digan's
theory as
to the
duty of a
cavalry
officer
placed in
his cir-
cumstan-
ces :

Even when in the midst of the narrative, I found
time to speak—although shortly—of what Lord Cardigan believes to be the true rule of cavalry practice.
His theory is, that a cavalry officer in command of two
or more lines when about to undertake a charge should
first give sufficient directions to the officers in command of his supports, and thenceforth address himself
specially (in the absence of exceptional circumstances)
to the leadership of his first line; the principle apparently being that, by reason of the impossibility of
transmitting verbal orders to a distance in the midst
of a cavalry charge, the movements of the first line
are in the nature of signalled directions, which offer
a continuous guidance to the squadrons advancing in

---

* That the theory was no mere afterthought, and that Lord Cardigan
really considered the leadership of the first line as the one task before
him is shown, I think, by the terms of the private memorandum which
he imparted to Lord Raglan on the second day after the battle, and
long before controversy began ; for he there described himself as having
been ordered to attack—not with the Light Brigade, but—with the 13th
Light Dragoons, and the 17th Lancers, *i.e.*, with the regiments constituting his first line. See note, *ante*, p. 203.

† As was said by the Lord Chief Justice, it would be well for men
forming opinions upon Lord Cardigan's conduct 'to ask themselves how
' they would have acted in a similar state of things ?'

their rear. The General does not of course cease to be in the actual and effective command of the whole force engaged in the charge, but he exerts his authority over the squadrons advancing in support first by giving them anticipatory directions, and afterwards by showing them through the means of their eyesight and without any further words the way in which he leads his first line.* If, in short, he gives proper instruction to his supports before the commencement of the charge, and then proceeding to lead his first line, takes care to lead it efficiently, he has done all that in ordinary circumstances could be required of him.

There is a defect in the argument by which Lord Cardigan applies this theory to his own case; for as soon as he had determined that (without first riding off a great way to the rear) there was nothing for, him to do towards rallying or otherwise governing the fragments of his first line, the exigency under which a General may be forced to leave his supports to take care of themselves would· seem to have lost its ·force. After the conclusion he had come to in regard to the hopelessness of attempting to rally his first line, or taking any farther part in its combats, Lord Cardigan was so circumstanced that he had leisure to look after his supports; and, indeed, there was no other public duty of a momentous kind that he well could attempt to discharge.

* Supposing the application of the theory to be confined within proper bounds, it seems to be based upon the necessity of the case, and to be, for that reason, sound; but I observe that infantry officers are at first much startled when they hear it propounded as a justification for leaving the supports to themselves.

Lord Cardigan, however, has reinforced this theory by an important assertion. He solemnly declares that when he retreated, he nowhere could see his supports; and after intimating a belief that he could not have reached them without pushing his search through bodies of Russian cavalry, he finally submits that any endeavour on his part to get to his supports under such circumstances would have been absolutely hopeless and therefore wrong.

His writ-
ten ex-
planations
of the
course he
took in
retiring.

In explanation of the course that he took in retiring, Lord Cardigan has made written statements, of which the following are a portion :—After stating that he 'gradually retreated' until he reached the battery into which he had led the first line, he goes on to say—' On arriving there I found no part of ' the first line remaining there; those which sur-' vived the charge had passed off to the left short ' of the Russian limber-carriages or retreated up ' the hill. I can upon my most solemn oath swear ' that in that position, and looking round, I could ' see none of the first line or of the supports. ' The supports ought to have followed me in the ' attack, instead of which they diverged to the right ' and left. . . . My aides-de-camp were prevented by different causes from being with me. I ' was consequently nearly or quite alone. I have ' already positively stated that when I got back to ' the battery which we had attacked and silenced, I ' could see none of the first line, and no troops formed ' either on the right or the left. I therefore found ' myself alone; and I ask, was it not my duty to retreat

' gradually and slowly in rear of the broken parties of
' the first line up the hill, rather than turn and ride
' through the Russian cavalry in search of my sup-
' ports, without knowing at the time which way they
' had gone, they not having followed the first line in
' the advance as they ought to have done? My humble
' opinion is, that it is quite sufficient for a General of
' Brigade to return with as well as lead the attack of
' the front line, unless he should by chance come in
' contact with his supports, in which case he would
' remain with them; but it may be observed that no
' general officer could have rendered any service or
' assistance in an affair like that of Balaclava, in which
' all the loss of men °and horses was sustained in
' twenty minutes, and there were no troops left with
' which to attack an overwhelming force like that of
'; the Russians in position on that day.' *   ' What was
' the duty of the Brigadier under such circumstances?
' In such a desperate *mêlée* to remain to be taken pris-
' oner, or was it his duty to retire?' †

When Lord Cardigan declares that at the time of Counter
his retiring he nowhere saw the supports, he places state-
himself in antagonism to a great body of sworn testimony.‡

Is it, can it be true that Lord Cardigan in his re-

---

* Paper furnished to me by Lord Cardigan.
† Another paper furnished to me by Lord Cardigan.
‡ The affidavits here referred to in *Cardigan v. Calthorpe* were not
regarded as being strictly relevant to the exact question *then* at issue,
and Lord Cardigan, I believe, had no opportunity of adducing evidence
in contradiction of them. The effect of the litigation was to *raise* the
question stated in the text, but not to *solve* it.

The definite question thus raised.

treat met a part of his supports then moving down towards the battery, and that in the face of their continued advance he pursued his way towards the rear, past the left of the 4th Light Dragoons ? *

I acknowledge the apparent weight and the general consistency of the evidence which has been adduced in support of an affirmative answer to this question, and I believe in the good faith of the witnesses. I also acknowledge that, supposing the supports to have reached the guns before Lord Cardigan retreated, it is hard to understand how he could have ridden back through the battery without becoming cognisant of the obstinate and boisterous combat which was there maintained for some time by the 4th Light Dragoons. But, on the other hand, there stands the solemn assertion of Lord Cardigan ; there is the mass of counter-evidence which he has adduced ; † there is a question of mistaken identity ; ‡ there is difficulty in seeing how Lord Cardigan, after his encounter with the Cossacks, could possibly have come back in time to be meeting the 4th Light Dragoons on the English

* This was the main question raised by the testimony adduced on behalf of Colonel Calthorpe.

† Not sworn and filed in a court of law, but verified by the witnesses as their solemn 'declarations,' and laid before me by Lord Cardigan.

‡ Nothwithstanding the great difference in the ages of the two men, an officer who was himself with the 4th Light Dragoons, and who could judge of the extent to which smoke and rapid movement might baffle the sight—I mean Captain E. W. Hunt—believed that Lieutenant Haughton of the 11th Hussars, who rode back mortally wounded, was mistaken for Lord Cardigan. From another source I have ascertained that Lieutenant Haughton (who wore the same conspicuous uniform as the leader of the brigade) rode a chestnut horse very like Lord Cardigan's.

side of the battery; and it will not be forgotten that the officer whose conduct at the time of his retreating has thus been brought into question, was the one who, a minute before, had been leading his brigade down the valley, and charging at its head through the guns with a firmness that was never surpassed.

The question is not ripe for conclusive decision.* Its issue is one of great moment to the military reputation of Lord Cardigan, but not, after all, essential to a due comprehension of the battle; because all agree that at the time of his retiring Lord Cardigan had become personally isolated; and was giving no orders. Still dwelling now upon the memory of the man who led the Light Cavalry charge—he has died since the last sentence was in type—I am unwilling to withhold all acknowledgment of what—as contradistinguished from a rigorously deduced conclusion— I will call the strong personal bias which my mind has received. I cannot, I do not believe that Lord Cardigan, when he retreated, met and saw his supports advancing.†

Down to the time of his extricating himself from

The question not yet ripe for decision.

---

* Some of those who, as is supposed, might throw much light on the question, have hitherto maintained silence. The proceeding in Cardigan v. Calthorpe was not one well calculated to probe the truth, for besides that the question was narrowed by technical rules, and that the evidence was not given orally, the disputants were without the means of obliging any witnesses to testify.

† It is the opinion of an officer of great authority who was so placed in the field as to be highly capable of forming a correct judgment of the effect of the smoke and other baffling causes, that whilst the three supporting regiments were advancing, it would have been quite possible for Lord Cardigan to ride back between two of those regiments without seeing either of them.

the Cossacks, Lord Cardigan's leadership of this extraordinary charge was so perfect as to be all but proof against even minute criticism. And to say this of his exploit is to say a great deal; for in the first place, his actions on the 25th of October have been subjected to a piercing scrutiny; and next, it is evident that his obedience had more the character of a soldier's martyrdom than of what men call 'desperate ' service.' Whilst he rode down the valley at the head of his splendid brigade with something like a foreknowledge of the fate to which he was leading it, he could not but feel that he was giving his chivalrous obedience to a wrongly-interpreted order; and there is nothing more trying to a soldier than the notion of being sacrificed by mistake.

The splendid machine which he had been trusted to wield was so perfectly constituted, and composed of men so resolute that although ever lessening and lessening in size as the squadrons advanced down the valley, they never broke up until they had entered the battery; and as long as it was possible for the attack to go on in that orderly, disciplined way, so long, notwithstanding all the havoc that round-shot, grape, and rifle-balls were making, and notwithstanding the slenderness of the thread on which his own life seemed each moment hanging, the leader performed what he believed to be his duty with an admirable exactness, and a courage so rigid, that almost one might call it metallic. I cannot but think that by a feat of devotion so brave, so desperate, and yet, during some eight or ten deadly minutes, so deliberately pushed on to extremity, he entitled himself to a generous interpre-

tation of what he next did when his peace-service
lessons all failed him.*

It has been said indeed that Lord Cardigan's attack
was deprived of the heroic character which might
otherwise have belonged to it by the fact of his having acted against his will, after actually remonstrating
against the decision which consigned him and his brigade to the fatal valley, and that he had no choice but
to charge like a hero or else become at his peril a
wilful disobeyer of orders which directed him at once
to advance.

But I imagine that this view is erroneous. In the
first place, it is not at all usual to strip a leader of the
glory naturally attaching to his enterprise by saying
that, though acting superbly, he only was brave under
orders ; but in point of fact no such dilemma as the
one supposed was really constituted. We saw what
Lord Lucan stated to have been the terms of his order,
and whether his version of the words or that of Lord
Cardigan be adopted, there was nothing in them
which would have caused an irresolute man to think
himself compelled to lead his brigade to destruction
by taking it down the length of the valley to the
mouths of the guns then distant a mile and a quarter.
It was only under the chivalrous construction which
Lord Cardigan chose to put on the words that he
could be compelled or even empowered to hazard the
attack which he made.

Besides, if I am rightly informed, there was nothing

* This, as I understand, was the ground on which the Lord Chief
Justice proceeded when he said that criticism of the man who led the
Light Cavalry charge 'should be a generous and liberal criticism.'—
Judgment of the Lord Chief Justice.

more easy than for Lord Cardigan to let his advance
down the valley come to an early end, not only without doing or omitting any act for which he could
have been blamed, but even without being forced to
confess to himself that he was so acting as to check
the advance. The rapid advance of a body of Cavalry
cannot of course be perfectly governed by orders like
the march of Foot soldiery, and the compactness of
squadrons when once fairly launched against the
enemy is so much dependent upon what may be
called the 'opinion' of the force and so liable to be
destroyed by the uncertainties, or the faltering, or the
impatience of even a few men that, upon the whole,
its principle of coherence is fragile and delicate in
the extreme. What the troops of the first line have
to do is to look carefully to the leader, and if his
bearing is such as to convey different impressions to
different men, a loosening of the ranks will begin.
Therefore, on the part of the leader, slight gestures,
slight movements in the saddle, slight changes of pace,
slight licence given to impatient horsemen are, in
general, but too likely to be followed by the further
loosening of the ranks, the angry objurgations of the
officers, and finally by that impotent fumbling after
carbines or pistols which proves that the attempt at
a charge has stopped short and will presently cease;
but in Lord Cardigan, during those minutes when
he silently rode down the valley, none could see that
one small sign of faltering or of doubt which alone
would have sufficed to arrest the attack. From the
first moment of the onset to the one when the battery
was entered the brigade felt the will of its leader.

APPENDIX.

No. I.

In answer to a letter which Mr Kinglake addressed to him, General Griffith wrote as follows :—

'Margaretta, Dundrum,
'County Dublin, *November* 5, 1868.

'Sir,—I have the honour to acknowledge the receipt of your
'courteous letter, and have much pleasure in answering your
'questions contained therein to the best of my ability. I com-
'manded and led the Greys into the midst of the Russian cavalry
'column at the battle of Balaclava, and, in charging back again
'with my men, got surrounded. In cutting my way out, I re-
'ceived a pistol-shot on my head, and, being stunned and stu-
'pefied from the effects of the blow, I can recollect little of what
'then passed around me, except remembering objecting strongly
'to Dr Ramsay Brush, the surgeon of the Greys, taking me off
'the field, but which, after an examination of my wound, he
'considered it his duty to do. On recovering from the imme-
'diate effects of the injury, I rejoined my regiment, and re-
'sumed the command.—I have the honour to be, Sir, very
'faithfully yours,

(Signed)   'H. DARBY GRIFFITH.'

I consider that this statement places the fact beyond all
question, and that no corroboration is needed ; but, nevertheless, I here give the statement which has been made on this
subject by an eyewitness—namely, Dr Ramsay Brush, late
Surgeon of the Scots Greys. The period of the combat at

which Colonel Griffith received his wound is indicated in the
footnote *ante*, p. 133; and *then* it was that Dr Ramsay Brush
seized the bridle of the Colonel's horse, and led him towards
the field-hospital.—*Note to 3d Edition.*

Dr Ramsay Brush's Narrative.

In a letter of the 17th August 1868, addressed to the
'Times,' Dr Brush (who was an officer of the Greys) says as
follows :—'I was present in this affair with my regiment, the
' Greys, and saw Colonel Griffith lead them into the dense
' mass of the Russian cavalry, go through them, and into their
' supports, when the regiment went about and cut their way
' back again, Colonel Griffith being still in command. Observ-
' ing that the Colonel was 'bleeding from the head, and suffer-
' ing from the stunning effects of the blow he had received, I
' ordered his trumpeter to go in search of Major Clarke, and tell
' him he had succeeded to the command ; and at the same time,
' perceiving that the Russian cavalry were again outflanking
' us, I seized the bridle of Colonel Griffith's horse, and endea-
' voured to reach my field-hospital in rear of the 93d High-
' landers. We had not gone many yards when the flank charge
' of the 4th and 5th Dragoon Guards was made, which, with a
' second charge of the Greys and Inniskillings, sent the Rus-
' sian cavalry flying a disorganised mass up the hill, and en-
' abled us to reach our destination. When the report arrived
' that the Light Cavalry had been destroyed, Colonel Griffith
' left the field-hospital without my knowledge, rejoined his
' regiment, and resumed the command, which he continued to
' hold throughout the day. The above, sir, is a brief state-
' ment of facts. Mr Kinglake does not seem to be aware that
' there were two distinct and separate charges of " Scarlett's
' " Dragoons "—the first in which the Greys and one squadron
' of the Inniskillings were alone engaged, and the second in
' which those regiments were assisted by a flank attack of the
' 4th and 5th Dragoon Guards and the Royals. In the inter-
' val between these two charges, the Russians retired a short
' way up the hill and re-formed, the Greys and Inniskillings
' following suit. Colonel Griffith led the Greys in the first

' charge, which was by far the most formidable one, and brought
' them out of it ; and it is the assertion on the part of Mr King-
' lake that he was prevented from doing this that I must re-
' quest you will permit me to contradict.'

In all he says respecting his Colonel, Dr Brush, I feel sure,
is perfectly accurate ; and I trust that he, no less than General
Griffith himself, will be satisfied with the corrections which I
have been careful to make in every one of the pages affected
by the error in question.—See pp. 112, 113, 114, 133.

With respect to the passage beginning 'Mr Kinglake does
' not seem, &c.,' I would refer Dr Brush to my narrative as
given in p. 133, and several subsequent pages. Further than
is there indicated, the information I have received does not
enable me to adopt Dr Brush's impression.

No. II.,

EXPLANATORY STATEMENTS LAID BEFORE MR KINGLAKE
BY LORD LUCAN.

*The circumstances under which the forces advancing from the
Baidar direction were suffered to occupy Kamara and
establish Batteries on the neighbouring heights ?*

It was not possible for Sir Colin Campbell to prevent the
enemy establishing themselves on the heights commanding
Kamara. It was very far from his base, and would have required a strong force of infantry and artillery. We had been
obliged to discontinue patrolling this pass a full week before
the 25th October, and the enemy were occupying Tchorgoun
village and heights between that village and Kamara.

*The grounds on which it was judged right for our cavalry
to avoid attacking the forces which assailed the Turkish
Redoubts ?*

Lord Raglan not having acted on the communication sent
to him the day previous by Sir Colin Campbell and myself

informing him of the approach of a considerable Russian army, and leaving us altogether without support, we considered it our first duty to defend the approach to the town of Balaclava; and as this defence would depend chiefly upon the cavalry, it was necessary to reserve them for this purpose. I therefore confined myself to cannonading the enemy so long as my ammunition lasted, and to threatening demonstrations. We only left the neighbourhood of the forts after they were already captured. My opinion was, that the advance upon Balaclava could only be assisted [qu. 'resisted'] by the cavalry on the plain, and I placed them in order of battle for that purpose until removed by Lord Raglan. The soundness of my opinion was established by the check and retreat of the enemy immediately on the repulse of their cavalry; and be it observed that their cavalry were attacked and repulsed on the very site I had prepared to meet them.

The circumstances under which it happened that the advance of the Russian Cavalry to the ground where it turned to engage our Heavy Dragoons was a surprise?

This advance of the Russian cavalry was *no* surprise, nor did I ever hear it so described. From the time that they descended into the valley they moved very slow, and should have been seen by General Scarlett when still one mile distant. I saw them before they crowned the heights, and found time to travel over double the extent of ground, and to halt, form, and dress the attacking line before it had traversed more than half the breadth of the valley.

The grounds on which it was thought necessary for the Heavy Brigade to desist from supporting the Light Brigade in its charge?

Be it remembered that I had carefully divided the Light Brigade into three lines, to expose as few men as possible in the first line, and that the first line should be efficiently supported. So soon as they had moved off, I instructed my aide-

de-camp to have me followed by the Heavy Brigade formed in
the same order of three lines. I then galloped on, and when
very far up [qu. 'down'] the valley I observed that the
Heavy Brigade in my rear were suffering severely from flanking batteries; and with the remark that they were already
sufficiently close to protect the Light Cavalry should they be
pursued by the enemy, and that I could not allow them to
be sacrificed as had been the Light Brigade, I caused them
to be halted. Had not the Chasseurs d'Afrique at this time
silenced one of these batteries, it is my opinion that the Heavy
Cavalry would have been destroyed.

When the Heavy Brigade was halted, no possible object
existed for further exposing them, they could only be useful
in protecting the retreat of the Light Brigade; and I am confident that from their position they materially did so.

*The purport of the Order given to Lord Cardigan after the
receipt of the Order brought by Nolan.*

With General Airey's order in my hand, I trotted up to
Lord Cardigan, and gave him distinctly its contents so far as
they concerned him. I would not on my oath say that I did
not read the order to him. He at once objected, on the ground
that he would be exposed to a flanking battery. When ordered
to take up his then position, he had expressed, through his
aide-de-camp, the same apprehensions. I told him that I was
aware of it. 'I know it,' but that 'Lord Raglan would have
' it,' and that we had no choice but to obey. I then said that
I wished him to advance very steadily and quietly, and that
I would narrow his front by removing the 11th Hussars from
the first to the second line. This he strenuously opposed ; but
I moved across his front and directed Colonel Douglas not to
advance with the rest of the line, but to form a second line
with the 4th Light Dragoons.

No. III.

The brigade was suddenly ordered to mount, upon which I sent one of my aides-de-camp to reconnoitre the ground.

Lord Lucan then came in front of my brigade and said, 'Lord Cardigan, you will attack the Russians in the valley.' I said, 'Certainly, my lord,' dropping my sword at the same time; 'but allow me to point out to you that there is a bat-'tery in front, a battery on each flank, and the ground is 'covered with Russian riflemen.'

Lord Lucan answered: 'I cannot help that; it is Lord Rag-'lan's positive order that the Light Brigade is to attack the 'enemy;' upon which he ordered the 11th Hussars back to support the 17th Lancers. After advancing about eighty yards, a shell fell within reach of my horse's feet, and Captain Nolan, who was riding across the front retreated with his arm up through the intervals of the brigade. I led straight down to the battery without seeing anybody else in front of me. I had to restrain some of the officers, who got very much excited within eighty yards of the battery by the heavy fire. I led into the battery, a shot being fired from one of the largest guns close by my right leg. I led into the battery and through the Russian gun limber-carriages and ammunition-waggons in the rear. I rode within twenty yards of the line of Russian cavalry. I was attacked by two Cossacks, slightly wounded by their lances, and with difficulty got away from them, they trying to surround me. On arriving at the battery through which I had led, I found no part of the brigade. I rode slowly up the hill, and met General Scarlett. I said to him, 'What do you think, General, of the aide-de-'camp, after such an order being brought to us which has de-'stroyed the Light Brigade, riding to the rear and screaming 'like a woman?' Sir J. Scarlett replied, 'Do not say any more, 'for I have ridden over his body.' Lord Lucan was present at this conversation. I then rode to the place from which we had moved off, and found all my brigade there; and, upon having them counted, there then were 195 mounted men out of 670. I immediately rode to Lord Raglan to make my report; who said, in a very angry way, 'What did you mean, sir, by 'attacking a battery in front, contrary to all the usages of war- 'fare and the custom of the service?' Upon which, I said: 'My Lord, I hope you will not blame me, for I received the 'order to attack from my superior officer in front of the 'troops.' I then narrated what I had done as described above.

Lord Lucan put in an affidavit upon oath that when I re- treated I passed eighty yards from him. He was close by when I spoke to General Scarlett. I came up to General Scarlett quite slowly. I afterwards galloped to the remains of the brigade re-forming.

No. IV.

STATEMENT LAID BEFORE MR KINGLAKE BY LORD CARDIGAN.

Having been kindly promised by Mr Kinglake that he will make me acquainted with the nature of the observations he intends to make in the third volume of his history of the Crimean war, I am anxious to give him the fullest informa- tion with regard to all which occurred connected with the charge of the Light Cavalry Brigade against the Russian bat- tery at Balaclava.*

* The promise above mentioned by Lord Cardigan was made under these circumstances : Several years ago—I believe in 1864 or 1865—I sought to allay in some measure Lord Cardigan's extreme anxiety by saying that, with respect to those points on which my opinion might be unfavourable to him I would call his attention to them before the publi- cation should take place, so that he might have an opportunity of sub- mitting to me any considerations tending to change my view, and I inti- mated that I would do this in the form of queries, asking whether he had any further explanation to offer upon such or such a point. During the years which followed, Lord Cardigan (in his anxiety to do himself justice) honoured me with visits so frequent and with a correspondence so ample (on his part) that I considered the subject as exhausted. Accordingly, when he adverted to my promise, I submitted to him that, considering

I commence by stating that the time occupied from the movement of the brigade to the attack to the time of reforming on the same ground did not exceed twenty minutes—the distance passed over was one mile and a quarter, at the lowest calculation—and in that space of time 300 men who had gone into action were killed, wounded, or missing, and 396 horses were put *hors de combat*. Of the 670 men who had gone into action, only 195 were mounted when the brigade reformed on the ground from which they had moved off, and during the engagement 24 officers were killed or wounded.

I presume that no one doubts that I led the first line of the brigade, consisting of the 13th Light Dragoons and 17th Lancers, through the Russian battery, and that, being the first man into the battery; that I pursued my course until I came up to the line of the Russian cavalry. That, being alone there, in consequence of the officers of my Staff being wounded or disabled, I was attacked by two Cossacks, slightly wounded, and nearly dismounted; that, on being nearly surrounded by Cossacks, I gradually retreated until I reached the battery into which I had led the first line; that, on arriving there, I found no part of the first line remaining there. Those which survived the charge had passed off to the left, short of the Russian gun limber-carriages, or retreated up the hill.

I can upon my most solemn oath swear that in that position, and looking round, I could see none of the first line or of the

the great extent to which I had given up my time to him since the period when the promise was made, it would be well for him to release me from it. He showed an indisposition to do this; and the slight feeling of anger which his persistency gave me tended much to counteract the pain that I felt in fulfilling the promise. I said I would fulfil it at once. Accordingly, I wrote the promised queries in Lord Cardigan's presence, read them out to him, and gave him a copy of them. This was on the 15th of February last. Lord Cardigan, under the pain which he thus brought upon himself, showed at the time a perfect command of temper ; and though he afterwards brought me a kind of written protest strongly questioning my impartiality, he offered to withdraw this before reading it, and after reading it, expressed a wish .that it should be considered as withdrawn. I said I wished that the paper should not be withdrawn, and upon Lord Cardigan's saying that he wished to take it away with him, I obtained from him a promise to let me have it afterwards. This he did.

APPENDIX. 365

supports. The supports ought to have followed me in the attack, instead of which they diverged to the right and left.

I have already stated that the first line did not follow me after I passed through the battery in leading the charge ; but whilst I was engaged with the Cossacks they passed off to the left, to avoid the Russian limber-carriages, or retreated up the hill.

My aides-de-camp were prevented by different causes from being with me; I was consequently nearly or quite alone.

I have already positively stated that when I got back to the battery which we had attacked and silenced, I could see none of the first line, except those returning up the hill, and no troops formed either on the right or the left.

I therefore found myself alone, and I ask, Was it not my duty to retreat gradually and slowly in rear of the broken parties of the first line up the hill, rather than turn and ride through the Russian cavalry in search of my supports, without knowing at the time which way they had gone, they not having followed the first line in the advance, as they ought to have done ?

My humble opinion is that it is quite sufficient for a general of brigade to return with as well as lead the attack of the front line, unless he should by chance come in contact with his supports, in which case he would remain with them ; but it may be observed that no general officer could have rendered any service or assistance in an affair like that of Balaclava, in which all the loss of men and horses was sustained in twenty minutes, and there were no troops left with which to attack an overwhelming force like that of the Russians in position on that day.

Twenty minutes being the time occupied in the affair, and the distance a mile and a quarter at the least, gives eight minutes for the advance, eight minutes for the retreat, and only four minutes for fighting or collision with the enemy.

Before concluding, I must revert to a subject already alluded to—viz., that the only point really to be considered is whether, after leading into the battery, and up to the Russian cavalry, and being wounded and nearly taken prisoner by the Cossacks, and having with difficulty got away from them—whether I was justified in returning slowly in rear of my own line, who were retreating up the hill, or whether it was my duty to turn and ride through the Russian cavalry in search of the supports, they not having led straight, but having separated in the advance, one to the right of the valley, and one to the left; whether I was bound to ride through the Russian cavalry in search of the supports, or to remain on the ground I have referred to, there being none of our troops formed there, or to be seen in any direction? As to my having retired, as it is asserted, under the Fedioukine Heights, the evidence of the non-commissioned officers in the printed pamphlet completely contradict such an assertion. The question is, Whether some officer of the 11th Hussars, wounded, was not seen by the men of the 4th Light Dragoons retiring in the rear of that regiment under the Fedioukine Heights?

References appended by Lord Cardigan to the above Statement, and by him headed 'Evidence in Proof.'

1. General Scarlett's evidence, from page 272 to 274 of printed appendix.

2. Lieutenant Johnston* of 13th Light Dragoons, from page 267 to page 272.

3. Extract from Colonel Jenyn's evidence: ' I, with one or ' two others, tried to rally the few men whom I saw left ' mounted, but it was utterly impossible to do so, and we re-' turned in broken detachments through the guns, which were ' then deserted.'

4. Extract from my own evidence: 'No general officer ' could have been of any use. The feeble remains of the lines ' of the brigade could have done nothing more under a general ' officer than they did under their own officers.'

5. Evidence of William Gray, trumpet-major of the 8th Hussars : 'The Earl of Cardigan led the charge against the ' Russian battery at the head of the first line of the brigade. ' The 8th Hussars and the 4th Light Dragoons formed the

* Lord Cardigan should have written this name ' Johnson.'

' rear line of the brigade; but very early in, the charge the
' 8th Hussars and the 4th Light Dragoons became gradu-
' ally separated, the 8th Hussars bearing to the right, and the
' 4th Light Dragoons to the left; and as we advanced farther,
' the distance between the two regiments increased very ma-
' terially.'

6. Extract of a letter written by Lord George Paget to
H.R.H. the Duke of Cambridge in 1856, the following passage
occurs : 'On the advance of the first line, I gave the word,
' " Second line will advance; 4th Light Dragoons direct." Soon,
' however, in the advance, I perceived that the 8th Hussars
' were bearing away to the right, and they kept gradually
' losing their intervals, and by the same process their align-
' ment, till they finally became separated from us. There are
' plenty of witnesses who could prove that during the whole of
' this time I was doing my best, and using the utmost exer-
' tions of my voice to keep them in their proper place, and to
' close them to the 4th; and at last Lieutenant Martin, 4th
' Light Dragoons, galloped to Colonel Shewell to assist me
' in my efforts.'

7. General Scarlett states : 'At the instant when the first
' line of the Light Brigade charged into the battery, it was
' almost impossible, from the dense smoke and confusion, to
' discover what took place; but a few minutes afterwards I ob-
' served the remnants of the Light Brigade, as well as the re-
' mains of the second line, retreating towards the ground which
' they had occupied immediately before the charge; whilst dis-
' mounted men, and horses without riders, were scattered over.
' the space which the brigade had just traversed. I recollect
' on this occasion pointing out to Lord Cardigan the broken
' remnants of his line as they were retreating up the hill. I
' firmly believe, from the information I received both at the
' time of the engagement and afterwards, that Lord Cardigan
' was the first to charge into the battery, and that he was
' amongst the last, if not the last, to return from behind the
' guns.' *

* General Scarlett afterwards explained that he meant 'among the
' last of the first line which he [Lord Cardigan] commanded in person.'—
Letter to Colonel Calthorpe, 1st May 1863.

8. Lieutenant George Johnston * of the 13th Hussars says:
' As to the opinion that we ought to have re-formed, &c., why,
' sir, there were none to form, had it been possible. Instance
' in my own regiment. We turned out 112 of all ranks, and
' lost 84 horses; in fact, there were only 10 of us assembled
' on the spot from whence we charged. We had 26 men
' wounded, 13 taken prisoners, and 12 killed; consequently
' all the generals in the Crimea would have been puzzled how
' to re-form us.'

No. V.

RECORD OF MILITARY SERVICES OF GENERAL WILLIAM FERGUSON BEATSON.

Entered the Bengal Army in 1820.

Being on furlough, he, with sanction of the British Government, served with the British Legion in Spain, in 1835-36, first as Major, afterwards as Lieutenant-Colonel, commanding a regiment, at the head of which he was severely wounded.

For services in Spain received Cross of San Fernando from Queen of Spain; and Her Britannic Majesty's permission to wear it, September 12, 1837.

Returned to India in 1837, and received thanks of Government of India for capture of Jignee, in Bundelkund, in 1840; and of Chirgong in 1841.

In February 1844 received thanks of Agent, Governor General, Scindia's dominions, for recovering, for Gwalior Government, forts and strongholds in Kachwahagar.

In March 1844 received thanks of Government for volunteering of Bundelkund Legion for Scinde; which volunteering, the Governor-General declared, placed the Government of India under great obligation.

* Lord Cardigan should have written this ' Thomas George Johnson.'

In March 1845 was mentioned in Sir Charles Napier's despatch regarding campaign in Boogtee Hills; which service called forth approbation of Government.

In July 1846 the conduct of Legion while in Scinde, of which he was Commandant, was praised in general orders by Governor-General Viscount Hardinge.

In July 1848 received approbation of Government of India for taking Jagheer and fort of Rymow from Rohillas.

In November 1850 recaptured Rymow from Arabs.

In February 1851 took the fort of Dharoor, one of the strongest in the Deccan.

In March 1851 the following General Order was issued by the Resident at Hyderabad:—

' Brigadier Beatson having tendered his resignation of the
' command of the Nizam's Cavalry, from date of his embarka-
' tion for England, the Resident begs to express his entire
' approval of this officer's conduct during the time he has
' exercised the important command°of the Cavalry Division.

' Brigadier Beatson has not only maintained but improved
' the interior economy and arrangement of the Cavalry Divi-
' sion; and the value of his active military services in the
' field has been amply attested, and rendered subject of record,
' in the several instances of Kamgoan, Rymow, Arnee, and
' Dharoor.'

Memorandum dated Headquarters, San Sebastian, March 4,
1837.—For his gallantry in the actions of the 28th of May and 6th of June 1836, Lieutenant-Colonel Beatson received the decoration of the first class of the Royal and Military Order of San Fernando.

From S. Fraser, Esq., Agent to the Governor-General, August
13, 1839.—A loyal spirit, so creditable to Captain Beatson as their Commanding Officer, pervades the force under his command.

From Captain D. Ross, Agent at Jansi, March 18, 1840.—
Commendation of Captain Beatson and the officers and men

under his command for their gallant conduct in overcoming the obstinate resistance at Jignee.

From the Officiating Secretary to Government N. W. P., March 21, 1840.—The thanks of the Government to Captain Beatson for the gallantry displayed in the attack upon Jignee.

From the Secretary to the Government of India, April 6, 1840.—The high satisfaction of the Governor - General in Council with the cool and gallant conduct of the officers and men of the Bundelkund Legion in the attack of the position at Jignee, which his Lordship in Council considers as reflecting the greatest credit on Captain Beatson and the officers who have acted under his authority, in bringing the Legion to its present state of discipline.

From the Secretary to Government N. W. P., May 1, 1841. —The Honourable the Lieutenant-Governor has received the highest gratification from the ability and gallantry displayed by Captain Beatson and the force under his command, in the reduction of that fortress.

From the Secretary to the Government of India, May 17, 1841. —I am directed to state that the Governor-General in Council warmly concurs in this tribute of praise to the Commanding Officer and the officers and men of the detachment lately employed against Chirgong; and has been pleased to direct a copy of Captain Beatson's report of his operations to be published in the official Gazette, a copy of which is enclosed. The steady gallantry of the young sepoys of the Bundelkund Legion, emulating that of the older troops employed on the occasion, has been alike creditable to them and to their commandant and other European officers. His Honour is requested to cause these sentiments to be communicated, through the Agent in Bundelkund, to Captain Beatson, and to the other officers and troops engaged in the service.

Extract of Letter from Lieutenant-Colonel W. H. Sleeman, February 9, 1844.—In conclusion, I beg to offer to you, and the officers and soldiers under your command, my best thanks for the services you have rendered in recovering possession of the forts and strongholds which had been taken by the insurgents from the Gwalior troops.

March 9, 1845.—Honourable mention in despatch from Major-General Sir C. Napier, G.C.B., to the Right Honourable the Governor-General of India in Council.

From the Secretary to Government of India, July 22, 1848. —Approbation of the efficient manner in which Brigadier Beatson performed the duty entrusted to him—that of taking possession of the Jagheer and Fort of Rhymow; and ridding the district of the Rohillahs after settling their claims.

Inscription on a sword presented after the Bundlelkund Legion was broken up :—To MAJOR W. S. BEATSON, late Commandant-in-Chief of the Bundelkund Legion, from his friends of the Legion, in token of their admiration of him as a soldier, and their esteem for him as an individual.—1850.

From General Sir Charles Napier, G.C.B., Commander-in-Chief in India, September 26, 1850.—Speaking of Beatson as ' one who did right good service when under my command, ' which I have neither forgotten, nor have I any disposition ' to forget.'

Extract from General Order by the Resident, on the part of the Nizam's Government, March 10, 1851.—The Resident begs to express his entire approval of this officer's conduct during the time he has exercised the important command of the Nizam's Cavalry Division.

Brigadier Beatson has not only maintained but improved the interior economy and arrangements of the Cavalry Division; and the value of his active military services in the field has been amply attested and rendered subject of record, in the several instances of Kamgaon, Arnee, Raemhow, and Dharoor.

The following accompanied the presentation of a piece of Plate from the officers of the Nizam's Cavalry, after BRIGADIER BEATSON *gave up command :*—' We have availed ourselves of ' this method of testifying our regard for you personally, and ' our admiration of your talents and abilities as a soldier, under ' whose command we have all served, and some of us have had ' opportunities of witnessing your gallant conduct in action ' with the enemy, and your sound judgment upon all occasions, ' when Brigadier in command of the Nizam's Cavalry, both in ' quarters and in the field.'

Extract from Minute by the Most Noble the Governor-General of India, September 1, 1851.—I was induced to appoint Major Beatson to the Nizam's service in consequence of the very energetic and able manner in which he had commanded the Bundelkund Legion for two years in Scinde, consisting of infantry, cavalry, and artillery.

Extract of Letter from the Earl of Ellenborough, G.C.B., April 24, 1852.—I remain impressed as strongly now as I was then with a sense of the obligation under which you and your noble Legion placed the Government when you volunteered for service in Scinde.

———

This was the officer who, notwithstanding his lengthened experience, his military rank, and the high commands he had held, was so animated by an honourable desire to render war-service that he was content to take his part in the campaign with no higher position than that of being attached (with Lord Raglan's consent) to the Staff of General Scarlett. And this was one of the two officers named with high commendation in that report of General Scarlett's which Lord Lucan thought fit to suppress.

———

No. VI.

GENERAL SCARLETT'S STAFF.

Report from General Scarlett to Lord Lucan, October 27, 1854.—*Extract.*

' My best thanks are due to Brigade-Major Conolly, and to
' my aide-de-camp, Lieutenant Elliot, 5th Dragoon Guards, who
' afforded me every assistance, and to Colonel Beatson of the
' Honourable E.I.C. service, who, as a volunteer, is attached to
' my Staff.'

General Scarlett to Lord Lucan, December 17, 1854.

Remonstrance against the omission of the names of Colonel Beatson and Lieutenant Elliot.

General Scarlett to the Military Secretary.—Extract.

' Lieutenant Elliot, till severely wounded in the head, was
' at my side in the charge, and previously displayed the great-
' est coolness and gallantry. Colonel Beatson also gave me
' all the assistance which his experience and well-known gal-
' lantry enabled him to do throughout the day.'

Lord Lucan to General Scarlett, December 18, 1854.—Extract.

' I did not consider it fitting specially to name him [Lieu-
' tenant Elliot] in my report. . . . I do not consider that it
' would have been justice towards regimental officers specially
' to name all Staff officers, and I think that the obvious con-
' sequences of such general and indiscriminate * recommenda-
' tions would be that but little value would be attached to
' general officers' requests, and that the claims of all would
' suffer.'

General Scarlett recommended Elliot for the Victoria Cross,
and the application was refused on the plea that to charge and
fight hand to hand was nothing more than the duty of a
cavalry officer.

No. VII.

*The Strength of the Body of Russian Cavalry under General
Ryjoff which engaged General Scarlett's Brigade.*

It is admitted by General de Todleben that the Russian
cavalry included in Liprandi's and Jabrokritsky's detachment
numbered 22 squadrons of regular cavalry, with a strength

* Certainly Lord Lucan discriminated, and discriminated, as I believe,
without acting from 'favour and affection,' but still so infelicitously that
he named and commended in his despatch his own first aide-de-camp, who
had not happened to be in any of the cavalry charges, and (suppressing
Scarlett's report) steadfastly refused to allow the name of Elliot to appear,
Elliot being a man who had charged at the side of Scarlett, and come out
with some fourteen wounds !

of 2200, and 12 'sotnias' of Cossacks, with a strength of
1200, making altogether 3400. Upon the question whether
Colonel Jeropkine's six squadrons of 'combined Lancers'
formed part of General Ryjoff's force, and also upon the question whether the squadron which advanced against the 93d
Highlanders rejoined the main body before Scarlett's charge,
the wording of Liprandi's official despatch is indecisive. On
the other hand, General de Todleben's statement is explicit
enough in giving a negative to both these questions; and the
General even seeks to cut down the force which engaged
Scarlett's dragoons to a strength of 1400 : but, as he discloses
the cause of the mistake which led him to that conclusion—
namely, the mistake of overrating the number of squadrons
opposed to Campbell—his error does not mislead. In support
of the opinion that puts Ryjoff's force at about 3500, I may
state that the body certainly included Lancers (other than
Cossacks), and that is a fact which could be well accounted
for if the six squadrons of Jeropkine's Lancers were present.
As tending to show that the estimate of 3500 might not be
excessive, I may mention that an accomplished artillery officer
(Colonel Hamley), who would be necessarily well skilled in
estimating distances and (by consequence) in inferring the
numerical strength of a column, was of opinion that Ryjoff's
force must have numbered no less than 6000. I consider that
a computation of from about 2000 (or, speaking more exactly
1900) to 3000 is the highest that could well be made by
any one who does not altogether discard the official Russian
accounts.

No. VIII.

PAPERS RELATING TO THE RECALL OF LORD LUCAN.

BALACLAVA, *Oct.* 26, 1854.

DEAR GENERAL AIREY,—I enclose a copy of the order
handed me by Captain Nolan yesterday, as desired by Lord
Raglan. When his Lordship is enabled to give it his atten-

tion, I anxiously hope that he will not still think 'I lost the 'Light Brigade' in that unfortunate affair of yesterday.—Believe me, &c.   (Signed)   LUCAN, *Lieut.-Gen.*

The Quartermaster-General.

Lord Raglan to the Secretary of State, October 28, 1854.—
Extract.

As the enemy withdrew from the ground which they had momentarily occupied, I directed the cavalry, supported by the Fourth Division under Lieutenant-General Sir George Cathcart, to move forward and take advantage of any opportunity to regain the heights; and not having been able to accomplish this immediately, and it appearing that an attempt was making to remove the captured guns, the Earl of Lucan was desired to advance rapidly, follow the enemy in their retreat, and try to prevent them from effecting their objects.

In the meanwhile, the Russians had time to re-form on their own ground, with artillery in front and upon their flanks.

From some misconception of the instruction to advance, the Lieutenant-General considered that he was bound to attack at all hazards, and he accordingly ordered Major-General the Earl of Cardigan to move forward with the Light Brigade.

This order was obeyed in the most spirited and gallant manner. Lord Cardigan charged with the utmost vigour, attacked a battery which was firing upon the advancing squadrons, and having passed beyond it engaged the Russian cavalry in its rear; but there, his troops were assailed by artillery and infantry as well as cavalry, and necessarily retired after having committed much havoc upon the enemy.

BALACLAVA, *Nov.* 30, 1854.

MY LORD,—In your lordship's report of the cavalry action of Balaclava of the 25th ultimo, given in the papers which have just arrived from England, you observe that, from some misconception of the instruction to advance, the Lieutenant-General considered that he was bound to attack at all hazards,

and he accordingly ordered Lord Cardigan to move forward
with the Light Brigade.　Surely, my lord, this is a grave
charge and imputation reflecting seriously on my professional
character. ·

I.cannot remain silent ; it is, I feel, incumbent on me to
state those facts which I cannot doubt must clear me from
what I respectfully submit is altogether unmerited.

The cavalry was formed to support an intended movement
of the infantry, when Captain Nolan, the aide-de-camp of the
Quartermaster-General, came up to me at speed, and placed
in my hands this written instruction :—

Copy.

　' Lord Raglan wishes the cavalry to advance rapidly to the
' front, follow the enemy, and try to prevent the enemy carry-
' ing away the guns.　Troop of horse-artillery may accompany.
' French cavalry is on your left.

　' Immediate.'　　　　　　　　(Signed)　　' R. AIREY.'

After carefully reading this order I hesitated, and urged the
uselessness of such an attack, and the dangers attending it ;
the aide-de-camp, in a most authoritative tone, stated that
they were Lord Raglan's orders that the cavalry should attack
immediately.　I asked him where? and what to do? as neither
enemy nor guns were within sight.　He replied in a most disrespectful but significant manner, pointing to the further end
of the valley, ' There, my lord, is your enemy ; there are your
' guns.'

So distinct in my opinion was your written instruction, and
so positive and urgent were the orders delivered by the aide-
de-camp, that I felt it was imperative on me to obey, and I
informed Lord Cardigan that he was to advance ; and to the
objections he made, and in which I entirely agreed, I replied
that the order was from your lordship.　Having decided
against my conviction to make the movement, I did all in my
power to render it as little perilous as possible.　I formed the
brigade in two lines, and led to its support two regiments of
heavy cavalry, the Scots Greys and Royals, and only halted

them when they had reached the spot from which they could protect the retreat of the light cavalry, in the event of their being pursued by the enemy; and when, having already lost many officers and men by the fire from the batteries and forts, any further advance would have exposed them to destruction.

My lord, I considered at the time—I am still of the same opinion—that I followed the only course open to me. As a lieutenant-general, doubtless I have discretionary power; but to take upon myself to disobey an order written by my Commander-in-Chief within a few minutes of its delivery, and given from an elevated position, commanding an entire view of all the batteries and the position of the enemy, would have been nothing less than direct disobedience of orders, without any other reason than that I preferred my own opinion to that of my general, and in this instance must have exposed me and the cavalry to aspersions, against which it might have been difficult to have defended ourselves.

It should also be remembered that the aide-de-camp, well informed of the intentions of his general, and the objects he had in view, after first insisting on an immediate charge, then placed himself in front of one of the leading squadrons, where he fell the first victim.

I did not dare so to disobey your lordship; and it is the opinion of every officer of rank in this army, to whom I have shown your instructions, that it was not possible for me to do so.

I hope, my lord, that I have stated the facts temperately, and in a becoming and respectful manner, as it has been my wish to do. I am confident that it will be your desire to do me justice. I will only ask that your lordship should kindly give the same publicity to this letter that has been given to your report, as I am sensitively anxious to satisfy my Sovereign, my military superiors, and the public, that I have not, on this unhappy occasion, shown myself undeserving of their confidence, or unfitting the command which I hold.—I have the honour, &c.   (Signed)   LUCAN, *Lieut.-Gen.*
Commanding Cavalry Division.

His Excellency the Commander
of the Forces.

Field-Marshal Lord Raglan to Duke of Newcastle.—
(Rec. Jan. 8, 1855.)

BEFORE SEBASTOPOL, *Dec.* 16, 1854.

MY LORD DUKE,—I regret to be under the necessity of forwarding to your Grace the copy of a letter which has been addressed to me by Lieutenant-General the Earl of Lucan.

When I received it, I placed it in the hands of Brigadier-General Airey, the Quartermaster-General, and requested him to suggest to his lordship to withdraw the communication, considering that it would not lead to his advantage in the slightest degree; but Lord Lucan having declined to take the step recommended, I have but one course to pursue—that of laying the letter before your Grace, and submitting to you such observations upon it as I am bound, in justice to myself, to put you in possession of.

Lieutenant-General the Earl of Lucan complains that, in my despatch to your Grace of the 28th of October I stated that, 'from some misconception of the instruction to advance, ' the Lieutenant-General considered that he was bound to ' attack at all hazards.' His lordship conceives this statement to be a grave charge, and an imputation reflecting seriously on his professional character, and he deems it incumbent upon him to state those facts which he cannot doubt must clear him from what he respectfully submits as altogether unmerited.

I have referred to my despatch, and, far from being willing to recall one word of it, I am prepared to declare, that not only did the Lieutenant-General misconceive the written instruction that was sent him, but that there was nothing in that instruction which called upon him to attack at all hazards, or to undertake the operation which led to such a brilliant display of gallantry on the part of the Light Brigade, and unhappily, at the same time, occasioned such lamentable casualties in every regiment composing it.

In his lordship's letter, he is wholly silent with respect to a previous order which had been sent him. He merely says that the cavalry was formed to support an intended movement of the infantry.

This previous order was in the following words :—' The
' cavalry to advance and take advantage of any opportunity
' to recover the heights. They will be supported by infantry,
' which has been ordered to advance on two fronts.'
This order did not seem to me to have been attended to,
and therefore it was that the instruction by Captain Nolan
was forwarded to him. Lord Lucan must have read the first
order with very little attention, for he now states that the
cavalry was formed to support the infantry, whereas he was
told by Brigadier-General Airey, ' that the cavalry was to
' advance, and take advantage of any opportunity to recover
' the heights, and that they would be supported by infantry,'
not that they were to support the infantry ; and so little had
he sought to do as he had been directed, that he had no men
in advance of his main body, made no attempt to regain the
heights, and was so little informed of the position of the
enemy that he asked Captain Nolan, 'Where and what he
' was to attack, as neither enemy nor guns were in sight ?'

This, your Grace will observe, is the Lieutenant-General's
own admission. The result of his inattention to the first
order was, that it never occurred to him that the second was
connected with, and a repetition of, the first. He viewed it
only as a positive order to attack at all hazards (the word
' attack,' be it observed, was not made use of in General
Airey's note) an unseen enemy, whose position, numbers, and
composition, he was wholly unacquainted with, and whom, in
consequence of a previous order, he had taken no step whatever to watch.

I undoubtedly had no intention that he should make such
an attack—there was nothing in the instruction to require it ;
and therefore I conceive I was fully justified in stating to
your Grace, what was the exact truth, that the charge arose
from the misconception of an order for the advance, which
Lord Lucan considered obliged him to attack at all hazards.

I wish I could say with his lordship that, having decided
against his conviction to make the movement, he did all he
could to render it as little perilous as possible. This, indeed,
is far from being the case, in my judgment.

He was told that the horse-artillery might accompany the cavalry. He did not bring it up. He was informed that the French cavalry was on his left. He did not invite their co-operation. He had the whole of the heavy cavalry at his disposal. He mentions having brought up only two regiments in support, and he omits all other precautions, either from want of due consideration, or from the supposition that the unseen enemy was not in such great force as he apprehended, notwithstanding that he was warned of it by Lord Cardigan, after the latter had received the order to attack.

I am much concerned, my Lord Duke, to have to submit these observations to your Grace. I entertain no wish to disparage the Earl of Lucan in your opinion, or to cast a slur upon his professional reputation; but having been accused by his lordship of having stated of him what was unmerited in my despatch, I have felt obliged to enter into the subject, and trouble your Grace at more length than I could have wished, in vindication of a report to your Grace in which I had strictly confined myself to that which I knew to be true, and had indulged in no observations whatever, or in any expression which could be viewed either as harsh or in any way grating to the feelings of his lordship.—I have, &c.

(Signed)   RAGLAN.

(*Copy.*)

WAR DEPARTMENT, *Jan.* 27, 1855.

MY LORD,—I have to acknowledge your lordship's despatch, dated the 16th December, inclosing the copy of a letter addressed to you by Lieutenant-General the Earl of Lucan, and submitting to me observations upon its contents.

Upon the receipt of that despatch, I felt that the public service, and the general discipline of the army, must be greatly prejudiced by any misunderstanding between your lordship as the general commanding her Majesty's forces in the field and the Lieutenant-General commanding the Division of Cavalry; but desiring to be fortified in all matters of this nature by the opinion of the General Commanding-in-Chief,

I submitted, without delay, your lordship's despatch, and the letter of the Earl of Lucan, for the consideration of General the Viscount Hardinge.

I have now the honour of inclosing, for your lordship's guidance, an extract from the reply which I have this day (26th January) received from Lord Hardinge, and which has been submitted to and approved by the Queen.

I have, therefore, to instruct your lordship to communicate this decision to the Earl of Lucan, and to inform his lordship that he should resign the command of the Cavalry Division, and return to England.

In performing this painful duty, I purposely abstain from any comments upon the correspondence submitted to me; but I must observe that, apart from any consideration of the merits of the question raised by Lord Lucan, the position in which he has now placed himself towards your lordship renders his withdrawal from the army under your command in all respects advisable,—I have, &c.

'(Signed)   NEWCASTLE.

Field-Marshal the LORD RAGLAN,
G.C.B. &c. &c. &c.

(*Extract.*)

HORSE GUARDS, *Jan.* 26, 1855.

MY LORD DUKE,—Lord Lucan, in his letter of the 30th November, objects to the terms used by Lord Raglan in his public despatch, that his orders for the Light Brigade to charge were given under a misconception of the written order, &c.

He declines to withdraw that letter, and adheres to the construction he has put upon the order, that it compelled him to direct a charge.

The papers having been referred by your Grace to me, I concur with Lord Raglan that the terms he used in his despatch were appropriate : and as a good understanding between the Field-Marshal commanding the forces in the field and the Lieutenant-General commanding the Cavalry Division are conditions especially necessary for advantageously carrying on the public service, I recommend that Lieutenant-General Lord Lucan should be recalled; and if your Grace and her Majesty's Government concur in this view, I will submit my recommendation to her Majesty, and take her Majesty's pleasure on the subject.—I have, &c.

(Signed)   HARDINGE.

His Grace the DUKE of NEWCASTLE,
&c. &c. &c.

BEFORE SEBASTOPOL, *February* 13, 1855.

MY DEAR LORD LUCAN,—It is with much concern that I fulfil the painful duty of transmitting to you a despatch which I received yesterday evening from the Duke of Newcastle.

I have anxiously considered how I could acquit myself of this task with most regard for your feelings; and I have arrived at the conclusion that the best way is to put you in possession of the Minister for War's communication and orders, without reserve or comment.

If you should desire to see me, I shall be happy to receive you at any time that may be most convenient to you.—Believe me, very faithfully yours,

(Signed)   RAGLAN.

Lieutenant-General the EARL of LUCAN.

20 HANOVER SQUARE, LONDON,
March 2, 1855.

SIR,—I have obeyed her Majesty's commands to resign the command of the cavalry of the Army of the East, and to return to England; and have now the honour to report my arrival, for the information of the General Commanding-in-Chief.

I consider it due to my professional honour and character to seize the earliest moment of requesting that my conduct in ordering the charge of the Light Cavalry Brigade at Balaclava, on the 25th October, and writing the letter addressed to Field-Marshal Lord Raglan, on the 30th November, may be submitted to, and investigated by, a Court-martial.

I make this appeal to General Lord Hardinge with the

greatest confidence, believing it to be the undoubted privilege, if not the positive right, of any soldier to be allowed a military inquiry into his conduct, when, as in my case, he shall consider it to have been unjustly impugned.—I have the honour, &c.

(Signed)   LUCAN, *Lieut.-Gen.*

The Adjutant-General.

HORSE GUARDS, *March* 5, 1855.

MY LORD,—I have had the honour to submit to the General Commanding-in-Chief your letter of the 2d March instant, reporting your arrival in London from the Army in the East, and requesting that your conduct in ordering the charge of the Light Cavalry Brigade at the action of Balaclava, on the 25th October last, and writing the letter you addressed to Field-Marshal Lord Raglan on the 30th November, may be submitted to, and investigated by, a Court-martial.

I am directed by the General Commanding-in-Chief to state in reply that, after a careful review of the whole correspondence which has passed, he cannot recommend to her Majesty that your lordship's conduct in these transactions should be investigated by a Court-martial.—I have the honour to be, &c.

(Signed)   G. A. WETHERALL.

Major-General the EARL of LUCAN.

HANOVER SQUARE, *March* 5, 1855.

SIR,—I have the honour to acknowledge the receipt of your letter informing me that the Commander-in-Chief cannot recommend that my conduct should be investigated by a Court-martial.

Until this day I have been kept uninformed of the letter from Lord Raglan, which appears to have been addressed by his lordship to the Minister of War, when forwarding mine of the 30th of November last.

This letter contains entirely new matter, and is replete with

new charges, reflecting more seriously than before on my professional judgment and character. There is now imputed to
me, and for the first time, inattention to, and neglect of,
another order; and again, a total incapacity to carry out my
instructions, and to avail myself of the means placed by his
lordship at my disposal.

Charges so grave, and of a character so exclusively professional, cannot, I submit, be properly disposed of without a
military investigation. I find myself, therefore, compelled to
express my anxious wish that the Commander-in-Chief will
be induced kindly to reconsider his decision, and consent to
my whole conduct on the day of the action of Balaclava (25th
of October 1854) being investigated by a Court-martial,—I
have the honour, &c.

(Signed)　　　LUCAN, Lieut.-Gen.

To the Adjutant-General.

March 12, 1855.

Letter from the Adjutant-General, stating that the Commander-in-Chief at the Horse Guards cannot recommend that
your conduct on the 25th October should be investigated by
a Court-martial.—I have the honour, &c.

(Signed)　　　G. A. WETHERALL, A.G.

Major-General LORD LUCAN, &c. &c.

No. IX.

The Nature of the Litigation in the Suit of the Earl of
Cardigan v. Lieutenant-Colonel Calthorpe.

The tenor of the litigation in Cardigan v. Calthorpe was of
this kind. In his 'Letters from Headquarters'—a book of
which the successive editions appeared in 1856, 1857, and
1858—Colonel Calthorpe had substantially maintained that

Lord Cardigan, after leading the Light Cavalry, retreated pre-maturely, and he had also stated in the same book that Lord Cardigan so retreated without having entered the battery.

In 1863, Lord Cardigan applied in the Court of Queen's, Bench for a criminal information against Colonel Calthorpe, and supported his complaint by affidavits which proved that he had not only entered the battery, but had passed on, some way, beyond it.

Colonel Calthorpe being satisfied with the proofs which his adversary had adduced upon this particular point, acknowledged his mistake so far as concerned the spot where Lord Cardigan's retrograde movement began, and declared himself 'satisfied 'that the Earl of Cardigan entered the Russian battery,' but he firmly persisted in maintaining that Lord Cardigan had retreated prematurely ;* and in support of that contention, he adduced a mass of evidence which went to show that whilst the 4th Light Dragoons and the 8th Hussars were in the act of advancing towards the battery, Lord Cardigan rode by, on his way to the rear. Moreover, to show at how early a moment Lord Cardigan had retired, he adduced an affidavit by no less a personage than the commander of the whole English Cavalry in the Crimea—that is, by the Earl of Lucan.

It was considered that Colonel Calthorpe, having thus partly shifted his ground, could not be allowed, in that suit, to sustain the charge of premature retreat in a new form; and Lord Cardigan was not called upon to refute, if he could, the evidence which had been adduced against him.

So, the change wrought by the litigation was substantially this :† On the one hand it had become clear from the proofs, nay it was even unanimously acknowledged that Lord Cardigan rode into the battery; and the highly favourable comments of the Lord Chief Justice added largely to the advantage thus gained by the plaintiff; but, on the other hand, the

* This he did by formally declaring in an affidavit his adherence to the following passage in his book: 'This was the moment when a general was ' most required, but unfortunately Lord Cardigan was not then present.'

† The actual decision was that the rule obtained by Lord Cardigan must be discharged; but not for reasons founded on anything that occur-red in the battle. The rule was discharged without costs.

substance of the charge which had been brought against Lord Cardigan—the charge of having prematurely retreated—remained still upheld against him as a charge deliberately persisted in by his adversary, and one which now rested no longer upon the mere assertion of an author narrating what he had heard from others, but—upon the testimony of numbers of men who (having at the time of the battle held various ranks in the army from that of the Lieutenant-General commanding the cavalry down to the private soldier) declared upon oath that they had seen with their own eyes, and heard with their own ears, the things to which they bore witness.

Upon the whole, the upshot of the litigation was that, ostensibly, and so far as concerned the immediate impression of the public, Lord Cardigan was clearly the gainer; and yet by the very process which brought him this advantage he had provoked into existence a mass of sworn and written testimony which, though judged to be out of place in the particular suit of Cardigan v. Calthorpe, might nevertheless be used against him with formidable effect in any other contention.

When I had imparted to Lord Cardigan my idea of the state in which his military reputation was left by all this sworn testimony, he caused to be prepared some 'statutory declara-'tions' by persons present in the combat, and laid these before me with great numbers of other documents. In fairness, these counter-declarations should be read as a sequel to the affidavits filed in Cardigan v. Calthorpe.*

* Accordingly, if a report of the trial with copies of the affidavits be published, I should wish, in justice to the memory of Lord Cardigan, to have the declarations which were laid before me printed in the same volume.

PRINTED BY WILLIAM BLACKWOOD AND SONS, EDINBURGH.

CPSIA information can be obtained
at www.ICGtesting.com
Printed in the USA
LVHW031550231220
674968LV00007B/625